Learning from Arguments
An Introduction to Philosophy

Daniel Z. Korman
UCSB

Published open access by the PhilPapers Foundation, 2022
Department of Philosophy, Stevenson Hall, Western University
1151 Richmond St, London, ON, N6A 5B8, Canada
https://philarchive.org/rec/KORLFA
ISBN 979-8-8442225-8-0

Contents

Preface for Students   i

Preface for Instructors   iv

INTRODUCTION   1
1. The Chapters
2. The Elements of Arguments
3. Premises and Conditionals
4. Common Argumentative Strategies
5. Counterexamples
6. Argument by Analogy
7. Thought Experiments
8. What is Philosophy?

CHAPTER 1: Can God Allow Suffering?   19
1. Introduction
2. The Argument from Suffering
3. Refining the Argument
4. The Appreciated Goods Defense
5. The Character Building Defense
6. The Free Will Defense
7. The Hidden Reasons Defense
8. Conclusion

CHAPTER 2: Why You Should Bet on God   32
1. Introduction
2. Practical Reasoning in an Uncertain World
3. The Expected Utility of Believing in God
4. Challenging the Decision Matrix
5. Is Belief Voluntary?
6. Conclusion

CHAPTER 3: What Makes You You   48
1. Introduction
2. Clarifying the Question of Personal Identity
3. Some Promising and Unpromising Answers
4. Against the Same Body Account
5. Against the Psychological Descendant Account
6. Souls
7. Combining the Psychological and Bodily Accounts
8. Conclusion

CHAPTER 4: Don't Fear the Reaper   74
1. Introduction
2. Hedonism
3. The Argument from Hedonism
4. Against Post-Mortem Consciousness
5. The Too Many Thinkers Argument
6. Irrational Fears

CHAPTER 5: No Freedom   86
1. Introduction
2. Freedom Unmotivated
3. The Desire Argument Against Free Action
4. The Argument from Undesired Actions
5. The Argument from Desire-Defeating Actions
6. Determinism
7. The Argument from Determinism
8. On Rejecting Determinism
9. Compatibilism
10. Freedom and Responsibility

CHAPTER 6: You Know Nothing   107
1. Skepticism about the Future
2. What It Takes to Know the Future
3. Why Believe the Future Will Be Like the Past?
4. No Inductive Argument for FLP
5. The Dreaming Argument
6. Why You Have to Rule Out the Dreaming Hypothesis
7. Why You Can't Rule Out the Dreaming Hypothesis
8. Can You Tell You're Not Dreaming?
9. No Useful Tests for Dreaming
10. Conclusion

CHAPTER 7: Against Prisons and Taxes   126
1. Taxation and Extortion
2. Morally Relevant Differences
3. The Social Contract
4. No Social Contract
5. Immigration
6. What Can the Government Do?

CHAPTER 8: The Ethics of Abortion   140
1. Preliminaries
2. Identifying Wrong-Making Features
3. Some Bad Pro-Choice Arguments
4. Some Bad Pro-Life Arguments

5. The Right to Life Argument
6. The Violinist Argument
7. Risk, Consent, and the Right to the Womb
8. The Future Like Ours Argument
9. Bad Objections to the FLO Argument
10. FLO-Overriding Factors
11. Making Exceptions
12. Making Laws

CHAPTER 9: Eating Animals   167
1. Introduction
2. The Argument from Precedent
3. The Argument from Naturalness
4. The Argument from Necessity
5. Meet Your Meat
6. Fred and His Puppies
7. Morally Relevant Differences
8. The No Impact Objection
9. Beyond Factory Farming

CHAPTER 10: What Makes Things Right   187
1. Utilitarianism
2. Why Accept Act Utilitarianism?
3. Killing One to Save Five
4. Rule Utilitarianism
5. The Trolley Argument
6. Conclusion

APPENDIX A: Logic   202
1. Valid Arguments
2. How to Check for Validity
3. Challenging Modus Ponens and Modus Tollens

APPENDIX B: Writing   214
1. Introducing Your Target
2. Advancing Your Argument
3. Anticipating Possible Responses
4. Editing
5. Likely Criteria for Grading
6. Citation and Plagiarism

APPENDIX C: Theses and Arguments   227

Preface for Students

I'm going to argue that you have no free will. I'm going to argue for some other surprising things too, for instance that death isn't bad for you, taxation is immoral, and you can't know anything whatsoever about the world around you. I'm also going to argue for some things you're probably not going to like: that abortion is immoral, you shouldn't eat meat, and God doesn't exist.

The arguments aren't my own. I didn't come up with them. I don't even accept all of them: there are two chapters whose conclusions I accept, three I'm undecided about, and five I'm certain can't be right. (I'll let you guess which are which.) This isn't merely for the sake of playing devil's advocate. Rather, the idea is that the best way to appreciate what's at stake in philosophical disagreements is to study and engage with serious arguments against the views you'd like to hold.

Each chapter offers a sustained argument for some controversial thesis, specifically written for an audience of beginners. The aim is to introduce newcomers to the dynamics of philosophical argumentation, using some of the arguments standardly covered in an introductory philosophy course, but without the additional hurdles one encounters when reading the primary sources of the arguments: challenging writing, obscure jargon, and references to unfamiliar books, philosophers, or schools of thought.

The different chapters aren't all written from the *same* perspective. This is obvious from a quick glance at the opening chapters: the first chapter argues that you shouldn't believe in God, while the second argues that you should. You'll also find that chapters 3 and 4 contain arguments pointing to different conclusions about the relationship between people and their bodies, and chapter 7 contains arguments against the very theory of morality that's defended in chapter 10. So, you will be exposed to a variety of different philosophical perspectives, and you should be on the lookout for ways in which the arguments in one chapter provide the resources for resisting arguments in other chapters.

And while there are chapters arguing both for and against belief in God, that isn't the case for other topics we'll cover. For instance, there's a chapter arguing that you don't have free will, but no chapter arguing that you *do* have free will. That doesn't mean that you'll only get to hear one side of the argument. Along the way you will be exposed to many of the standard objections to the views and arguments I'm advancing, and you can decide for yourself whether those objections are convincing. Those who need help finding the flaws in the reasoning (or ideas for paper topics) can look to the reflection questions at the end of each chapter for some clues.

As I said, the arguments advanced in the book are not my own, and at the end of each chapter I point out the original sources of the arguments. In some chapters, the central arguments have a long history, and the formulations I use can't be credited to any one philosopher in particular. Other chapters, however, are more directly indebted to the work of specific contemporary philosophers, reproducing the contents of their books and articles (though often with some modifications and simplifications). In particular, chapter 7 draws heavily from the opening chapters of Michael Huemer's *The Problem of Political Authority*; chapter 8 reproduces the central arguments of Judith Jarvis Thomson's "A Defense of Abortion" and Don Marquis's "Why Abortion is Immoral"; and the arguments in chapter 9 are drawn from Dan Lowe's "Common Arguments for the Moral Acceptability of Eating Meat" and Alastair Norcross's "Puppies, Pigs, and People." The quote from Delia Graff Fara at the end of the introduction is from Steve Pyke's *Philosophers, Volume II*.

I'm grateful to Jeff Bagwell, Jacob Berger, Matt Davidson, Nikki Evans, Jason Fishbein, Bill Hartmann, Colton Heiberg, Will Huesser, İrem Kurtsal, Leo Iacono, Jeonggyu Lee, Clayton Littlejohn, Neil Manson, David Mokriski, Charles Perkins, Seán Pierce, Ryan Ross, David Shoemaker, Neil Sinhababu, Dan Sturgis, Joshua Tepley, and Travis Timmerman for helpful suggestions, and to the Facebook Hivemind for help selecting the further readings for the various chapters. Special thanks are due to Chad Carmichael, David King, Jonathan Livengood, and Daniel Story for extensive feedback on earlier drafts of the textbook, and to the students in my 2019 Freshman Seminar: Shreya Acharya, Maile Buckman, Andrea Chavez, Dylan Choi, Lucas Goefft, Mino Han, PK Kottapalli, Mollie Kraus, Mia

Lombardo, Dean Mantelzak, Sam Min, Vivian Nguyen, Ariana Pacheco Lara, Kaelen Perrochet, Rijul Singhal, Austin Tam, Jennifer Vargas, Kerry Wang, and Lilly Witonsky. Finally, thanks to Renée Jorgensen for permission to use her portrait of the great 20th century philosopher and logician Ruth Barcan Marcus on the cover. You can see more of her portraits of philosophers here: www.reneebolinger.com/portraits.html

Preface for Instructors

Learning from Arguments is a novel approach to teaching Introduction to Philosophy. It advances accessible versions of key philosophical arguments, in a form that students can emulate in their own writing, and with the primary aim of cultivating an understanding of the dynamics of philosophical argumentation.

The book contains ten core chapters, covering the problem of evil, Pascal's wager, personal identity, the irrationality of fearing death, free will and determinism, Cartesian skepticism, the problem of induction, the problem of political authority, the violinist argument, the future-like-ours argument, the ethics of eating meat, utilitarianism (both act and rule), and the trolley problem. Additionally, there is an introductory chapter explaining what arguments are and surveying some common argumentative strategies, an appendix on logic explaining the mechanics and varieties of valid arguments, and an appendix providing detailed advice for writing philosophy papers.

Each of the ten core chapters offers a sustained argument for some controversial thesis, specifically written for an audience of beginners. The aim is to introduce newcomers to the dynamics of philosophical argumentation, using some of the arguments standardly covered in an introductory philosophy course, but without the additional hurdles one encounters when reading the primary sources of the arguments: challenging writing, specialized jargon, and references to unfamiliar books, philosophers, or schools of thought.

Since the book is aimed at absolute beginners, I often address objections that would only ever occur to a beginner and ignore objections and nuances that would only ever occur to someone already well-versed in these issues. Theses defended in the chapters often are not ones that I myself accept. Instead, decisions about which position to defend in each chapter were made with an eye to pedagogical effectiveness.

Instructors will find the book easy to teach from. The chapters are self-standing with no cross-referencing, and may be taught in any order. The central arguments of each chapter are already extracted in valid, premise/conclusion form, ready to be put up on the board or screen and debated. The chapters also contain plenty of arguments that haven't been extracted in this way, but that are self-contained in a single paragraph, making for moderately challenging—but not *too* challenging—argument reconstruction exercises. The reflection questions at the end of each chapter can easily be incorporated into class discussion.

The book can be used in different ways in the classroom. Instructors may decide to take on the persona of the author of the chapter, leaving it to the students to find a way of resisting the arguments—which I have found to be an enjoyable and effective way of teaching the material. Or they may use the arguments in the chapter as a jumping-off point for presenting the standard positions and responses. They may wish to supplement the chapters with the original sources of the arguments or with readings representing competing philosophical positions, possibly drawn from the list of further readings at the end of each chapter.

Don't worry about *Learning from Arguments* being too "one-sided." It's true that whichever view is being defended in the chapter always gets the last word. But along the way, students are exposed to clear and charitable presentations of the standard objections to the views and arguments advanced in the chapter, and can decide for themselves whether the chapter's responses to those objections are convincing. Students who need help finding the flaws in the reasoning (or ideas for paper topics) can look to the reflection questions at the end of each chapter for clues about the most promising places to resist the arguments.

Additionally, I think instructors will find there to be significant pedagogical advantages to a "one-sided" approach. When beginners are presented with a full menu of available views, surveying the pros and cons of each, this can sometimes give the wrong impression: that, in philosophy, all views are equally defensible, that it's all a matter of opinion, and that one can simply pick and choose whichever view one likes best. What the approach in *Learning from Arguments* emphasizes is that it's not that easy. If you want to say that abortion is permissible or that people have free will, you have to work for it, identifying some flaw in the arguments for the opposite conclusion. In my experience, students find this sort of challenge *exciting*.

Introduction

The aim of this book is to introduce you to the topics and methods of philosophy by advancing a series of arguments for controversial philosophical conclusions. That's what I'll do in the ten chapters that follow. In this Introduction, I'll give you an overview of what I'll be arguing for in the different chapters (section 1), explain what an argument is (sections 2-3), and identify some common argumentative strategies (sections 4-7). I'll close by saying a few words about what philosophy is.

1. The Chapters

As I explained in the preface, each chapter is written in character, representing a specific perspective (not necessarily my own!) on the issue in question. This is not to say that they are all written from the *same* perspective. You should not expect the separate chapters to fit together into a coherent whole. I realize that this may cause some confusion. But you should take this as an invitation to engage with the book in the way that I intend for you to engage with it: by *questioning* the claims being made and deciding for yourself whether the reasons and arguments offered in support of those claims are convincing.

In chapter 1, Can God Allow Suffering?, I advance an argument that an all-powerful and morally perfect God would not allow all the suffering we find in the world, and therefore must not exist. I address a number of attempts to explain why God might allow suffering, for instance that it's necessary for appreciating the good things that we have, or for building valuable character traits, or for having free will. I also address the response that God has hidden reasons for allowing suffering that we cannot expect to understand.

In chapter 2, Why You Should Bet on God, I advance an argument that you should believe in God because it is in your best interest: you're putting yourself in the running for an eternity in heaven without risking losing anything of comparable value. I defend the argument against a variety of objections, for instance that it is incredibly unlikely that God exists, that *merely* believing in God isn't enough to gain entry into heaven, and that it's impossible to change one's beliefs at will.

In chapter 3, What Makes You You, I criticize a number of attempts to answer the question of personal identity: under what conditions are a person at one time and a person at another time one and the same person? I reject the suggestion that personal identity is a matter of having the same body, on the basis of an argument from conjoined twins and an argument from the possibility of two people swapping bodies. I also reject the suggestion that personal identity can be defined in terms of psychological factors on the strength of "fission" cases in which a single person's mental life is transferred into two separate bodies.

In chapter 4, Don't Fear the Reaper, I advance an argument that death cannot be bad for you, since you don't experience any painful sensations while dead, and that since death is not bad for you it would be irrational to fear it. I argue that you don't experience any painful sensations while dead by way of arguing that physical organisms cease to be conscious when they die and that you are a physical organism. I also address the suggestion that what makes death bad for you is that it deprives you of pleasant experiences you would otherwise have had.

In chapter 5, No Freedom, I advance two arguments for the conclusion that no one ever acts freely. The first turns on the idea that all of our actions are determined by something that lies outside our control, namely the strength of our desires. The second turns on the idea that our actions are all consequences of exceptionless, "deterministic" laws of nature. In response to the concern that the laws may not be deterministic, I argue that undetermined, random actions wouldn't be free either. Finally, I address attempts to show that there can be free will even in a deterministic universe.

In chapter 6, You Know Nothing, I argue for two skeptical conclusions. First, I advance an argument that we cannot know anything about the future. That's so, I argue, because all of our reasoning about the future relies on an assumption that we have no good reason to accept, namely that the future will resemble the past. Second, I advance an argument that we cannot know anything about how things presently are in the world around us, since we cannot rule out the possibility that we are currently having an incredibly vivid dream.

In chapter 7, Against Prisons and Taxes, I argue that it is wrong for governments to tax or imprison their citizens, on the grounds that these practices are not relevantly different from a vigilante locking vandals in her basement and robbing her neighbors to pay for her makeshift prison. I address a variety of putative differences, with special attention to the suggestion that we have tacitly consented to following the law and paying taxes and thereby entered into a "social contract" with the government.

In chapter 8, The Ethics of Abortion, I examine a number of arguments both for and against the immorality of abortion. I argue that the question cannot be settled by pointing to the fact that the embryo isn't self-sufficient or conscious or rational, nor by pointing to the fact that it has human DNA, that it is a potential person, or that life begins at conception. I then examine the argument that abortion is immoral because the embryo has a right to life, and I show that the argument fails since having a right to life doesn't entail having a right to use the mother's womb. Finally, I advance an alternative argument for the immorality of abortion, according to which this killing, like other killings, is wrong because it deprives its victim of a valuable future. I close the chapter by arguing that, although immoral, abortion should not be illegal.

In chapter 9, Eating Animals, I defend the view that it is immoral to eat meat that comes from so-called "factory farms." I begin by criticizing three common reasons for thinking that eating meat is morally acceptable: because people have always eaten meat, because eating meat is necessary, and because eating meat is natural. I then argue that eating factory-farmed meat is immoral, on the grounds that it would be immoral to raise and slaughter puppies in similar ways and for similar reasons.

In chapter 10, What Makes Things Right, I advance a "utilitarian" theory of morality, according to which the rightness or wrongness of an action is always entirely a matter of the extent to which it increases or decreases overall levels of happiness in the world. I defend the theory against the objection that it wrongly permits killing one person to save five. Along the way, I consider the ways in which morality is and isn't subjective and variable across cultures, and what to say about the notorious "trolley cases."

3

In appendix A, Logic, I examine one of the features that makes an argument a good argument, namely *validity*. I explain what it means for an argument to be valid, and I provide illustrations of different types of valid arguments.

In appendix B, Writing, I present a model for writing papers for philosophy courses: introduce the view or argument you plan to criticize (section 1), advance your objections (section 2), and address likely responses to your objections (section 3). I explain the importance of clear and unpretentious writing that is charitable towards opposing viewpoints; I offer advice for editing rough drafts; I identify some criteria that philosophy instructors commonly use when evaluating papers; and I explain the difference between consulting online sources and plagiarizing them.

In appendix C, Theses and Arguments, I collect together the key arguments and theses discussed in the book. Readers may find it helpful to have a printed copy of this appendix at hand, or have it open in a separate tab, while reading through the chapters.

2. The Elements of Arguments

Let's begin by having a look at what an argument is. An *argument* is a sequence of claims, consisting of premises, a conclusion, and in some cases one or more subconclusions. The *conclusion* is what the argument is ultimately trying to establish, or what's ultimately being argued *for*. The *premises* are the assumptions that, taken together, are meant to serve as reasons for accepting the conclusion. A *subconclusion* is a claim that is meant to be established by some subset of the premises but that isn't itself the ultimate conclusion of the argument.

As an illustration, consider the following argument:

Against Fearing Death
(FD1) You cease to be conscious when you die
(FD2) If you cease to be conscious when you die, then being dead isn't bad for you
(FD3) So, being dead isn't bad for you
(FD4) If being dead isn't bad for you, then you shouldn't fear death
(FD5) So, you shouldn't fear death

The argument has three premises: FD1, FD2, and FD4. FD5 is the conclusion of the argument, since that's what the argument is ultimately trying to establish. FD3 is a subconclusion. It isn't *the* conclusion, since the ultimate goal of the argument is to establish that you shouldn't fear death, not that being dead isn't bad for you (which is just a step along the way). Nor is it a premise, since it isn't merely being assumed. Rather, it's been *argued* for: it is meant to be established by FD1 and FD2.

In this book, you can always tell which claims in the labeled and indented arguments are premises, conclusions, and subconclusions. The conclusion is always the final claim in the sequence. The subconclusions are anything that begins with a "So" other than the final claim. Any claim that doesn't begin with "So" is a premise.

However, when it comes to unlabeled arguments—arguments appearing in paragraph form—all bets are off. For instance, I might say:

> Death isn't bad for you. After all, you cease to be conscious when you die, and something can't be bad for you if you're not even aware of it. And if that's right, then you shouldn't fear death, since it would be irrational to fear something that isn't bad for you.

The paragraph begins with a subconclusion, the conclusion shows up right in the middle of the paragraph, and neither of them is preceded by a 'So'. Here, you have to use some brain-power and clues from the context to figure out which bits are the basic assumptions (the premises), which bit is the conclusion, and which bits are mere subconclusions.

All of the labeled arguments in the book are constructed in such a way that the conclusion is a *logical consequence* of the premises—or, as I sometimes put it, the conclusion "follows from" the premises. You may or may not agree with FD1, and you may or may not agree with FD2. But what you can't deny is that FD1 and FD2 together entail FD3. If FD3 is false, then it must be that either FD1 or FD2 (or both) is false. You would be contradicting yourself if you accepted FD1 and FD2 but denied FD3. Because all the arguments are constructed in this way, you cannot reject the conclusion of any of the labeled arguments in the book while agreeing with all of the premises. You must find some premise to deny if you do not want to accept the conclusion. (See appendix A for more on how to tell when a conclusion is a logical consequence of some premises.)

3. Premises and Conditionals

There are no restrictions on which sorts of statements can figure as premises in an argument. A premise can be a speculative claim like FD1 or a conceptual truth like FD4. A premise can also be a statement of fact, for instance that a six-week-old embryo has a beating heart, or it can be a moral judgment, for instance that a six-week-old embryo has a right to life. Arguments can have premises that are mere matters of opinion, for instance that mushrooms are tasty. They can even have premises that are utterly and obviously false, for instance that the sky is yellow or that 1+1=3. Any claim can be a premise.

That said, an argument is only as strong as its premises. The *point* of giving an argument is to persuade people of its conclusion, and an argument built on dubious, indefensible, or demonstrably false premises is unlikely to persuade anyone.

Arguments frequently contain premises of the form 'if… then…', like FD2 and FD4. Such statements are called *conditionals*, and there are names for the different parts of a conditional. The bit that comes between the 'if' and the 'then' is the *antecedent* of the conditional, and the bit that comes after the 'then' is the *consequent* of the conditional. Using FD2 as an illustration, the antecedent is *you cease to be conscious when you die*, the consequent is *being dead is not bad for you*, and the conditional is the whole claim: *if you cease to be conscious when you die then being dead is not bad for you*.

(Strictly speaking, conditionals don't *have* to be of the form 'if… then…'. They can also be of the form '… only if…', as in 'You should fear death only if being dead is bad for you', or of the form '… if …', as in 'You shouldn't fear death if being dead isn't bad for you'.)

Conditionals affirm a link between two claims, and you can agree that some claims are linked in the way a conditional says they are, even if you don't agree with the claims themselves. To see this, consider the following argument:

The Drinking Age Argument
(DK1) Kristina is twenty years old
(DK2) If Kristina is twenty years old, then Kristina is not allowed to buy alcohol in the US
(DK3) So, Kristina is not allowed to buy alcohol in the US

You might object to this argument because you think that Kristina is 22 and that she *is* allowed to buy alcohol. Still, you should agree with the conditional premise DK2: you should agree that being 20 years old and buying alcohol are linked in the way DK2 says they are. You should agree that DK2 is true even though you disagree with *both* its antecedent *and* its consequent. To deny DK2, you'd have to think, for instance, that the legal drinking age in the US was 18. But if you agree that the legal drinking age is 21, then your quarrel is not with DK2; it's with DK1.

Likewise, you can agree with the conditional premise FD4 even if you think that being dead *is* bad for you. To disagree with FD4, you'd have to think that it's sometimes rational to fear things that *aren't* bad for you.

4. Common Argumentative Strategies
Arguments can play a variety of different roles in philosophical debates. Let's have a look as some common argumentative strategies that you'll encounter in the book.

First, an argument can be used to defend a premise from another argument. Premise FD1 of the Against Fearing Death argument—that you cease to be conscious when you die—is hardly obvious. So, someone who likes the Against Fearing Death argument might try to produce a further argument in defense of that premise, like the following:

The Brain Death Argument
(BD1) Your brain stops working when you die
(BD2) If your brain stops working when you die, then you cease to be conscious when you die
(FD1) So, you cease to be conscious when you die

Notice that in the context of the Brain Death Argument FD1 is a *conclusion*, whereas in the context of the Against Fearing Death argument it's a *premise*. Which role a given statement is playing can vary from one argument to the next. And whenever one wants to deny a claim that's a conclusion of an argument, one must identify some flaw in that argument. That means that anyone who planned to resist the Against Fearing Death argument by denying FD1 now has to reckon with this Brain Death Argument.

Second, an argument can be used to *challenge* another argument. There are two ways of doing so. One would be to produce an argument for the opposite conclusion. For instance, one might advance the following argument against FD5:

The Uncertain Fate Argument
(UF1) You don't know what will happen to you after you die
(UF2) If you don't know what will happen to you after you die, then you should fear death
(UF3) So, you should fear death

Notice that UF3 is a denial of the conclusion of the Against Fearing Death argument. Thus, if the Uncertain Fate Argument is successful, then *something* must go wrong in the Against Fearing Death argument, though it would still be an open question where exactly it goes wrong.

Another way to challenge an argument is to produce a new argument against a *premise* of the argument you wish to challenge. Here, for instance, is an argument against FD1 of the Against Fearing Death argument:

The Afterlife Argument
(AF1) You go to heaven or hell after you die
(AF2) If you go to heaven or hell after you die, then you don't cease to be conscious when you die
(AF3) So, you don't cease to be conscious when you die

Unlike the Uncertain Fate Argument, The Afterlife Argument challenges a premise of the Against Fearing Death argument, and does indicate where that argument is supposed to go wrong.

I don't mean to suggest that these are especially good arguments. Not all arguments are created equal! People who believe in the afterlife aren't likely to be convinced by the Brain Death Argument, and people who don't believe in the afterlife aren't likely to be convinced by the Afterlife Argument. As you read on, you'll discover that a lot of the work in philosophy involves trying to construct arguments that *will* be convincing even to those who aren't initially inclined to accept their conclusions.

5. Counterexamples

Arguments often contain premises which contend that things are *always* a certain way. For instance, someone who is pro-life might advance the following argument:

The Beating Heart Argument
(BH1) A six-week-old embryo has a beating heart
(BH2) It's always immoral to kill something that has a beating heart
(BH3) So, it's immoral to kill a six-week-old embryo

The second premise, BH2, says that killing things that have beating hearts is always immoral. Put another way, the fact that something has a beating heart is *sufficient* for killing it to be immoral.

Arguments also often contain premises which contend that things are *never* a certain way. For instance, someone who is pro-choice might advance the following argument in defense of abortion:

The Consciousness Argument
(CN1) A six-week-old embryo isn't conscious
(CN2) It's never wrong to kill something that isn't conscious
(CN3) So, it isn't wrong to kill a six-week-old embryo

The second premise, CN2, says that killing things that aren't conscious is never wrong. Put another way, in order for a killing to be wrong, it's *necessary* for the victim to be conscious at the time of the killing.

When a premise says that things are always a certain way or that they're never a certain way, it's making a very strong claim. And one can challenge such a claim by coming up with *counterexamples*, examples in which things aren't the way that the premise says things always are, or in which things are the way that the premise says things never are. For instance, you might challenge BH2 by pointing out that worms have hearts, and it isn't immoral to kill them. And you might challenge CN2 by pointing out that it's wrong to kill someone who's temporarily anesthetized, even though they're unconscious. In other words, worms are counterexamples to BH2 and anesthetized people are counterexamples to CN2.

These counterexamples can then be put to work in arguments of their own, for instance:

The Worm Argument
(WA1) If it's always immoral to kill something that has a beating heart, then it's immoral to kill worms
(WA2) It isn't immoral to kill worms
(WA3) So, it isn't always immoral to kill something that has a beating heart

The Temporary Anesthesia Argument
(TA1) If it's never wrong to kill something that's unconscious, then it isn't wrong to kill a temporarily anesthetized adult
(TA2) It is wrong to kill a temporarily anesthetized adult
(TA3) So, it is sometimes wrong to kill something that's unconscious

Argument by counterexample is a very common argumentative strategy, and we'll see many examples in the different chapters of the book.

It's important to realize that these arguments do not require saying that embryos are in every way analogous to worms or to temporarily anesthetized adults, or that killing an embryo is the moral equivalent of killing a worm or a temporarily anesthetized adult. The arguments from counterexamples formulated above don't say anything at all about embryos. Rather, they're giving independent reasons for rejecting the general principles (BH2 and CN2) being employed in the Beating Heart Argument and the Consciousness Argument.

One last thing. You'll sometimes encounter claims in the book that include the phrase "if and only if." For instance, later on in the book we'll address the question of what makes something bad for you. Breaking your leg is bad for you, and relaxing in a hot tub isn't bad for you. Those are just some examples of things that are and aren't bad for you, but suppose we wanted to give a more general answer to the question of what makes something bad for you. Here's a first stab at doing so, which we'll encounter in chapter 4:

(HD) Something is bad for you if and only if it's painful

HD gives the right results in the cases we just considered: it says that breaking your leg is bad for you, since that's painful, and that relaxing in a hot tub isn't bad for you, since that's not painful.

HD can be seen as two claims packed into one. First, it's saying that something is bad for you *if* it's painful. In other words, if something is painful, that's sufficient for it to be bad for you; painful things are always bad for you. Second, it's saying that something is bad for you *only if* it's painful. In other words, something's being painful is necessary for it to be bad for you; non-painful things are never bad for you.

So, HD is saying that being painful is necessary and sufficient for being bad for you. Accordingly, it can be challenged in two different ways. First, you might try to show that being painful isn't sufficient, by producing examples of things that are painful but aren't bad for you. Second, you might try to show that being painful isn't necessary, by producing examples of things that aren't painful but that are still bad for you. An example of *either* sort would count as a counterexample to HD and would be enough to show that HD is incorrect. Can you think of one?

11

6. Argument by Analogy

Another common argumentative strategy is argument by analogy. We'll encounter such arguments repeatedly in this book. Here is an example from chapter 7, which is meant to show that it's wrong for the government to tax and imprison its citizens:

VIGILANTE

Jasmine discovers that some con men have set up a fake charity and are conning some people in her neighborhood. She captures them at gunpoint, takes them to her basement, and plans to keep them there for a year as punishment. Quickly realizing how expensive it is to take care of them, Jasmine goes to her neighbors and demands $50 from each of them, at gunpoint. She explains that half the money will go towards taking care of her prisoners and that the rest will go towards a community gym to help keep troubled kids off the street. Those who do not comply are locked up in her basement with her other prisoners.

Thinking about this scenario is meant to elicit the intuition that Jasmine is doing something wrong. But what Jasmine is doing seems entirely analogous to what the government does when it taxes and imprisons its citizens. If that's right, then we should think that taxation and imprisonment by the government are wrong as well.

What really drives an argument by analogy isn't so much the presence of similarities between the two cases being compared, but rather the *absence* of a certain kind of difference. With VIGILANTE, the idea is that there's no morally relevant difference between what Jasmine does and what the government does, that is, no difference between them that could explain why the one is wrong while the other is okay. The argument can be framed as follows:

Against Taxation and Imprisonment

(TX1) If there is no morally relevant difference between two actions A and B, and A is wrong, then B is wrong

(TX2) It is wrong for Jasmine to extort and kidnap her neighbors

(TX3) There is no morally relevant difference between Jasmine extorting and kidnapping her neighbors and the government taxing and imprisoning its citizens

(TX4) So, it is wrong for the government to tax and imprison its citizens

The idea behind TX1 is that, if one action is immoral and another isn't, there has got to be *some* explanation for that, some difference between them that accounts for the moral difference. To put it another way, it would be *arbitrary* to hold that one action is right and another is wrong unless one can point to some difference between the actions to explain why they differ morally. TX2 is meant to strike you as obvious after reading the VIGILANTE case. And the idea behind TX3 is that there are no differences between what Jasmine does and what the government does that could make for a moral difference.

The challenge for those who don't want to accept the conclusion of the argument, TX4, is to identify some morally relevant difference, and defenders of the argument must then either argue that the indicated differences aren't morally relevant, or else modify the story so that the indicated differences are no longer present.

7. Thought Experiments

The VIGILANTE case is what's called a *thought experiment*. In a thought experiment, a fictional scenario is presented—some more realistic than others—and then readers are asked for their intuitive reactions to the case. We'll see many more examples throughout the book.

Thought experiments can be put to work in defending or challenging an argument in a number of different ways. We just saw how they can play a role in argument by analogy. They also often play a supporting role in arguments by counterexample. In chapter 5, for instance, we'll encounter the following argument for the idea that we sometimes do things of our own free will:

The Argument for Freedom
(FR1) Sometimes you perform an action after deciding to
       perform that action
(FR2) If one performs an action after deciding to perform it,
       then one performs that action freely
(FR3) So some of your actions are performed freely

The second premise, FR2, says that so long as someone does what they decided to do, that by itself suffices for it to count as a free action. Later on, in chapter 5, I try to cast doubt on this premise with the following thought experiment:

HYPNOTIC DECISION
Tia is on the run from the law and knows the cops are hot on her trail. She is also a master hypnotist. As she passes Colton on the street, she hypnotizes him and plants an irresistible post-hypnotic suggestion: whenever he hears someone shout *Freeze!* he will grow very angry with the person, decide to tackle them, and then tackle them. Just then, Kabir the cop arrives on the scene, sees Tia, and shouts *Freeze!* As a result of the hypnotic suggestion, Colton gets angry at Kabir, consciously decides to tackle him, and then tackles him.

Colton did do exactly what he decided to do, namely tackle Kabir. But when we think about this case, it seems to us, intuitively, that Colton did not *freely* tackle Kabir; this isn't something he did of his own free will. So HYPNOTIC DECISION looks to be a counterexample to FR2, which is reason to reject FR2 and think that the Argument for Freedom fails.

When it comes to thought experiments, the details matter, and the cases we'll use in this book are carefully constructed with an eye to the work they're intended to do. HYPNOTIC DECISION, for example, is carefully constructed to serve as a counterexample to FR2, and in order for it do so it's crucial that Colton tackles Kabir as a result of Tia's hypnotic suggestion.

At times, you might naturally wonder what happens if we vary the details of a case. For instance, you may wonder: what if Colton snaps out of Tia's hypnotic control at the last second, but still decides to tackle Kabir? Well, that's a different case. Let's call it HYPNOTIC BREAK. HYPNOTIC BREAK isn't a counterexample to FR2, since intuitively Colton *is* acting freely in this new case. But that doesn't change the fact that the original case, HYPNOTIC DECISION, *is* a counterexample to FR2. And so long as there's *one* counterexample to FR2, that's enough to show that it's false.

At times, you may find that the description of the thought experiment leaves out some important details, and you may be tempted to fill in the details in ways that make them more interesting. For instance, in chapter 10 you'll be asked whether Corrine did the right thing in the following case:

TROLLEY LEVER

A runaway trolley with no driver is hurtling down the tracks towards five pledges from a local fraternity. Corrine is an onlooker, standing beside the tracks. Next to her is a lever which can divert the trolley onto a side track. She could do nothing, and let the pledges die. But if she pulls the lever and diverts the trolley, it will kill the pledge master, who is asleep on the side track. Corrine decides to pull the lever, killing the pledge master and saving the pledges. She then unties the pledges, and they all go on to lead long, happy lives.

You might be tempted to ask, "what if the pledge master is Corrine's brother?" or "what if he has the cure for cancer?", turning the case into an exciting moral dilemma. And you may be frustrated and confused when your instructor insists upon a boring interpretation of the scenario, where the people on the tracks are all equally unremarkable people whom Corrine has never met. Understand the reason for this. To do their intended work—to serve as clear counterexamples, for example, or as illuminating analogies—thought experiments often *need* to be boring. The more discussion-worthy they are, and the less obvious it is what we ought to say about them, the less able they are to serve their argumentative purpose.

After reading a few of the chapters, you might begin to get suspicious of all this reliance on thought experiments. In particular, you might wonder how purely fictional, unrealistic cases could be relevant to the questions we're trying to answer. If a zoologist says that zebras have black and white stripes, it would be no objection to say that you can imagine a zebra with purple and orange stripes. Why, then, when a philosopher affirms FR2, is it supposed to be an objection that we can imagine a case (like HYPNOTIC DECISION) in which someone isn't acting freely despite doing what they decided to do?

Here's the difference. When a zoologist says that zebras have black and white stripes, she only means to be claiming that, normally, zebras are like this. Neither my imaginary purple and orange zebra, nor even actual albino zebras, are any objection to a claim like that. The philosopher, by contrast, means to be making a stronger claim. She isn't just saying that, normally, people are acting freely when they do what they decide to do. Rather, she is saying that doing what one decides to do is what *makes* an action free, or that that's just *what it is* for an action to be free. And a claim like that is true only if it is absolutely exceptionless, both in actual cases and in merely possible cases.

To see this, suppose I wanted to know what makes someone a bachelor. And suppose you reply: what makes someone a bachelor is that they are an unmarried man under eighty feet tall. That's obviously a terrible account of what it is to be a bachelor. But why? All actual unmarried men under eighty feet tall are bachelors, and all actual bachelors are unmarried men under eighty feet tall. So, there are no actual counterexamples. Still, it's clear that being under eighty feet tall isn't *required* for being a bachelor; height has nothing to do with what makes someone a bachelor. The in-principle possibility of a ninety-foot-tall bachelor is enough to show that this is an unsatisfactory account of bachelorhood. Likewise, the mere possibility of doing what one decided to do without acting freely is enough to falsify a philosophical thesis about what makes actions free.

Why, though, do philosophers make such strong claims—especially if that opens them up to refutation by imaginary cases? The answer (at least in part) is that philosophers want the claims they defend to be *definitive*: they are trying to definitively settle the philosophical questions at issue. For instance, think about the Beating Heart Argument from section 5, according to which the fact that something has a beating heart makes it wrong to kill that thing. Suppose, though, that this were put forward merely as a useful, but not exceptionless, rule of thumb: that it's typically wrong to kill things with beating hearts. In that case, even if I could convince you beyond any doubt that it's typically wrong to kill things with heartbeats and that six-week-old embryos have a heartbeat, that would not yet settle the question of whether it's wrong to kill them. After all, maybe embryos are one of the exceptions to the rule, one of the atypical cases where it's okay to kill something that has a beating heart.

Philosophical principles would have no "bite" unless these are meant to be absolutely exceptionless. So, it is for good reason that philosophers are searching for absolutely exceptionless principles. But this is precisely what opens them up to refutation by thought experiments; one possible exception would be enough to show that the principle is false.

8. What is Philosophy?
As you can see, this book is going to cover a wide array of topics, including whether you should fear death, whether abortion is immoral, whether God exists, and whether we ever do things of our own free will. So, what do these topics all have in common, that makes them all *philosophical* topics?

It's hard to say. Philosophy is sometimes characterized as the study of life's most fundamental questions. That does capture some of the topics we'll cover, like the true nature of morality and the existence of God. But the question of whether we should have to pay taxes hardly seems like one of "life's most fundamental questions." And other questions that we'd naturally describe as being among life's most fundamental questions, like whether we're alone in the universe or how many generations the human race has left, aren't exactly philosophical. So, this won't do as a definition of philosophy, since there are counterexamples: being one of life's fundamental questions is neither necessary nor sufficient for being a philosophical topic.

Honestly, I'm not sure how to give necessary and sufficient conditions for a topic's being philosophical. Philosophers have lots of interesting things to say about biology, physics, sociology, and psychology, and it can be difficult (and probably unnecessary) to say where the science ends and the philosophy begins.

Perhaps a more promising approach to saying what makes some inquiries and not others philosophical would be to look, not for what unites the topics studied, but rather at *how* they are studied. Philosophers try to answer questions and make sense of things just by thinking carefully about them, attempting to resolve controversial questions and assess challenges to commonsense assumptions using rational argumentation alone. (Though this doesn't mean that philosophical argumentation *can't* be informed by scientific discoveries and other worldly observations.) As Delia Graff Fara put it,

> "By doing philosophy we can discover eternal and mind-independent truths about the nature of the world by investigating our own conceptions of it, and by subjecting our most commonly or firmly held beliefs to what would otherwise be perversely strict scrutiny."

After finishing this book, I think you'll have a pretty good sense of what Professor Fara means by "perversely strict scrutiny." And I don't think she meant this as a criticism. Done well, philosophy can sometimes feel like thinking in slow motion. Even when an idea or argument seems clear enough, philosophers like to break it down into its component parts; separate out all of the different premises and assess the plausibility of each individually; identify challenges to the premises and break *them* down into their component parts; see whether arguments can be strengthened by small changes to how they are formulated; and so on. Some things can only be figured out by paying the closest attention to the smallest details.

CHAPTER 1
Can God Allow Suffering?

Views and arguments advanced in this chapter are not necessarily endorsed by the author of the textbook, nor are they original to the author, nor are they meant to be consistent with arguments advanced in other chapters. Different chapters represent different philosophical perspectives.

1. Introduction

Imagine that you are a tourist, visiting the distant country of Nornia. You see some wondrous sights: stunning skyscrapers, beautiful parks, galleries full of masterpieces. You also see extreme poverty and injustice, poorly designed highways, grossly corrupt government agencies, innocent people serving life sentences in prison, and many other terrible things. After seeing all this, suppose you are told that Nornia is run by a wise and compassionate ruler with limitless power, who keeps careful track of everything that goes on in his country. You wouldn't believe it for a second.

Now look around the world. You'll see some wondrous sights: stunning mountain peaks, beautiful prairies, staggering artistic and athletic talent. But you will also find poverty and injustice, a planet afflicted by extreme weather and natural disasters, bodies afflicted by all manner of diseases and injuries, and many other terrible things. Now, suppose you are told that this is the work of a maximally powerful, all-knowing, and morally perfect deity. You shouldn't believe it for a second.

There is no God, and we can know that there is no God simply by reflecting on the impressive variety of evils and sufferings we encounter in the world. Or so I shall argue. After laying out the argument (sections 2-3), I address three attempts to explain why God would allow the sorts of suffering we endure: because suffering enables us to appreciate the good things we have (section 4), because suffering is necessary for acquiring valuable character traits (section 5), or because God must permit suffering in order for us to have free will (section 6). I then consider the response that God has his reasons for allowing suffering, but that those reasons are kept hidden from us (section 7).

2. The Argument from Suffering

My argument that God doesn't exist is easy to state and highly intuitive:

The Argument from Suffering
(AS1) There is suffering in the world
(AS2) If there is suffering in the world, then God does not exist
(AS3) So, God does not exist

By 'suffering', here, I mean any pain or discomfort that living beings experience—large or small, physical or emotional.

The first premise, AS1, is entirely uncontroversial. Even if your life has gone pretty smoothly, you could still fill a book with the pains and sufferings—large and small, physical and emotional—that you have experienced. And that's just *one* life.

To see the idea behind the second premise, AS2, note that God is supposed to be a perfect being. In particular, he is supposed to be omnipotent (that is, maximally powerful), omniscient (all-knowing), and omnibenevolent (morally perfect). Let's call a being with all three of these qualities an *omnibeing*.

Now, consider how an omnibeing would react to any suffering that might crop up in the world. Since she is omnipotent, there are no bounds whatsoever on what she is able to do. So, if she noticed some suffering occurring, it would be entirely within her power to stop it if she wanted to. Since she is omnibenevolent, she would want the best for everyone. So, if she noticed some suffering occurring, she would want to prevent. It follows that she would prevent any suffering that she notices. But since she is omniscient, she knows absolutely everything; nothing that happens in the universe escapes her notice, and that includes all of our suffering. So, being an omnibeing, she would notice our suffering, she would prevent it if she were able to, and she *would* be able to. So she would prevent it.

Put another way, the only way for there to be suffering if there were an omnibeing around is if the omnibeing wanted there to be suffering, couldn't prevent it, or didn't realize it was happening—none of which seems possible given the definition of 'omnibeing'. So, *if* there is suffering, it must be because there is no omnibeing around to stop it. That is the idea behind AS2.

What I expect most believers to say in response to the Argument from Suffering is that God allows suffering because there is some greater good that can be obtained only by those who

20

have endured certain kinds of suffering. But in trying to identify what that greater good *is*, it's important to use your imagination. For instance, you might be tempted to say that God allows people to die—despite all the suffering involved both for the victim and for those left behind—because if no one ever died, then the world would quickly become overpopulated, and there would be even *more* suffering due to our limited resources. But it's not as if an *omnibeing* would have to choose between death and overpopulation. With limitless power, an omnibeing could easily have created a world for us with unlimited space and unlimited resources, a world that would never be in danger of becoming overpopulated.

Accordingly, an adequate account of why an omnibeing would allow suffering must identify some greater good that would be *absolutely unobtainable* in the absence of suffering. I'll examine three different proposals—that suffering is necessary for appreciating the good things we have, that suffering is necessary for building valuable character traits, and that allowing suffering is necessary for free will—and I will argue that none provides an adequate response to the argument.

3. Refining the Argument
Before getting into these specific proposals, however, let me make two concessions.

First, my defense of AS2 presupposed that God is an omnibeing. But some people who believe in God may be willing to admit that God is not an omnibeing. You might say that God isn't omnipotent: he knows all about your toothache, and he wishes he could do something about it, but he just isn't able to. Or you might say that God isn't omniscient: he would end the toothache if he knew about it, but he genuinely has no idea that you have a toothache right now. Or you might say that God isn't omnibenevolent: he knows about your toothache and could stop it if he wanted to, but he really couldn't care less about you and your toothache.

Admittedly, the Argument from Suffering will be ineffective against someone who believes in an imperfect God like this. At the same time, I suspect that a great many believers will be unwilling to admit that God is imperfect, which means the argument is still a problem for them. For the sake of clarity, I will reformulate the argument below, so that it explicitly targets only those who believe in an omnibeing.

Second, it's hard to deny that there are *some* good things that truly are unobtainable without at least some suffering. For instance, there's something valuable about the sense of accomplishment you feel after overcoming some obstacle. That sense of accomplishment would arguably be impossible unless there was some struggle, and there can be no struggle without suffering. In cases like these, we can see why an omnibeing might allow certain sorts of suffering.

I want to concede that even an omnibeing could and would sometimes allow people to suffer. This suggests (once again) that AS2 is overstated: even if there is an omnibeing, that doesn't necessarily mean that we shouldn't expect to see *any* suffering. That said, all I really need in order to show that there is no omnibeing is that *some* of the suffering we endure serves no conceivable purpose.

Let us then replace the Argument from Suffering with the following Argument from *Pointless* Suffering:

The Argument from Pointless Suffering
(PS1) There is pointless suffering in the world
(PS2) If there is pointless suffering in the world, then there is no omnibeing
(PS3) So, there is no omnibeing

PS1 is admittedly more controversial than AS1, since PS1 says not just that there is suffering but that some of that suffering serves no purpose. Still, PS1 is highly plausible. For instance, even if some amount of struggle can add a good deal of value to a life, it is hard to imagine what purpose could possibly be served by the insurmountable and demoralizing challenges that so many people face, simply trying to find food and shelter. The idea behind PS2 is that an omnibeing can allow suffering *only if* there is some good reason for allowing it. But, by definition (of 'pointless'), there is no good reason for allowing pointless suffering. So, if there is pointless suffering, it must be because there is no omnibeing around to prevent it.

22

Notice that in the original Argument from Suffering the first premise (AS1) was entirely uncontroversial and the second premise (AS2) was the one to challenge. Now the reverse is true. The second premise (PS2) is now uncontroversial—an omnibeing can't allow suffering *for no reason*—and it's the first premise that I expect believers to challenge.

Notice also that I've rephrased the argument so that the conclusion is that there is no omnibeing, leaving open that God exists but that he is weak, ignorant, or morally imperfect. For simplicity, I'll continue to use the term 'God' below, but that should be understood as shorthand for 'a God who is an omnibeing'.

4. The Appreciated Goods Defense

Let's turn now to the suggestion that the point of suffering—the reason that God allows suffering—is to enable us to *appreciate* good things. After all, the idea goes, if we were in a constant state of pleasure and contentedness, that would just strike us as a normal, unremarkable baseline. And it's better for us to appreciate the good things we have than merely to have the good things without in any way appreciating them. So, since God wants the best for us, he would want us to appreciate the good things we have, and he would therefore permit all of the suffering necessary for attaining that appreciation. Call this *The Appreciated Goods Defense*.

On closer inspection, however, it just isn't plausible that no one could appreciate the good things they have without suffering. Again, you have to use your imagination. Suppose God wanted to create beings who experience nothing but pleasure but also wanted them to be able to appreciate that pleasure. He could do so by arranging for their pleasure to keep increasing at every moment. That way, they can always look back on their earlier states of pleasure and feel appreciative that they are now so much better off. With this sort of possibility in mind, it is hard to see why there would have to be *any* suffering in order for people to appreciate good things.

One might object that there's a limit to the amount of pleasure that human beings are capable of experiencing, perhaps connected to the quantity of serotonin our brains are capable of generating. But even if we *actually* have these psychological or neurological limitations, surely there's nothing to prevent an omnibeing like God from removing those limitations if he wanted to.

Moreover, even if it were true that *some* suffering is needed in order to appreciate good things, there surely is no need for *all* the suffering we endure. A chilly, overcast day now and then can help one appreciate warm sunny days, but there is surely no need for endless, soul-crushing Midwest winters. A bit of back pain now and then can help one appreciate a healthy body, but there is surely no need for debilitating, chronic back pain and other such maladies. If God's intention in allowing suffering is just to make it possible for us to appreciate good things, then so much of the suffering we endure still seems entirely *pointless*; it serves no purpose. Accordingly, even if the Appreciated Goods Defense were able to account for some of our suffering, it gives us no reason to reject PS1 of the Argument from Pointless Suffering.

5. The Character Building Defense

Let's try out a different objection to PS1. Here the idea is that there are certain highly valuable character traits that can be developed only in the face of adversity, failure, temptation, and other sources of suffering. Take courage, for instance. If there were no suffering, then nothing could be dangerous, and in a world without danger no one has the opportunity to become courageous. Similar points can be made for empathy, loyalty, perseverance, self-control, forgiveness, and trustworthiness. In short, building character requires a potential for suffering. And, the idea goes, these character traits are sufficiently valuable to justify allowing all of the suffering necessary for cultivating them. Call this *The Character Building Defense*.

What's nice about the Character Building Defense is that it's able to account for such a wide range of bad things, including some extreme forms of suffering. Without profound acts of betrayal, there could be no profound acts of forgiveness. Without the horrors and hardships of war, no one could reach the levels of courage and selflessness that soldiers attain. Since these sufferings are necessary in order to have the best kind of world—one with courageous and forgiving people—we can see why God would allow them. Furthermore, the Character Building Defense seems equipped to handle the alleged examples of pointless suffering mentioned in the previous section: by enduring chronic back pain and brutal winters, one learns perseverance and endurance.

Ultimately, though, the Character Building Defense fails to account for all apparent cases of pointless suffering. For while some soldiers find that the horrors of war strengthen their moral character, others are pushed to their breaking point and return home with debilitating PTSD. Or take someone who is tortured mercilessly and then killed before the experience can help them build character. The Character Building Defense seems unable to explain the purpose of the suffering in such cases.

Proponents of the Character Building Defense may insist that at least the *friends and family* of the traumatized soldier or torture victim get to develop valuable character traits as a result of their own grief and sadness. But it seems deeply at odds with the omnibenevolence of an omnibeing to allow someone to suffer terribly for *someone else's* benefit. In any event, we can sidestep this response by focusing on cases where the people suffering have no friends or family whose moral character is enhanced by the suffering, or cases where the tragedy pushes the friends and family of the victim beyond their breaking points. All it takes is one such case to show that PS1 is true.

6. The Free Will Defense
Let's consider one last version of the appeal to greater goods, which turns on the idea that allowing suffering is a necessary condition for *free will*. Here, the idea is that a world in which people have the ability to do things of their own free will has to be a world in which suffering is permitted. God could force us to always do the right thing, but being forced to perform an action is incompatible with doing it freely. And free will is plausibly a very valuable thing: a world in which people are able to freely choose to do the right thing is superior to a world in which everyone is an automaton, performing only kind and wholesome actions but never because they freely choose to do so. This, the idea goes, is why God decided to give us free will, even though that requires allowing some suffering. Call this *The Free Will Defense*.

The Free Will Defense is well equipped to handle many of the alleged cases of pointless suffering considered above. No one can ever *freely* make good choices unless God steps back and permits people to sometimes make bad choices, including warring and torturing. So, the Free Will Defense does look more promising than the Character Building Defense. Even so, we shouldn't be satisfied by the Free Will Defense either.

First, the Free Will Defense only accounts for suffering caused by other humans. It goes no way towards explaining how an omnibeing could allow suffering caused by disease or scarcity or natural disasters or animals. There could still be free will in a world without earthquakes, droughts, dog bites, back pain, and cold winters.

Second, it's not even clear that the Free Will Defense can account for all the *human*-caused suffering in the world. Certainly, there could still be plenty of valuable freedom in the world if, now and then, God discreetly intervened to prevent a genocide or a terrorist attack or a third-degree burn. By analogy, a loving parent can allow their toddler the freedom to make their own mistakes, but would still intervene if the kid is about to step off a cliff or fire up a chainsaw.

Third, it's not even clear that there *could* be free will in a world in which God exists. After all, since God is supposed to be omniscient, he already knows everything you're going to do before you do it. To see how this causes trouble for the Free Will Defense, let's focus on just one example of an alleged free action. You see a fifty-dollar bill fall out of someone's pocket. You grab it, and you're pretty confident that no one would notice if you kept it for yourself. But you decide to do the right thing and return it.

If God is an omnibeing, he must already know what you were going to do with the money. Otherwise, there'd be something he doesn't know, and he wouldn't be omniscient. But in order for God to know in advance that you'd return the money, it had to already have been settled that you were going to return the money. God couldn't have known what you were going to do if it was still an open possibility that you were going to keep the money. But if it was already settled in advance that you were going to return it, then it's not true that you could have kept it.

And if you couldn't have behaved any differently from how you actually behaved, then what you did wasn't really up to you. It wasn't a free action after all!

Of course, there's nothing special about the particular example I chose. The same problem arises for *any* allegedly free action. What that shows is that the Free Will Defense is a complete nonstarter. Suffering can't be explained as something God permits in order to make room for free will, since any world with an omnibeing—who already knows in advance everything that's going to happen—is already a world without free will.

7. The Hidden Reasons Defense
We have been unable to identify any greater good that could justify an omnibeing in allowing all the different kinds of suffering people endure. But perhaps theists will insist that we shouldn't *expect* to be able to identify that greater good. We inhabit a universe unfathomably larger than the small corner of it we've observed, they'll say, with human concerns that are infinitesimally smaller than those of a deity with an entire universe to look after. Accordingly, the idea goes, it would be absurd to think that we'd be able to discern or even comprehend God's reasons for allowing this or that kind of suffering. In other words, what God sees as good may be different from what we are able to recognize as good, given our limited perspective.

I find this response deeply unsatisfying. True, it's *possible* that every last bit of suffering we find in the world is an indispensable part of some magnificent plan that we can't even begin to imagine. We can't be one hundred percent certain that it isn't. I admit that. But just because we can't be certain that the suffering isn't all part of some secret plan, that doesn't mean we should believe that *there is* some such secret plan. Rather, the reasonable thing to believe, even though we can't be absolutely certain that it's true, is that the suffering people endure is often exactly what it seems to be: pointless suffering.

To help see this, let's return to the example from the beginning of the chapter. You are touring the country of Nornia and observe a mix of wondrous and terrible sights. Having seen all the poverty, injustice, pollution, road hazards, corruption, inefficiency, cruelty, etc., you laugh off the suggestion that the ruler of the country has limitless power, perfect compassion, and complete knowledge of everything that goes on in his country.

Now suppose that your tour guide reminds you that Nornia is a *very* large country, most of which you haven't seen. She reminds you that the ruler is privy to classified information and has concerns and projects that you know nothing about. She reminds you that, for all you know, the poverty, pollution, and so on are all a necessary part of his master plan for creating the best of all possible countries. Reminded of all this, should you now believe what your tour guide says, that the country has a ruler with unchecked power, knowledge, and compassion? Of course not. You should continue laughing.

This suggests the following argument against appealing to hidden reasons:

The Argument for Disbelief
(DB1) You should not believe that all the suffering in Nornia is necessary for some unknown greater good that its ruler has in mind
(DB2) If you should not believe that all the suffering in Nornia is necessary for some unknown greater good that its ruler has in mind, then you should not believe that all the suffering in the actual world is necessary for some unknown greater good that an omnibeing has in mind
(DB3) So, you should not believe that all the suffering in the actual world is necessary for some unknown greater good that an omnibeing has in mind

DB1 is plausible. You can of course admit that it's *possible* that the ruler knowingly allows all the corruption and cruelty and poverty as an ingenious means to some benevolent end, just as you can admit that it's *possible* that the earth is flat and that all the evidence to the contrary is part of some elaborate hoax. You can admit that there's a remote possibility that flat-earthers are right, but that obviously doesn't mean you should believe that they *are* right. Likewise, even if you admit that there's a remote possibility that the tour guide is telling the truth, that doesn't mean you should believe what she says.

As for DB2, the idea is that we ought to give similar answers to the question of whether the ruler has good, hidden reasons for all the suffering in Nornia and the question of whether God has good, hidden reasons for all the suffering in the universe. There is no difference between what we know about Nornia and what we know about the universe that could make it reasonable to believe in hidden reasons in the one case but not the other.

Think of it this way. Try to explain *why* all the apparent defects of Nornia justify disbelief in what the tour guide said. I bet that any explanation you give would serve equally well as an explanation for why the apparent defects of the universe justify disbelief in an omnibeing with hidden reasons. Or try to explain why it's reasonable to believe that the apparent defects of the universe are part of an omnibeing's secret plans. I bet that your explanation would serve equally well as an explanation for why it's reasonable to believe your tour guide, that the apparent defects of Nornia are all part of its benevolent ruler's ingenious plans.

Just to be clear, I'm not saying that the cases are exactly analogous. God is supposed to be an omnibeing, whereas the ruler is a mere mortal. My point is just that the *reasons* for dismissing the suggestion that the ruler must have some secret plan for all the suffering are equally reasons for dismissing the suggestion that some omnibeing has a secret plan for all the seemingly pointless suffering we see around us.

8. Conclusion

I have argued that the sorts of suffering we find in the world cannot be reconciled with the existence of an omnipotent, omniscient, and omnibenevolent God. We have examined a number of attempts to reconcile them, which involved pointing to one or another purpose that might be served by the suffering, but we found that these attempts cannot make sense of the full range of suffering that people endure. Finally, I argued that it is not reasonable to believe that the suffering is all in service of some unknown greater good that, due to our limited perspective, we have been unable to identify.

Reflection Questions

1. Is it possible to escape the objections raised in sections 4, 5, and 6 by *combining* the Appreciated Goods Defense, the Character Building Defense, and/or the Free Will Defense?

2. God is widely believed to reward people with eternal happiness in heaven. Could this be turned into a response to the Argument from Pointless Suffering? Why or why not?

3. One might respond to the Argument from Pointless Suffering by insisting that God *has to* allow bad things to happen to certain people, because they deserve it and—being perfectly just—God has to give people what they deserve. Is this an adequate response? How about bad things that happen to good people? Or animals?

4. Can the Hidden Reasons Defense be defended against the objections raised in section 7? In particular, what do you think about the claim that "there is no difference between what we know about Nornia and what we know about the universe that could make it reasonable to believe in hidden reasons in the one case but not the other"?

Sources

The Argument from Suffering (often called "The Problem of Evil") traces back at least as far as the ancient Greek philosopher Epicurus. A classic discussion can be found in David Hume's *Dialogues on Natural Religion* (parts X and XI). See J. L. Mackie's "The Problem of Evil" for a more recent defense of the argument. A version of the Character Building Defense can be found in John Hick's *Evil and the God of Love*, and a version of the Free Will Defense can be found in Alvin Plantinga's *God, Freedom, and Evil*. The problem of divine foreknowledge is advanced in Nelson Pike's "Divine Omniscience and Involuntary Action." Here are some additional resources:

- Marilyn McCord Adams on Evil (philosophybites.com)
- Marilyn McCord Adams: Horrendous Evils and the Goodness of God

- Louise Antony: For the Love of Reason
- Ted Chiang: Hell is the Absence of God
- Beverley Clack: Feminism and the Problem of Evil
- Laura Ekstrom: Suffering as Religious Experience
- Bryan Frances: *Gratuitous Suffering and the Problem of Evil*
- Sally Haslanger: The Problem of Evil (wi-phi.com)
- Mohammed Ali Mobini: Earth's Epistemic Fruits for Harmony with God: An Islamic Theodicy
- Franklin Perkins: The Problem of Evil in Classical Chinese Philosophy
- John Perry: *Dialogue on Good, Evil, and the Existence of God*
- William Rowe: The Problem of Evil and Some Varieties of Atheism
- Eleanore Stump: The Problem of Evil

CHAPTER 2

Why You Should Bet on God

Views and arguments advanced in this chapter are not necessarily endorsed by the author of the textbook, nor are they original to the author, nor are they meant to be consistent with arguments advanced in other chapters. Different chapters represent different philosophical perspectives.

1. Introduction

I am going to try to convince you that you should believe in God. But I'm going to do it in a different way than you might expect. I'm not going to give you an argument that God exists. I won't try to convince you, for instance, that there has to be a God in order to serve as a first cause of the universe (what's sometimes called "the cosmological argument"), or that we have to posit an intelligent designer in order to explain all the forms of life and other complex systems we find in the world (what's sometimes called "the design argument"). Rather, I'm going to argue that you should believe in God because it's in your best interest to do so.

Here's an analogy, to give you a feel for the sort of argument I'm going to give. Imagine that you're at a casino and you're deciding whether to bet your $10 on red or on black at the roulette table. But it's not a regular game of roulette. The way it works is that if you bet on red and win you walk away with $20, and if you bet on black and win you walk away with a million dollars. You don't know whether it will land on red or black. And yet you know exactly what to do: bet on black. Why? Because you stand to gain so much if it comes up black and stand to lose so little if it doesn't. Similarly, you have no way of knowing whether or not God exists. Still, you should believe in God. Why? Because you stand to gain so much by believing in God and stand to lose so little. Indeed, only by betting on God do you stand a chance of winning the ultimate jackpot: eternal afterlife in heaven.

In sections 2-3, I'll give a more careful and rigorous presentation of this argument. Then, in section 4, I'll address some potential objections to the argument, for instance that it's extremely unlikely that God exists or that belief alone is not enough to guarantee entrance into heaven. Finally, in section 5, I address the worry that it's impossible to make yourself believe in God through sheer force of will, no matter how convincing you find the argument.

2. Practical Reasoning in an Uncertain World

In this section, I will take a big step back from the question of whether you should believe in God, and look more generally at how we make rational decisions about what to do in situations of uncertainty. After looking informally at the sorts of factors we take into account when making such decisions (section 2.1), I lay out a more rigorous way of thinking about rational decision-making, in terms of "expected utility calculations" (section 2.2).

2.1 Costs, Benefits, and Likelihoods

Let's shift from the roulette-wheel example to something more realistic. You're at a party and you spot your crush across the room. You're trying to decide whether to go talk to him (or her, but let's go with "him") and confess your feelings. The night is young and you've still got your wits about you, and you want to make a smart decision. What sorts of things do you need to take into account?

First, you need to think about your options and the possible outcomes. Your options are telling him that you're crushing on him or saying nothing. (What about flirting without blurting? We'll get to that; let's keep it simple for now.) And the possible outcomes are that he likes you back or that he's not into you.

Second, you need to consider the costs or benefits of each eventuality, that is, each way things might unfold. If you confess your feelings to him and he's into you too, you get to date your crush and you've won big. If you confess your feelings and he's not into you, you'll probably have some mix of embarrassment that he turned you down but maybe also pride that you had the courage to take a risk. If you don't confess your feelings but actually he is into you, you've missed a huge opportunity. And finally, if you don't confess your feelings and he isn't into you, you've dodged a bullet.

Third, you need to think about *how* good or bad the different costs and benefits are, relatively speaking. What's worse: the embarrassment of getting turned down or missing out on the opportunity? Probably the missed opportunity is worse. Then again, if you've got a new crush every weekend, you're incredibly sensitive about being rejected, and you have plenty of other interested suitors, maybe the embarrassment is worse. It's going to vary from person to person, and what you ought to do will depend in part on how good or bad the different eventualities are for you.

Finally, you need to take into account the *likelihood* of each of the possible outcomes. Obviously, it makes a difference whether the chances that he likes you back are very good or very slim. If there's virtually no chance that he's into you, then it's not worth the risk of embarrassment. If it's more or less certain he *is* into you—if he's been sending you heart emojis all day and keeps winking at you from across the room—then it's not worth worrying about the insignificant chance of embarrassment.

Somehow or other, you weigh all these different factors and make a smart decision about what to do. In fact, you do this sort of thing all the time: deciding whether to lug around an umbrella all day when you're not entirely sure if it's actually going to rain; deciding whether to turn back when you remember you forgot to lock the front door and you're already five minutes away; deciding whether to go see a certain movie when you're not sure if it's going to be any good; and so on. And you do it without the help of a calculator and without having to write out a pro/con list. But there is a more rigorous way of thinking about such decisions, and it will prove to be a useful tool for thinking about them—and, in particular, for thinking about whether to believe in God.

2.2 Expected Utility Calculations

We can model the decision about talking to your crush by using a certain sort of "decision matrix." The matrix will represent the options available to you (as rows), the possible outcomes (as columns), and the likelihood of each outcome. And it will use numerical values to represent your rankings of the different eventualities (that is, option/outcome pairs).

To make this a bit more concrete, let's suppose that in the crush case the eventualities are ranked from best to worst as follows (where a higher number represents a better eventuality):

4: Confess your feelings and he's into you
3: Don't confess your feelings and he's not into you
2: Confess your feelings and he's not into you
1: Don't confess your feelings and he is into you

And let's suppose you think there's about a 75% chance that he likes you back. Then the matrix would look like this:

Matrix 2.2.1

	He's into you 75%	He's not into you 25%	Expected Utility
Confess your feelings	4	2	3.5
Don't confess your feelings	1	3	1.5

I've snuck in an extra column for *expected utility*. This is the column we'll use to crunch the numbers, calculating what the smart choice is for you, given your preferences and the likelihoods of the different outcomes. Before I explain where these numbers (3.5 and 1.5) are coming from, let me say something about how to think about these expected utilities.

In effect, the expected utility of an option tells you how well you'd do, on average, if you kept choosing that option over and over again. Imagine that you're in an infinite loop. You choose an option, and then time rewinds and you choose that same option again and again—and 75% of the time he's into you and 25% of the time he isn't. The fact that confessing has an expected utility of 3.5 and not confessing has an expected utility of 1.5 tells you that on average you'd do a little over twice as well by repeatedly choosing to confess your feelings than by repeatedly choosing not to (since 3.5 is a little over twice as much as 1.5). And what *that* tells you is that the smart thing to do is to confess your feelings.

But where exactly are these numbers coming from? To calculate the expected utility of a given option, you multiply the value of each possible outcome of the action by the likelihood of that outcome, and add together the results. Or put in terms of the rows and columns of Matrix 2.2.1: to calculate the expected utility of the top row, you multiply the value in the top row of the first column by the likelihood associated with that column, multiply the value in the top row of the second column by the likelihood associated with *that* column, and add the results together. So, we get:

Confess your feelings = (.75 x 4) + (.25 x 2) = 3.5
Don't confess your feelings = (.75 x 1) + (.25 x 3) = 1.5

The specific numbers themselves don't have much significance. It's not as if you get 3.5 "units" of happiness by confessing your feelings, or anything like that. What matters is the relative differences between the expected utilities for different actions: the expected utility of telling your crush how you feel (3.5) is over two times as big as the expected utility of not telling him (1.5).

This gives us an argument for confessing your feelings:

The Argument for Confessing Feelings
(CF1) One should always choose the option with the greatest expected utility
(CF2) Confessing your feelings has a greater expected utility than not confessing
(CF3) So, you should confess your feelings

Premise CF1 is justified by the fact that, in ordinary cases like this, these decision matrices and expected utility calculations do such a good job of reflecting the rational thing to do in situations with uncertain outcomes. And premise CF2 is reasonable to the extent that we have filled in the matrix correctly, ranking the eventualities and assigning probabilities to the outcomes in a sensible way.

There are two more things I want to point out about this model of decision-making before I (finally) bring us back around to the question of believing in God. First, by using 1 for the worst eventuality and 2 for the second-worst, that means that the worst-case scenario is only twice as bad as the second-worst. But sometimes the worst-case scenario is *way* worse than any other eventuality. Suppose for instance that you do very badly with humiliation, and that for you a rejection is about 100 times worse than a missed opportunity. We can represent that by using a weighted ranking, giving the eventuality of confessing and getting rejected a value that's 100 times lower than the others:

Matrix 2.2.2

	He's into you 75%	He's not into you 25%	Expected Utility
Confess your feelings	100	1	75.25
Don't confess your feelings	98	99	98.25

Now, the expected utility of confessing is less than the expected utility of not confessing, and so the calculations tell us that you ought to hold your tongue—which is the right result if you really do take rejection *that* hard.

Second, I've obviously oversimplified the example by pretending that there are only two possible outcomes. Really, there are at least three different ways things could turn out: he's into you, he's not into you and he rejects you in front of everyone, or he's not into you but he discreetly and privately rejects you. We can get more fine-grained about your options too: confess your feelings, flirt a little, or completely avoid him. Our model for decision-making can easily accommodate this simply by adding extra rows and columns to our decision matrix:

Matrix 2.2.3

	He's into you --%	He privately rejects you --%	He publicly rejects you --%	Expected Utility
Confess your feelings				
Flirt with him				
Avoid him				

All you have to do is figure out a weighted ranking of the different eventualities, estimate the likelihood of each of the different outcomes, crunch the numbers, see which option has the greatest expected utility, and—*voilà!*—now you know what you should do.

3. The Expected Utility of Believing in God

This same sort of reasoning from expected utilities can be put to work in an argument that you ought to believe in God:

The Argument for Betting on God
(BG1) One should always choose the option with the greatest expected utility
(BG2) Believing in God has a greater expected utility than not believing in God
(BG3) So you should believe in God

Premise BG1—which is exactly the same as CF1 above—is justified by the fact that it is so sensible to rely on expected utility calculations in the sorts of ordinary examples considered above. If you thought the option with the greatest expected utility is the smart choice in all other cases, it would be weird and unprincipled to think it *isn't* the smart choice in just this one case of deciding whether to believe in God.

To justify BG2, we have to construct the decision matrix. And that's going to look something like this:

Matrix 3.0

	God exists 50%	God doesn't exist 50%	Expected Utility
Believe in God	∞	2	∞
Don't believe in God	1	3	2

Since we don't know one way or the other whether God exists, I've assigned a probability of 50% to God existing and 50% to God not existing. I've given the lowest score (1) to the eventuality of not believing he exists when he in fact does, since that presumably means you're going to hell. The second lowest (2) goes to the eventuality in which you do believe in God but he doesn't exist, since in that case you've been wasting your time going to church, praying, and living an upstanding religious life. Slightly better (3) is being an atheist and being right about it, since then you get all the benefits of an atheist lifestyle (for instance skipping church) without any punishment at the end. Top score goes to the eventuality in which you believe in God and God does turn out to exist, and this gets a value of infinity (∞) rather than 4, since the amount of pleasure and fulfillment you receive in an eternal afterlife in heaven is infinitely greater than what you get in any of the other eventualities.

We then calculate the expected utilities in just the way we did in section 2.2. The calculation in the second row is straightforward arithmetic: $(.5 \times 1) + (.5 \times 3) = 2$. As for the first row, the expected utility of believing in God $= (.5 \times \infty) + (.5 \times 2)$. What's $(.5 \times \infty)$? In other words, how many things do you have left if you take infinitely many things and then remove half of them? Answer: ∞. (Take all the numbers and remove all the odd ones. You're still left with infinitely many even numbers.) Now add 1 (that is, $.5 \times 2$), and you still get ∞. After all, if you add one thing to infinitely many things, you still have infinitely many.

Finally, we need to compare the expected utilities of the two options. Which is greater: ∞ or 2? Obviously ∞. So, the expected utility of believing in God is greater than the expected utility of not believing in God. And that's the argument for BG2.

4. Challenging the Decision Matrix

The argument for BG2 relies on a number of assumptions I made about how to fill in the decision matrix (Matrix 3.0): the range of possible options and outcomes, the likelihood of the different outcomes, and the relative goodness or badness of the different eventualities. Thus, one way of challenging BG2 is to insist that, in one way or another, I've constructed or filled in the decision matrix incorrectly. In this section, we'll consider a variety of different challenges of this kind.

But before turning to that, let me quickly dispense with a different line of objection, which some readers may find tempting. People sometimes object that the argument rests on some sort of conceptual error *simply* because it invokes the notion of infinity. They say that it doesn't make any sense to talk about infinity, or to compare infinite quantities with finite quantities, or something to that effect. But surely that's not right. Suppose you're choosing between two offers for free movie tickets. One gives you free entry to twenty movies. The other gives you limitless free entry: no matter how many times you go for free, you can always go for free again. Do you throw your hands up and say "How could I possibly decide?? It makes no sense to talk about limitless tickets!" No, you accept the second offer. And it makes perfect sense why you would: because the second offer, despite involving an infinite quantity, gives you more of a good thing than the first.

4.1 Wrong Probabilities

One might complain that I've grossly overestimated the probability that God exists, by assuming that it's a 50/50 chance that he exists. Perhaps you think it's extremely unlikely that God exists. Surely, though, you'll admit that it's at least *possible* that God exists. If you die and are ushered into God's presence, you'll be surprised, but not in the way that you'd be surprised if you were ushered into the presence of something you think is genuinely impossible, like a round square.

So, let's say it's a 1% chance that God exists (though the response I'm about to give will work even if you think it's a .00000001% chance). In that case, we need to update a couple of the boxes in the original decision matrix:

Matrix 4.1

	God exists 1%	God doesn't exist 99%	Expected Utility
Believe in God	∞	2	∞
Don't believe in God	1	3	2.98

Changing the probabilities required us to recalculate the expected utility of not believing in God. It shot up almost a whole point! But the expected utility of believing in God doesn't change at all. Why is that? Let's crunch the numbers. What's $.01 \times \infty$? In other words, what do you get when you have infinitely many things, and you take away 99 out of every 100 of them? Answer: ∞. Now add 1.98 (= $.99 \times 2$) to that, and you get ∞. The expected utility of believing in God doesn't change and is still greater than the expected utility of not believing in God. Thus, so long as there is *some* chance that God exists, however small it may be, the argument for BG2 still works.

4.2 Belief Isn't Enough

You might object that believing in God isn't all by itself enough to get into heaven. You might think that you also have to meet some further conditions, for instance that you led a good, moral life and followed God's commandments. I might ask you how you know that, but then again you might ask me how I know that badly-behaved believers go to heaven. (Touché.) So, let me just grant the point for the sake of argument: only well-behaved believers get into heaven. What that means is that the original decision matrix is inadequate, since it runs together two importantly different options: being a well-behaved believer and being a badly-behaved believer.

The fix is to expand our matrix so that each of these options has a row of its own.

Matrix 4.2

	God exists 50%	God doesn't exist 50%	Expected Utility
Believe in God and be good	∞	3	∞
Believe in God and be bad	2	4	3
Don't believe in God	1	5	3

The new row introduces new eventualities, which means we have to redo the rankings. I gave a 1 to the eventuality in which you don't believe in God and yet he does exist, and a 2 to being a badly-behaved believer, on the assumption that God will punish you for that too but will be a little more lenient since you at least believed in him. I've scored being an atheist in a Godless world (5) higher than being a badly-behaved believer in a Godless world (4), and I've ranked both ahead of the life of a well-behaved believer in a Godless world (3). Finally, the eventuality in which you're a well-behaved believer and God does exist gets ∞, since this is what will get you into heaven, and that's infinitely better than any of the other eventualities.

So, what does this all mean? What it means is that—assuming that you have to be a well-behaved believer to get into heaven—being a well-behaved believer has greater expected utility than either being a badly-behaved believer or not believing in God at all. It's still true, then, that the option with the greatest expected utility requires you to believe in God. So, we have not yet found a reason to reject BG2.

It may be that I haven't gotten all the scores exactly right. Maybe I'm wrong, and God gives exactly the same punishment to both nonbelievers and badly-behaved believers. In that case, you could make it a tie and change the 2 in the first column to a 1. Or maybe I'm wrong that the life of an atheist in a Godless world is more rewarding than the life of a believer in a Godless world. Fine, we can lower the score for "God does not exist" in the bottom row. It doesn't matter. The argument still goes through, since the expected utility of being a nonbeliever or a badly-behaved believer still comes out to be some finite number, whereas the expected utility of being a well-behaved believer will be infinite.

4.3 Heaven May Be Finite

The reasoning behind BG2 takes for granted that God rewards believers with something that's infinitely valuable, for instance an eternal afterlife filled with an infinite amount of pleasure. But I haven't offered any evidence or argument for that. For all we know, God rewards believers only with some finite amount of pleasure—maybe ten years in heaven. And one might object that this imperils the argument: if we can't be sure that believers stand to receive something of infinite value, then there's no guarantee that the expected utility of believing will be infinite, and thus no guarantee that it will come out greater than the expected utility of disbelief.

But that's the wrong way to look at it. Let's just acknowledge that we can't be sure whether God is generous and rewards believers with something of infinite value or whether God is stingy and rewards believers with something of finite value. That means that Matrix 3.0 is oversimplified, and that we need to expand the decision matrix to include three columns: one for the possibility of a generous God who offers infinite rewards, one for the possibility of a stingy God who offers only finite rewards, and one for the possibility that there's no God.

42

Matrix 4.3

	Generous God exists 25%	Stingy God exists 25%	No God 50%	Expected Utility
Believe in God	∞	1,000,000	2	∞
Don't believe	1	1	3	2

I've valued the eventuality in which you're a believer and God turns out to be stingy at 1,000,000 to reflect the idea that it's still many orders of magnitude better than the next best eventuality, in which you're a nonbeliever and God doesn't exist. Again, though, the exact values don't really matter, nor do the exact probabilities. All that matters is the ∞ on the top left, since that's going to ensure an infinite expected utility for believing in God. So, even if we can't be sure that God rewards anyone with an infinitely valuable afterlife, we still get the result that we ought to believe in God.

4.4 Many Gods to Choose From

Let's consider one last objection to BG2. You might worry that getting into heaven isn't simply a matter of believing in God. You've got to believe in the *right* God. If the true God is the Christian God and you believe in Zeus (or vice versa), you're going to hell. And the decision matrix can't tell you which God is the right God to believe in.

I think that's right. But it's no objection to BG2. Once again, what this shows us is that Matrix 3.0 was oversimplified. We need additional rows reflecting the different gods we can choose to believe in, and additional columns reflecting the different gods that might turn out to exist. So, let's rectify that:

Matrix 4.4

	Christian God exists 25%	Zeus exists 25%	No God 50%	Expected Utility
Believe in Christian God	∞	1	3	∞
Believe in Zeus	1	∞	3	∞
Don't believe	2	2	4	3

Once again, I've done my best to assign probabilities and score the non-infinite eventualities, and once again it doesn't much matter whether I've gotten the rankings of the non-infinite eventualities exactly right. And we can, if you like, expand the matrix to include more and more possible gods, but that shouldn't affect the argument either.

What we get now is a tie for greatest expected utility. This means that the objection under consideration is right as far as it goes: we aren't told whether to believe in the Christian God or whether to believe in Zeus. But notice that believing in *some God or other* continues to have greater expected utility than not believing at all. So, the decision matrix still tells us that the greatest expected utility is attained by (and only by) believing that there is a God. So, there is no successful challenge to BG2 here.

5. Is Belief Voluntary?
I have examined a number of ways one might challenge my decision matrix, and in each case we've seen that the matrix can be modified without jeopardizing the Argument for Betting on God. I can't claim to have surveyed *every* possible way of challenging the matrix, but we must stop somewhere, and I think that our success in handling the objections discussed above gives us reason to be optimistic that the argument can withstand further challenges to the matrix. But let us move on to an importantly different style of objection.

Suppose you find my reasoning entirely convincing. You decide that—despite all of your many reasons for doubting that God exists—it's time to start believing in God. You say to yourself: okay, *believe!!* Nothing changes, you still don't believe in God. You clench your fists, furrow your brow, and try again: *believe!!!* Nothing changes. You still don't believe in God.

What you've just discovered is that belief is not voluntary. You don't get to decide what to believe in the way that you get to decide what to imagine or what to say. And that's potentially a problem for the argument, for two reasons. First, it threatens to make the argument ineffective: if the point of the argument is to get you to believe in God, then it can't get the job done. Second, it threatens to undermine BG1. BG1 says you should always go with the option that has the greatest expected utility. But saying that you *should* do something implies that you *can* do it. Accordingly, if you can't choose the option with the greatest expected utility—in this case, believing in God—then it's not true that you should choose it, in which case BG1 is false.

The problem with this objection is that furrowing your brow and trying really hard to believe something different isn't the *only* possible way of changing your beliefs. By way of comparison, alcoholics can't change whether they have intense cravings for alcohol merely by willing themselves to stop craving it. But what they can do is check themselves into rehab, steer clear of their old haunts and friends who may rekindle their drinking habit, join an AA program, and so on.

Similarly, changing your beliefs isn't something you can do directly, on the spot, by merely willing it to be so. But if you want to change your mind about God, you can do so indirectly. Go to church, read some scripture and other religious literature, surround yourself with the smartest and most inspirational believers you can find, steer clear of clever atheists, and so on. It does sometimes happen that nonbelievers find the Lord. Figure out how they did it, and follow their lead. Changing what you believe may be difficult, but that doesn't mean it can't be done.

We can now revise the original Argument for Betting on God to reflect the fact that changing your beliefs takes some effort.

The Argument for Trying to Believe
(TB1) One should always choose the option with the greatest expected utility
(TB2) Making an effort to believe in God has greater expected utility than not making an effort to believe in God
(TB3) So, one should make an effort to believe in God

We have already seen the argument for TB1 (a.k.a. BG1), and I'll leave it as an exercise for the reader to construct the decision matrix for TB2. Suffice it to say that making that effort puts you in the running for an afterlife of infinite happiness, and it is the *only* way to be in the running for an afterlife of infinite happiness. So, even though you cannot be entirely sure in advance whether your efforts to believe will succeed, the expected utility calculations are bound to deliver the result that making the effort has infinite expected utility and that not making the effort merely has a finite expected utility.

6. Conclusion

I have argued that, faced with a decision between believing in God and not believing in God, the smart choice—the one with the greatest expected utility—is to believe. I defended the idea that one should prefer the option with the greatest utility by showing that it yields the right result in everyday cases (like whether to confess your feelings to your crush). I then showed how the possibility of attaining something of infinite value ensures that belief in God has the greatest expected utility. And we saw that the argument is resilient: it still works even if we suppose it's very unlikely that God exists, even if we grant that God only rewards well-behaved believers or may only reward believers with a finitely valuable afterlife, and even once we acknowledge that entry into heaven requires betting on the right God.

Reflection Questions

1. For all we know, disbelief in God or belief in the wrong God will result in being sent to hell and enduring something *infinitely* bad. How might the introduction of negative infinite values into the decision matrices affect the Argument for Betting on God?

2. For all we know, God rewards only those who believe in him for wholesome reasons, and won't reward those who believe in him purely out of a self-interested desire to get into heaven. Can this be used to underwrite an effective argument against BG2?

3. For all we know, there is no God but rather an evil deity who *punishes* believers and *rewards* atheists. Can this observation be used to challenge BG2?

4. In section 4.4, we considered the objection that there are many Gods to choose from. Can that objection be strengthened by arguing that there are *infinitely* many Gods to choose from?

5. Suppose that you are given the opportunity to enter a lottery to win an unlimited amount of money. The thing is, there's only a one-in-a-million chance of winning, and the cost of a lottery ticket is every last dollar you have in your bank account and all of your worldly possessions. Would it be rational to enter the lottery? If not, is that a problem for BG1?

Sources
Versions of the Argument for Betting on God, also known as "Pascal's Wager", can be found in Abū Hāmid Muhammad Al-Ghāzāli's *The Alchemy of Happiness* and Blaise Pascal's *Pensées*. Here are some additional resources:

- Mohammad Shahid Alam: Pragmatic Arguments for Belief in the Qur'ān
- Nick Bostrom: Pascal's Mugging
- Lara Buchak: When is Faith Rational?
- Tom Donaldson: The Will to Believe (wi-phi.com)
- Daniel Garber: *What Happens After Pascal's Wager? Living Faith and Rational Belief*
- Alan Hájek: Pascal's Ultimate Gamble
- Elizabeth Jackson and Andrew Rogers: Salvaging Pascal's Wager
- William G. Lycan and George N. Schlesinger: You Bet Your Life: Pascal's Wager Defended
- Susanna Rinard: Pascal's Wager (wi-phi.com)
- Michael Rota: *Taking Pascal's Wager: Faith, Evidence and the Abundant Life*

CHAPTER 3

What Makes You You

Views and arguments advanced in this chapter are not necessarily endorsed by the author of the textbook, nor are they original to the author, nor are they meant to be consistent with arguments advanced in other chapters. Different chapters represent different philosophical perspectives.

1. Introduction

In this chapter, I address the question of what makes you the person that you are. In particular, is it your physical aspects or, rather, your psychological aspects that make you the person that you are? I will argue that neither facts about your body, nor facts about your mental life, nor any combination of the two can answer the question of what makes you you, and that this remains an open and challenging—and perhaps unanswerable—question.

In section 2, I clarify the question that I mean to be asking, and I explain what a satisfactory answer would have to look like. In section 3, I present a variety of potential answers to the question, some more promising than others. In section 4, I closely examine an account according to which it is having the body that you do that makes you the person that you are, and I advance two arguments against that account: an argument from conjoined twins and an argument from the possibility of body swaps. In section 5, I show that psychological accounts of personal identity face problems of their own, involving abrupt changes to one's mental life and cases in which one person's psychology is replicated in two different bodies. In section 6, I address the suggestion that your soul is what makes you the person that you are. Finally, in section 7, I consider and reject the idea that the bodily and psychological accounts can somehow be *combined* to yield a satisfactory answer to the question of personal identity.

2. Clarifying the Question of Personal Identity

Let me begin by clarifying what it is that I am asking when I ask what makes you the person that you are. What I am looking for is a theory that will tell us who's who at different times. Suppose we're looking at a picture from a five-year-old's birthday party.

You point at one of the kids in the picture and tell me that it's you. My question is: what makes that one you? There's some resemblance, but on the whole you're physically very different from that little kid. You're also psychologically very different from the kid, who (judging from the picture) thinks crayons are the most incredibly interesting thing on the face of the earth. You probably have more in common with the adults in the picture than with that kid. So, what is it about that kid that makes her (or him) you?

More precisely, an answer to the question I'm asking will provide a way to fill in the blank in the following sentence:

A at time t is the same person as B at time t* if and only if ___

In other words, when we're looking at or thinking about a person at one time, under what conditions should we say that this person and a person who exists at another time are one and the same person? In section 3, we'll consider a number of possible ways of filling in the blank, which will further clarify what it is I'm after. But before we get there, let me head off two potential confusions.

First, the word 'same' is ambiguous, and if you don't keep an eye on the ambiguity you are liable to get very confused. To see the ambiguity, let's think about a couple examples. Suppose that Jade buys a Honda Civic, and then Tanner goes out and buys one too. Is it true that Jade and Tanner drive the same car? There are multiple ways of taking that question. I could be asking whether the car that Jade drives and the car that Tanner drives are the same color and make and model, in which case the answer is yes. Alternatively, I could be asking whether there's a single car that Jade and Tanner share and take turns driving, in which case the answer is no. Another example: Suppose you saw some shirt at the GAP, and you liked it so much that you bought two of them. You wore one yesterday, and the other today. I see you today and say: 'isn't that the same shirt you were wearing yesterday?' In one sense, yes: they're exactly the same design. In another sense, no: you have changed your shirt since I last saw you.

To put a label on it, I'll say that two things, A and B, are *qualitatively* the same when A and B are very similar to one another. I call this sort of sameness 'qualitative' because the idea is that A and B have a lot of the same qualities (color, shape, design, etc.). A and B are *numerically* the same when A *is* B. I call this sort of sameness 'numerical' because it's saying that A is the same as B in the way that numbers are sometimes said to be the same number. '$2^2 = 4$' isn't just saying that the number 2^2 and the number 4 are incredibly similar; it's saying that '2^2' and '4' are two names for one and the same number. The cars Jade and Tanner drive are qualitatively the same, but not numerically the same. The shirts you bought are qualitatively the same, but not numerically the same.

The same ambiguity arises when talking about whether one person is the same as another. When we're looking at identical twins and say "you two are exactly the same," what we mean is that they're qualitatively the same, not that they're one and the same person. But when we say that Marilyn Monroe is the same person as Norma Jean Baker, or that Muhammad Ali is the same person as Cassius Clay, we *are* saying that they are one and the same person; they're numerically the same.

The question I am asking in this chapter is a question about numerical sameness, not qualitative sameness. So, whenever I say "A is the same person as B," that means that A and B are numerically the same. When I do want to talk about qualitative sameness, I'll describe things as "very similar" or "exactly alike" or "indistinguishable."

Here's how failing to track the distinction between numerical and qualitative sameness is going to get you in trouble. You might think: "Wait a minute! I'm not the same as that kid in the photo. We're different in all sorts of ways. In fact, I'm changing every second, so I'm not even the same from one *moment* to the next. I'm not even the same person as the person who started this sentence!" The problem with this line of reasoning is that it runs together qualitative and numerical sameness. Yes, the way you are now isn't the way the kid in the picture was, and isn't even exactly the way you were a moment ago. You are not (qualitatively) exactly the same as you were before. But it's *you* that was one way then and is a different way now. There's numerical sameness despite the lack of perfect qualitative sameness from one time to the next.

The second thing I want to clarify is that I'm looking for an answer that's more than just a mere *rule of thumb* for telling who's who. If that were all that I wanted, then answering the question of personal identity would be easy: A at t is the same person as B at t* when A's fingerprints and B's fingerprints are exactly alike. But since I want something absolutely exceptionless, this Fingerprints Account won't do. To see why that is, consider the following case:

LEAVE NO TRACE

After robbing the mansion, Bekah realizes that she may have left some fingerprints behind. To help ensure that the police can't prove that she was the burglar, she soaks her fingers in acid, completely searing off her fingerprints. The police track her down and, just as she hoped, they are unable to prove that she committed the burglary.

It's the same person, Bekah, both before and after the fingerprints are seared off. But the Fingerprints Account gets it wrong: it says that the fingerprintless person with the seared fingertips is not the same person as the person who burglarized the mansion.

Moreover, because I'm after an account of what *makes* people at different times the same person, it's not enough for an account of personal identity just to get the right result in all *actually existing* cases. Here's an analogy to help see why that is. Suppose I wanted to know what makes someone a bachelor, and you say: Person A is a bachelor if and only if A is an unmarried man who is under eighty feet tall. That would not be an accurate account of what a bachelor is. And yet it's true that every actually existing unmarried man under eighty feet tall is a bachelor, and every actually existing bachelor is an unmarried man under eighty feet tall. So, what's wrong with your account? The problem is that being under eighty feet tall clearly isn't *required* for being a bachelor; height has nothing to do with what makes someone a bachelor. The in-principle, hypothetical possibility of a ninety-foot-tall bachelor is enough to show that this is not a satisfactory account of bachelorhood.

Likewise, even if no one has *actually* ever successfully burned off their fingerprints, the mere possibility of a case like LEAVE NO

TRACE is enough to show that the Fingerprints Account is no good. That's because what we're looking for is an account of personal identity which has no exceptions even in principle. The same is true for other accounts which we will consider below: even merely hypothetical examples can serve as counterexamples to those accounts. (For more on how merely hypothetical cases can still be relevant when assessing philosophical claims, see section 7 of the Introduction to this textbook.)

3. Some Promising and Unpromising Answers

3.1 Physical Answers
We have already seen one possible answer to the question of personal identity, the Fingerprints Account:

> #### The Fingerprints Account
> A at time t is the same person as B at time t* if and only if A and B have indistinguishable fingerprints

And we have already seen one good reason to reject the Fingerprints Account: someone with fingerprints can be the same person as someone (at a later time) with no fingerprints at all. That shows that having indistinguishable fingerprints isn't necessary for being the same person, which makes this a counterexample to the Fingerprints Account.

Another reason for rejecting the Fingerprints Account is that, at least in principle, two different people could have indistinguishable fingerprints—by sheer coincidence or, more gruesomely, because one person grafts another person's fingerprints onto their own fingertips for some nefarious purpose. That shows that having indistinguishable fingerprints isn't even sufficient for being the same person.

What if we focused on DNA instead of fingerprints?

> #### The DNA Account
> A at t is the same person as B at t* if and only if A and B have indistinguishable DNA

The DNA Account does get around some of the problems that arise for the Fingerprints Account. Bekah's DNA doesn't change at all before and after searing off her fingerprints, so the DNA Account delivers the correct verdict that pre-searing Bekah is the same person as post-searing Bekah.

But the DNA Account has problems of its own. Identical twins have indistinguishable DNA, but this doesn't make them the same person. (Any identical twins reading this are now nodding along vigorously. In unison.) So, having indistinguishable DNA isn't sufficient for being the same person. Nor is it necessary. There could, at least in principle, be a medication or performance-enhancing drug you can take that would make some small change to the DNA in every cell of your body. But it would still be *you* after you took the medication, even though your DNA would be somewhat different.

Still, these answers may be on the right track by focusing on some physical aspect of you. Perhaps, instead of focusing on some small part of your body, like your fingerprints or DNA, we would do better to focus on the body as a whole:

The Same Body Account
A at t is the same person as B at t* if and only if A has the same body as B

'Body' is sometimes used to mean just the torso, not including the head and limbs. That's not how I'm using it. When I say 'body', I mean the *whole* body, including the head and all the other body parts. And when I say that A and B have the same body, I mean that they have *numerically* the same body. Bodies obviously can change over time—indeed, your body was composed of almost entirely different cells seven years ago—but that's not to deny that the body you have now is numerically the same as the body you had seven years ago. It's not as if you used to have some other arms and legs and now you have entirely new ones!

The Same Body Account is going to avoid all the other problems we mentioned, since you have the same body even if your fingerprints or DNA change, and separate people with indistinguishable DNA or fingerprints don't have numerically the same body. It's true that your body won't be exactly the same *qualitatively* after your DNA changes, but what's required by the Same Body Account is numerical sameness, not qualitative sameness. The body *is* numerically the same after the DNA changes.

3.2 Psychological Answers

We'll see in the next section that the Same Body Account has problems of its own. But before getting there, we should also consider a different sort of account, one framed in terms of people's psychological features as opposed to their physical features. By 'psychological features', I mean to include any features of a person's mental life: their memories, their personality, their likes and dislikes, their beliefs, their emotions, and even their current perceptual experiences (how things look, sound, smell, and feel to them).

So how should we formulate an answer to the question of personal identity in terms of psychological features? As a first stab, we might consider the following account:

The Psychological Matching Account
A at t is the same person as B at t* if and only if A's psychological features are exactly the same as B's psychological features

But this Psychological Matching Account is obviously far too demanding. Every second that passes, you are forming new memories. For instance, you now have a memory of reading the previous sentence, but you had no memory of it a minute ago (since you hadn't yet read it a minute ago). You also have slightly different visual experiences now than you had a minute ago, since you're now looking at different words on the page. Accordingly, the Psychological Matching Account is going to say that the person sitting in your chair a minute ago and the person sitting in your chair now are two different people. But that's absurd! It was *you* that was sitting in the chair a minute ago.

To get around this problem, we might try to loosen things up, so that the account doesn't require people at different times to have *all* the same psychological features, but only that they have *mostly* the same psychological features.

The Psychological Overlap Account

A at t is the same person as B at t* if and only if A's psychological features are mostly the same as B's psychological features

The Psychological Overlap Account avoids the previous problem. You may not have *all* the same psychological features you had a moment ago, but you do have mostly the same psychological features (beliefs, memories, personality, etc.).

But the Psychological Overlap Account gets the wrong results when we reach back further into the past. You and that kid in the photo are the same person. That's you in the photo. But your current psychological features and the kid's psychological features when the photo was taken *aren't* mostly the same. The kid's personality and likes and dislikes are completely different from yours. You have very few of the same memories, since you've forgotten much of what the kid remembers at that time, and the kid at that time hasn't yet formed most of the memories you now have. So, the Psychological Overlap Account is going to yield the wrong verdict: it says that the kid in that photo isn't you.

What we need is something even *more* flexible, something that can accommodate the fact that, over a long period of time, a person can gradually undergo a massive change in their psychological features. But we don't need to abandon the notion of psychological overlap entirely. Rather, we can use it to define the new, more flexible notion that we need.

To see the way forward, notice that, even though there isn't much overlap between your current psychological features and your psychological features at the time the photo was taken, there is a great deal of psychological overlap between you now and you a year ago. And there's a great deal of overlap between you a year ago and you *two* years ago. And between you two years ago and you three years ago. And so on, going all the way back, year-by-year, to you at age six and the five-year-old in the photo. We can picture this as a long chain—running from you now to that five-year-old—where each link represents a "snapshot" of your psychological features at some time, and each link in the chain has mostly the same psychological features as the links immediately before and after it. And the chain needn't be year-by-year; it can be day-by-day or even moment-by-moment.

When there is such a moment-by-moment chain of overlap linking a person at one time to a person at a later time, I'll say that the person at the earlier time is a *psychological ancestor* of the person at the later time, and that the person at the later time is a *psychological descendant* of the ancestor. This gives us:

The Psychological Descendant Account
A at t is the same person as B at t* if and only if A is either a psychological ancestor or a psychological descendant of B

This gives us the right results in all of the cases we have been considering. You are a psychological descendant of the kid in the photo, despite sharing very few psychological features with that kid; Bekah pre-searing is a psychological ancestor of Bekah post-searing; and so on.

We now have two different, initially promising answers to the question of personal identity: the Same Body Account and the Psychological Descendant Account. It may seem like an embarrassment of riches. They both look great, so how are we supposed to choose between them? As we are about to see, however, both answers are deeply flawed, and we should not accept either of them.

4. Against the Same Body Account
According to the Same Body Account, having the same body is sufficient for being the same person. In other words, it is impossible for two different people to have the same body. The account also entails that having the same body is necessary for being the same person. In other words, it is impossible for the same person to have different bodies at different times. In what follows, I develop two arguments against the Same Body Account: an argument from the actual case of conjoined twins, which shows that having the same body isn't sufficient for personal identity, and an argument from the hypothetical case of swapping bodies, which shows that it isn't necessary either.

Some may be tempted by a different kind of argument against the Same Body Account, an argument from dissociative identity disorder, a.k.a. "multiple personality disorder." Isn't this a case of more than one person having numerically the same body? Perhaps. But it's not entirely clear to me that that's right way to understand the disorder. Another way of thinking about such cases is that there is a single person with a highly disunified mind, a single person who feels and behaves dramatically differently at different times. In any event, I would want to know a lot more about what it is like "from the inside" for those suffering from this disorder before I am prepared to say that such cases literally involve multiple people inhabiting a single body. For that reason, I will set such cases aside and focus on cases that much more clearly pose a problem for the Same Body Account.

4.1 Conjoined Twins

The first objection I'll raise against the Same Body Account involves conjoined twins. Abby and Brittany Hensel are dicephalic parapagus twins, which means there are two heads on a single torso. They are alive and well and are currently about 30 years old. It's easy to see why conjoined twins pose a problem for the Same Body Account. We would naturally describe Abby and Brittany as two people sharing a single body. But the Same Body Account rules that out, since it says that sharing a body is sufficient for being the same person.

We can make the argument more explicit as follows:

The Conjoined Twins Argument
(CT1) If the Same Body Account is true, then *either* Abby and
        Brittany have different bodies or Abby and Brittany
        are the same person
(CT2) Abby and Brittany have the same body
(CT3) Abby and Brittany are not the same person
(CT4) So, the Same Body Account is false

CT1 is merely reporting an implication of the Same Body Account. If *same body* entails *same person*, then that either means that Abby and Brittany are two different people in two different bodies or the same person in the same body. Those are the only two ways it can be according to the Same Body Account. CT2 seems true: what we have here is a single, two-headed human organism. (Indeed, there's a documentary on Abby and Brittany titled, "The Twins Who Share a Body.") And CT3 seems right as well: Abby and Brittany are different people. Among other things, they have different preferences in food and they excelled in different subjects in school. I bet you didn't even flinch when I said 'they' as opposed to 'she'.

I can imagine someone denying CT2 and insisting that, actually, there are *two* bodies there, split down the middle. First, there's Abby's body, consisting of the right arm, right leg, right lung, the right head (the one that says "my name is Abby") and so on. Second, there's Brittany's body, consisting of the left arm, left leg, left lung, left head, and so on.

I find that completely implausible. For one thing, it would entail that Brittany has no liver (since the liver is on the right side). But surely the correct thing to say is that they *share* a liver, which requires that the body parts on right side are also parts of Brittany's body. Additionally, upon encountering a two-headed snake or a two-headed turtle, you would never say that there were two bodies there. There's just a single animal with two heads; it's a single, two-headed body. Since that's what we'd say about nonhuman animals, we should say the same about human animals. To be clear, I am not saying there is only one *person* there; indeed, I say just the opposite in premise CT3. Rather, the claim is that there's a single, two-headed body, which is both Abby's body and Brittany's body.

What about denying CT3 and saying that Abby and Brittany are the same person? That's certainly a strange thing to say. But maybe what I said above about multiple personalities can be applied to the case of conjoined twins as well: there is just one person there, but her mind is disunified and as a result she behaves in peculiar ways, for instance saying (out of one of her mouths) "I'm good at math" and then saying (out of her other mouth) "I'm terrible at math."

But this seems entirely implausible when applied to Abby and Brittany. To see this, consider the following case:

CONJOINED DRAMA
Abby is dating Arie. Brittany is secretly in love with Arie and has always been jealous of their relationship. One night, while

Abby is sleeping, Brittany confesses her feelings to Arie, and Arie kisses her. Later, when Abby finds out, she strangles Brittany.

Here's how we'd naturally describe what happened: Arie cheated on Abby and then Abby killed Brittany. Yet someone who denies CT3, and therefore says that Abby and Brittany are the same person, would have to say that this description is completely inaccurate. Arie didn't cheat on anyone, since the person he was kissing that night was his own girlfriend Abby (a.k.a. Brittany). Furthermore, the CT3-denier would have to say that Abby didn't kill anyone, because no one was killed: she strangled herself and she survived (albeit with one fewer functioning head). But surely that's not the right way to describe what happened.

4.2 *Body Swaps*

Here's a second argument against the Same Body Account. This one involves an imaginary case, one which may seem familiar if you've read John Locke's chapter on Identity and Diversity in his *Essay Concerning Human Understanding*. Or if you've seen *Freaky Friday* on the Disney Channel. The case is far-flung, but the fact that nothing like it has ever actually happened and perhaps never will (though I wouldn't be so sure) is neither here nor there. For, as I explained in section 2, an account of personal identity cannot admit of any exceptions, even in principle.

Now for the case:

BODY SWAP

Rachel is a neurotechnologist. Using an fMRI, a supercomputer, and advanced laser technology, she has devised a way to get a complete neuron-for-neuron scan of one person's brain, and then rewire a second person's brain to be an exact duplicate of it. She recruits a pair of volunteers to have their wiring "swapped" for a day: a man named Raúl and a woman named June. Rachel's team performs the procedure on Tuesday night, and the volunteers are awakened on Wednesday. Both stare down at their bodies in disbelief. The person with the male body says 'my name is June' and can recount all of June's memories but knows nothing at all about Raúl's past. The person with the female body says 'my name is Raúl' and can tell you all about Raúl's past but nothing about June's.

I think we can all agree on how we ought to describe what is happening on Wednesday. June is now walking around with a male body, and Raúl is walking around with a female body. The alternative would be to say that June is still the person with the female body but that she is completely delusional: she mistakenly thinks her name is 'Raúl', and recalls doing all sorts of things that she has never actually done (but all of which Raúl has done). But that's not what happened. No one is delusional. Rather, two sane people have switched bodies.

If that's right, then the Same Body Account is incorrect. Before stating the argument against the Same Body Account, it will be helpful to introduce some terminology to help us talk and think clearly about the case. I'll use "Male$_T$" to refer to the person with the male body on Tuesday; "Female$_T$" for the person with the female body on Tuesday; "Male$_W$" for the person with the male body on Wednesday, and "Female$_W$" for the person with the female body on Wednesday. Here, then, is the argument:

The Body Swap Argument
(BS1) Male$_T$ and Male$_W$ have the same body
(BS2) If Male$_T$ and Male$_W$ have the same body, then: if the Same Body Account is true, then Male$_T$ and Male$_W$ are the same person
(BS3) Male$_T$ and Male$_W$ are not the same person
(BS4) So, the Same Body Account is false

BS1 is true: it's the same male body that enters the lab on Tuesday and leaves the lab on Wednesday. No doubt, rewiring its brain to resemble a woman's brain is going to affect the chemistry of that body in all sorts of ways. But that doesn't make it a numerically different body, any more than medically modifying all your DNA gives you a numerically different body (see section 3.1). BS2 is just reporting an implication of the Same Body Account: that account entails that having the same body suffices for being the same person. And BS3 is reporting what we all find

60

perfectly obvious when we think about this case or when we watch a movie like *Freaky Friday*.

The Same Body Account yields the wrong verdict about who's who in BODY SWAP. It wrongly entails that Male$_T$ is the same person as Male$_W$. It also wrongly entails that Male$_T$ (i.e., the one who was calling himself 'Raúl' on Tuesday) and Female$_W$ (i.e., the one insisting "I'm Raúl!" on Wednesday) are different people. So, the Same Body Account must be rejected.

The Psychological Descendant Account, by contrast, gets the right answers in this case. Female$_W$ is a psychological descendant of Male$_T$: there is massive overlap between the psychological features of the person who woke up with a female body on Wednesday and the person who walked in with a male body on Tuesday. Additionally, Male$_W$ is *not* a psychological descendant of Male$_T$: Male$_T$ has virtually nothing in common psychologically with Male$_W$, nor is there any gradually changing chain of overlap (of the sort described in section 3.2) linking Male$_T$ to Male$_W$. So, the Psychological Descendant Account again gives us the right result, that Male$_T$ is not Male$_W$.

Getting one wrong result is enough to show that the Same Body Account is false. But getting a couple correct results is not enough to show that the Psychological Descendant Account is true. So, let us turn now to see whether the Psychological Descendant Account has some problematic consequences of its own. (Spoiler: it does.)

5. Against the Psychological Descendant Account

5.1 Arguments from Discontinuity

According to the Psychological Descendant Account, A is the same person as B only if one is a psychological descendant of the other. One way to put pressure on this account is to look at cases involving dramatic psychological discontinuities, breaks in the moment-by-moment chain of overlapping psychological features. I'll look at two such cases: one that I *don't* think is conclusive against the Psychological Descendant Account, and then a second case that does seem to be conclusive.

Our first case involves dramatic memory loss:

TOTAL AMNESIA

Jiwoo is stranded on a deserted island. Adding injury to insult, a coconut fell on Jiwoo's head at noon today, instantly resulting in total amnesia. She can't remember how she got on the island or anything else about her past. She can't even remember her own name.

To see why this case is supposed to pose a problem for the Psychological Descendant Account, notice that the non-amnesiac immediately before the coconut strike has very different psychological features from the amnesiac immediately after the coconut strike. This would seem to imply that the amnesiac is not a psychological descendant of the non-amnesiac, in which case the Psychological Descendant Account implies that the amnesiac isn't the same person as the non-amnesiac. But the amnesiac clearly *is* the same person as the non-amnesiac. After all, the coconut doesn't *kill* Jiwoo. But if she's still around after noon, that means someone on the island after noon must be the same person as her. And the only person on the island after noon is the amnesiac. Jiwoo *is* the amnesiac.

I've just argued that TOTAL AMNESIA is a counterexample to the Psychological Descendant Account. But I can imagine a plausible reply from a defender of the Psychological Descendant Account. Such a defender might say that the amnesiac *is* a psychological descendant of the non-amnesiac. To be a descendant, the idea goes, it's enough for their psychological features to be "mostly the same" before and after the coconut strike. But, differences in memory notwithstanding, there is still a great deal of overlap. The amnesiac and the non-amnesiac both love crossword puzzles, both are afraid of sharks, both have slightly blurry vision (since both are near-sighted), both have an easygoing temperament, and so on. All this similarity in their other psychological features, the idea goes, is enough for their psychological features to count as "mostly the same."

Rather than trying to challenge the claim that there is sufficient overlap in TOTAL AMNESIA to count as a case of descendance, I'll instead shift to a new case, one in which there is *no* overlap in the mental states, thus rendering this response unavailable. Here is the new case:

Total Blackout

Minjun is stranded on a deserted island. Adding injury to insult, a coconut fell on Minjun's head at noon today, temporarily knocking him unconscious. While unconscious, he is not dreaming, nor does he have any thoughts or experiences or any physical sensations whatsoever. He is completely blacked out. When he finally awakens hours later, it will feel as if no time has passed.

Here is how to turn the case into an argument against the Psychological Descendant Account:

The Blackout Argument

(BL1) The unconscious man is not a psychological descendant of the conscious man

(BL2) If the unconscious man is not a psychological descendant of the conscious man, then: if the Psychological Descendant Account is true, then the conscious man is not the same person as the unconscious man

(BL3) The conscious man is the same person as the unconscious man

(BL4) So, the Psychological Descendant Account is false

The idea behind BL1 is that the conscious man has a wealth of sensations and emotions and thoughts and desires, whereas the unconscious man has no mental states at all. So, there is no overlap whatsoever in their psychological features. BL2 is reporting an implication of the Psychological Descendant Account: in order to be the same person, on this account, one must be a psychological descendant of the other. And BL3 seems obviously true. One would be right to point to the unconscious man lying on the island and say: that's Minjun, the very person who was wandering the island earlier today.

5.2 The Argument from Fission

I turn now to a second argument against the Psychological Descendant Account, for which I will once again recruit the help of our neurotechnologist from section 4.2:

> **DOUBLE TROUBLE**
>
> Rachel's rewiring program has been tremendously successful, and she is now performing dozens of body swaps a day. But she's starting to get a little sloppy. Today, after rewiring Chad's brain to duplicate JoJo's, Rachel then accidentally rewires Alex's brain to duplicate JoJo's as well. As a result, both the person with Chad's original body and the person with Alex's original body wake up and say 'my name is JoJo'. Both can tell you all about JoJo's past; neither can tell you anything about Chad or Alex's past. Rachel's team also accidently obliterates JoJo's original body.

Figuratively speaking, JoJo's mind has "fissioned" like an amoeba, into two separate bodies. But strictly speaking, how are we supposed to describe what's happened? In particular, who's who after the procedure, and which person (if any) is JoJo?

I'm honestly not sure what to think about the case. But one thing I *am* sure of is that the Psychological Descendant Account provides us with an incoherent account of what's happened, and therefore must be incorrect. The problem, in short, is that *both* of the people who wake up after the procedure are psychological descendants of JoJo. If the Psychological Descendant Account is right, then that means that both of them *are* JoJo. But that, I contend, is impossible.

Before we state the argument more explicitly, it will again be helpful to introduce some abbreviations. Let's use "$Chad_{RW}$" to refer to the person with the rewired brain in Chad's original body and "$Alex_{RW}$" for the person with the rewired brain in Alex's original body. Now we can state the argument against the Psychological Descendant Account as follows:

The Fission Argument

(FS1) If the Psychological Descendant Account is true, then JoJo is the same person as Chad$_{RW}$ *and* is the same person as Alex$_{RW}$

(FS2) If JoJo is the same person as Chad$_{RW}$ and the same person as Alex$_{RW}$, then Chad$_{RW}$ is the same person as Alex$_{RW}$

(FS3) So, if the Psychological Descendant Account is true, then Chad$_{RW}$ is the same person as Alex$_{RW}$

(FS4) Chad$_{RW}$ is not the same person as Alex$_{RW}$

(FS5) So the Psychological Descendant Account is false

Let's take the premises one at a time.

FS1 is indisputable. The psychological features of Chad$_{RW}$ and Alex$_{RW}$ when they first wake up are virtually indistinguishable from those of JoJo, that is, the woman calling herself 'JoJo' just prior to the rewiring. In the minutes and hours that follow, Chad$_{RW}$ and Alex$_{RW}$ will of course begin to diverge psychologically from one another. Indeed, they'll likely begin diverging from one another the moment they wake up! But they will remain psychological *descendants* of JoJo, linked by an ever-growing, moment-by-moment chain, with each "link" in the chain exhibiting massive psychological overlap with the preceding link. And that's all we need in order to get FS1. For, so long as each is a psychological descendant of JoJo, the Psychological Descendant Account will entail that each of them is the same person as her.

FS2 follows from a highly plausible logical principle: the transitivity of identity. According to this principle, if A = B and B = C, then it follows that A = C. (Here, the '=' symbol signifies numerical sameness.) That's true no matter what you plug in for 'A', 'B', and 'C'. Suppose you find out that Chadwick Boseman is the actor who played the Black Panther, and you also find out that the actor who played the Black Panther was also the star of *Ma Rainey's Black Bottom*. You wouldn't then wonder whether Chadwick Boseman is the same person as the star of *Ma Rainey's Black Bottom*. That's because you already have all the information you need in order to *deduce* that it's the same guy: if Chadwick Boseman = the actor who played the Black Panther, and the actor who played the Black Panther = the star of *Ma Rainey's Black*

Bottom, then (by the transitivity of identity) Chadwick Boseman = the star of *Ma Rainey's Black Bottom*. By that same indisputable logic, if $Chad_{RW}$ = JoJo and JoJo = $Alex_{RW}$, then $Chad_{RW}$ = $Alex_{RW}$. That's what gives us FS2.

Premise FS4 is motivated by a different logical principle, which I'll call 'The No Difference Principle', or 'NDP' for short:

> (NDP) If A is numerically the same as B, then at any given time, anything that's true of A at that time is also true of B at that time

To illustrate the principle, consider Cassius Clay and Muhammad Ali. Cassius Clay *is* Muhammad Ali, they're numerically the same. Here's something that was true of Ali: he was in a boxing ring on October 30, 1974 at 10pm. So, by NDP, the same must be true of Clay: he too was in a boxing ring at that time. And that's just as it should be. 'Cassius Clay' and 'Muhammad Ali' are just two names for one and the same guy, so it can't very well be that "one of them" is in the boxing ring and "the other one" isn't. There's just the one guy, and he either was or wasn't in the boxing ring at that time.

This principle, NDP, is also a useful tool for demonstrating that two people *aren't* numerically the same. NDP tells us that if, at a given time, you can find even a single difference between A and B, then A and B cannot be numerically the same. If you're wondering whether Emily and Haley are the same person, just notice that Emily is skydiving right now and Haley isn't, and that settles it: they must be two different people. If they *were* numerically the same, then anything true of the one would have to be true of the other. But it's true of Emily that she's skydiving and that isn't true of Haley. So, by NDP, they must be two different people.

Exactly the same logic applies in the case at hand. If you're wondering whether $Chad_{RW}$ and $Alex_{RW}$ are the same person, just notice that $Chad_{RW}$ is currently walking down the street and $Alex_{RW}$ isn't currently walking down the street. ($Alex_{RW}$ is still in Rachel's lab, staring at the ceiling.) That settles it: no one person can both be and not be walking down the street. So $Chad_{RW}$ and $Alex_{RW}$ must be two different people, just as FS4 says.

I can imagine someone objecting to FS4 by saying that after the rewiring, JoJo is a single person with two bodies. If that were true, that would mean that she has four eyes, two of which are looking down at the sidewalk and two of which are looking up at the ceiling. If you ask her "are you walking down the street right now?" she might say yes or she might say no, depending on which of her two bodies you ask. But when Alex's original body (which is in the lab) answers 'no', that's a mistake according to the view in question. For on this view, $Alex_{RW}$ *is* walking down the street, since $Alex_{RW}$—the person with Alex's original body—is a person who has two bodies, one of whose bodies—the one that used to belong to Chad—is walking down the street. So, the idea goes, we don't have a case of a single thing with conflicting properties after all, thus clearing the way to denying FS4 and insisting that $Chad_{RW}$ and $Alex_{RW}$ are the same person, namely JoJo.

This is an incredibly weird way of thinking about the DOUBLE TROUBLE case. And it can't be right, for the very same reasons that it can't be right to say that conjoined twins Abby and Brittany are the same person (see section 4.1). Suppose that $Chad_{RW}$ goes on to marry a man named 'Emir'. Emir later kisses $Alex_{RW}$, and then kills $Chad_{RW}$ so he can be with $Alex_{RW}$. If $Chad_{RW}$ and $Alex_{RW}$ were the same person, then Emir isn't cheating on $Chad_{RW}$, since Emir *was* kissing $Chad_{RW}$ (a.k.a. $Alex_{RW}$); and Emir didn't kill anyone, since $Chad_{RW}$ is $Alex_{RW}$, and $Chad_{RW}$ is still alive (all Emir did, on this view, is destroy one of $Chad_{RW}$'s two bodies). But surely that's wrong. Emir did cheat on $Chad_{RW}$, and the district attorney would be right to charge him with homicide—all of which presupposes that FS4 is right, and that $Chad_{RW}$ and $Alex_{RW}$ are two different people.

6. Souls

Some may feel that I have overlooked an obvious answer to the question of personal identity, namely that it's your *soul* that makes you the person that you are. In other words, one might embrace the Same Soul Account of personal identity:

The Same Soul Account
A at t is the same person as B at t* if and only if A has the same soul as B

The Same Soul Account could then be put to work in addressing the various challenging cases we have been discussing. Abby and Brittany, one might say, are different people because they have two different souls. The conscious and unconscious man on the island are the same person because they have the same soul. Male$_T$ and Male$_W$ in the BODY SWAP case are different people because Raúl's soul left the male body and now inhabits the female body.

But what exactly is "a soul"? I suspect that when people talk about their souls, this is just a roundabout way of talking about themselves. For instance, if you're talking about souls in the first place, you probably think that your soul is something that will eventually come apart from your body and that will (if you have behaved yourself) go to heaven. Certainly, though, you don't think it's something *other than you* that goes to heaven. It's you yourself who will go to heaven. In that case, saying "my soul will go to heaven" is just another way of saying "I will go to heaven," and maybe calling yourself "a soul" is just a way of signaling that you take yourself to be a ghostly thing that merely inhabits—but isn't the same thing as—your physical body.

Let's suppose that's what you mean: you are your soul. But then the Same Soul Account doesn't actually answer the question of personal identity. For suppose that "A's soul" is just a fancy way of referring to A herself, and "B's soul" is just a fancy way of referring to B herself. In that case, all that the Same Soul Account is saying is: A is the same person as B if and only if A is the same person as B. And while that's true, it's also completely trivial and uninformative. It's like answering the question of what makes someone a bachelor by saying that A is bachelor if and only if A is a bachelor. That's true, but it's trivial, and it certainly doesn't tell us anything about what *makes* someone a bachelor.

Nor, in that case, does the Same Soul Account actually shed light on the cases we have been discussing. You say that Abby and Brittany are different people because they have different souls. But that's just a fancy way of saying that Abby and Brittany are different people because they're different people, which isn't much of an explanation at all. The same goes for TOTAL BLACKOUT: saying that the conscious and unconscious man are the same person because they have the same soul is just a roundabout way of making the utterly uninformative claim that they are the same person because they're the same person. The Same Soul Account is particularly unhelpful in DOUBLE TROUBLE. The Same Soul Account says that whether JoJo is Chad$_{RW}$ or Alex$_{RW}$ depends on which of those two people has JoJo's soul. But that just means that whether JoJo is Chad$_{RW}$ or Alex$_{RW}$ depends on which of them is JoJo—which is exactly what we're trying to figure out!

Perhaps you *don't* want to say that a person is the same thing as their soul. Suppose, instead, you want to say that the soul is merely one *part* of the person (their body being the other part). In that case, saying that Abby and Brittany are different people because they have different souls *would* be saying something nontrivial, namely that they are different people in virtue of failing to share a certain special immaterial part. Still, there are problems with the account, so understood.

The first problem is that it's still entirely unhelpful for settling questions of personal identity. Even if you think JoJo and her soul are two different things, what could possibly determine whether JoJo's soul went into Chad$_{RW}$'s body or Alex$_{RW}$'s body? Both of them think and act just like JoJo, so there would seem to be nothing at all to settle the question of which one acquired her soul. Indeed, the account leaves us with no way to assure ourselves that *we* persist from one moment to the next. You can check whether you are a psychological descendant of the person who was reading this page a moment ago, or whether you have the same body as that person, but there's no way to check whether you have the same immaterial part as that person—and therefore (if the Same Soul Account is right) no way to know that you are the same person who was reading this page a moment ago!

The second problem involves the separability of the soul from the body. If these really are different parts of a person, there should be nothing in principle to stop the immaterial part of one person from coming apart from that person and combining with another body at a later time. Suppose it turns out that your immaterial part (your "soul") is the same one that used to be part of Harriet Tubman. You don't look like her. You didn't inherit any of her memories and personality traits. All that's happened is that an immaterial thing that used to be part of her is now a part of you. Certainly, we shouldn't say in that case that you *are* Harriet Tubman. Finding out that your immaterial part used to be a part of her may be exciting, just as it would be exciting to find out that a surprisingly large number of carbon atoms in your body used to be part of her. But neither of these would show that you're the same person as her.

For these reasons, I don't think that the Same Soul Account is any improvement on the physical and psychological accounts we have already considered and dismissed.

7. Combining the Psychological and Bodily Accounts

I argued in sections 4 and 5 that neither the Same Body Account nor the Psychological Descendant Account can serve as an adequate theory of personal identity. One might suspect that we ran into all this trouble only because we were focusing too narrowly on just physical aspects or just psychological aspects. Perhaps the problems can all be avoided if we had considered hybrid theories of personal identity that involve a *combination* of physical and psychological factors.

To quiet these concerns, I'll conclude this chapter by considering two ways of incorporating physical and psychological considerations into a single account: a Body-And-Mind Account and a Body-Or-Mind Account.

> *The Body-And-Mind Account*
> A at t is the same person as B at t* if and only if A has the same body as B *and* A is a psychological ancestor or descendant of B

> *The Body-Or-Mind Account*
> A at t is the same person as B at t* if and only if A has the same body as B *or* A is a psychological ancestor or descendant of B

Let's begin with the Body-And-Mind Account. This account does have certain advantages over the earlier accounts. For instance, whereas the Same Body Account wrongly entails that conjoined twins Abby and Brittany are the same person, the Body-And-Mind Account rightly entails that they're two different people, since Abby isn't a psychological descendant of Brittany (or vice versa). And whereas the Psychological Descendant Account gets into trouble with DOUBLE TROUBLE on account of having to say that JoJo is numerically the same as two separate people, the Body-And-Mind Account is able to avoid the problem by denying that JoJo is numerically the same as *either* of those people (since neither has the same body as JoJo).

But the Body-And-Mind Account does fall victim to some of the other objections we considered. For instance, it gets the wrong result in TOTAL BLACKOUT. The conscious man at the earlier time is neither a psychological ancestor nor a psychological descendant of the unconscious man at the later time. So trivially, it's not true that the conscious man *both* has the same body and is an ancestor or descendant of the unconscious man. The Body-And-Mind Account therefore wrongly says that he isn't the same person as the unconscious man. Or take BODY SWAP. The person with the male body before the rewiring is the same person as the person with the female body after the rewiring. But they don't have the same body, and thus the Body-And-Mind Account wrongly implies that they aren't the same person.

How about the Body-*Or*-Mind Account? Here we get exactly the opposite results: the Body-Or-Mind Account escapes the problems that plagued the Body-And-Mind Account but is plagued by the problems that the Body-And-Mind Account does escape. The Body-Or-Mind Account correctly says that the conscious man is numerically the same as the unconscious man, since they do at least have the same body, and it correctly says that in BODY SWAP the person with male body on Tuesday is numerically the same as the person with the female body on Wednesday, since the one is at least a psychological descendant of the other. But now we get the wrong results in DOUBLE TROUBLE. The Body-Or-Mind Account says that being a psychological ancestor is enough for personal identity, which is all we need to get the problematic result that JoJo is the same person as two separate people. And it says that having the same body is enough for personal identity, which is all we need to get the problematic result that Abby and Brittany are the same person.

In a way, it's no surprise that neither of these hybrid accounts work. The Body-And-Mind Account says that both sameness of body and psychological descendance are necessary for personal identity, but we already knew (from BODY SWAP and TOTAL

BLACKOUT) that *neither* is necessary. The Body-Or-Mind Account says that sameness of body and psychological descendance are each sufficient for personal identity, but we already knew (from CONJOINED TWINS and DOUBLE TROUBLE) that neither is sufficient. It's no wonder that these hybrid accounts inherit the problems of the "pure" accounts they're meant to replace.

8. Conclusion

We have seen that neither physical factors, nor psychological factors, nor appeals to souls can yield a satisfactory answer to the question of personal identity. And that's puzzling, since it is hard to see what *else* could be involved in making a person the person that they are.

Not only is it puzzling; it's also troubling. For there are pressing ethical and life-and-death issues that seem to turn on the question of what makes you you. Is it true that a person's life begins at conception? In other words, was that fertilized egg cell in your mother's womb *you*? If you are in a horrific accident, is that brain-dead person on life support in the hospital bed *you*? And let's not kid ourselves: we will get to a point, possibly even in your own lifetime, where we have the technology to replicate a person's mind in a computer simulation. Would that simulated person—with all of your memories, preferences, and personality traits—be you? Would uploading your consciousness into such a simulation be a way of surviving the death of your body, or would that be a numerically different person—very much like you, but not actually you? It is hard to see how to answer any of these questions without an answer to the question of personal identity.

Reflection Questions

1. Can you defend the Same Body Account against the Conjoined Twins argument from section 4.1?

2. Would a Same *Brain* Account be any improvement on a Same Body Account? Why or why not?

3. Can the Psychological Descendant Account be defended against the Blackout Argument (section 5.1)? If so, how?

4. In section 7, I considered two different hybrid accounts of personal identity and raised problems for both. Can you articulate a superior hybrid account that avoids some of these problems?

Sources
The debate over personal identity largely traces back to John Locke's *Essay Concerning Human Understanding*, which advances a psychological account of personal identity and presents a version of the Body Swap Argument as well as an argument against the Same Soul Account. See Derek Parfit's "Personal Identity" for a classic discussion of fission cases, and see Heather Demarest's "Fission May Kill You" for an exploration of the "one person, two bodies" strategy. Here are some additional resources:

- "The Twins Who Share a Body" (youtube.com)
- Elizabeth Camp: The Narrative Self (wi-phi):
- Tim Campbell and Jeff McMahan: Animalism and the Varieties of Conjoined Twinning
- Robert Casati and Achille Varzi: *Insurmountable Simplicities* (pp.17-23)
- Crash Course Philosophy: Personal Identity (youtube.com)
- Clarence Darrow: The Myth of Immortality
- Michael Della Rocca: Locke on Personal Identity (wi-phi.com)
- Daniel Dennett: Where Am I?
- Amy Kind: *Persons and Personal Identity*
- Ifeanyi A. Menketi: Person and Community in African Traditional Thought
- John Perry: *A Dialogue on Personal Identity and Immortality*
- Marya Schechtman: *Staying Alive: Personal Identity, Practical Concerns, and the Unity of the Life*
- Mark Siderits: Personal Identity and Buddhist Philosophy
- Nina Strohminger: The Essential Self (wi-phi.com)

CHAPTER 4
Don't Fear the Reaper

Views and arguments advanced in this chapter are not necessarily endorsed by the author of the textbook, nor are they original to the author, nor are they meant to be consistent with arguments advanced in other chapters. Different chapters represent different philosophical perspectives.

1. Introduction

My aim in this chapter is to argue for the surprising conclusion that you shouldn't fear death. In short, the idea is that the only things that can be bad for you, ultimately speaking, are pains and other such unpleasant sensations. Accordingly, since you won't be experiencing any unpleasant sensations once you're dead, being dead isn't bad for you, and you shouldn't fear things that aren't bad for you. In other words:

Against Fearing Death
(FD1) You cease to be conscious when you die
(FD2) If you cease to be conscious when you die, then being dead is not bad for you
(FD3) So, being dead is not bad for you
(FD4) If being dead is not bad for you, then you should not fear death
(FD5) So, you should not fear death

I should emphasize that I am not denying that *dying* is bad. The process of dying can of course be quite painful—both physically and emotionally—and, thus, bad for you. If you're going to be torn apart by piranhas tomorrow, that's certainly bad for you and something to be afraid of. But you should fear it because the dying will be painful, not because you will be dead at the end of it. On the other hand, if you are about to be anesthetized for some surgery and there is a very good chance that you will die painlessly while under anesthesia, this is not bad for you and there is nothing to fear.

I'll defend the opening premises in reverse order, first arguing (in sections 2-3) that *if* it's true that you cease to be conscious when you die *then* being dead is not bad for you, and then arguing (in sections 4-5) that it indeed is true that you cease to be conscious when you die. Then, having established that being dead isn't bad for you, I defend FD4 (in section 6) on the grounds that it is irrational to fear things that aren't bad for you.

Let me make one last preliminary remark before launching into the defense of FD2. Some readers may be strongly inclined to reject the first premise, FD1, because they think that they will go on, after death, to have conscious experiences in the afterlife. Perhaps pleasant experiences, or perhaps painful experiences, depending on the will of their Creator. But even such readers have reason to think carefully about FD2. For the Creator may instead decide to punish sinners and nonbelievers, not by sending them to hell, but by permanently snuffing out their consciousness after they die. You probably think that this would be bad for you. But if FD2 is true, then it wouldn't in any way be bad for you (and thus wouldn't be any sort of punishment). So if you are inclined to say that being snuffed out by your Creator is bad for you, then you'll need to find some way to resist my argument below for FD2.

2. Hedonism

My argument for FD2 turns on the idea—sometimes known as "hedonism"—that, ultimately speaking, experiencing pleasant sensations is the only thing that's good for you, and experiencing painful sensations is the only thing that's bad for you. And when I say 'painful', that should be understood in a broad sense, to include psychological and emotional pain, in addition to physical pain and discomfort.

It's easy to see the appeal of hedonism. Why is it bad for you if someone kicks you? Because it's painful. Why it is bad for you not to brush your teeth? Because you might get plaque. Why is that bad for you? Because plaque leads to cavities. Why is that bad for you? Because cavities are painful.

Still, we must be careful in how exactly we formulate our hedonistic account of what's bad for you. For instance, suppose we tried the following:

(HD) Something is bad for you if and only if it's painful

There are multiple problems with HD. First, there are all sorts of things that are bad for you that aren't themselves painful. For instance, eating a whole large pizza in one sitting isn't painful, but it is bad for you. Second, there are all sorts of painful things that aren't bad for you. For instance, a deep-tissue massage isn't bad for you, but it can be somewhat unpleasant while it's happening.

Thinking a bit more about these examples can help us see what's missing from HD. Why is eating the whole pizza bad for you? Because, later in the day, you'll have a painful stomach ache. Why isn't the deep-tissue massage bad for you? Because working out the knots in your muscles results in your having less discomfort later on. What we're seeing is that what makes something bad for you isn't just whether it itself is painful but also its connection to the presence or absence of future pains. With this in mind, we can revise the principle as follows:

(HD*) Something is bad for you if and only if it results in more pain than you would otherwise have had

This is still true to the core hedonist insight stated above. Eating the whole pizza in one sitting is bad for you because it results in a painful stomach ache that you wouldn't otherwise have had. Massages aren't bad for you because, even if they're painful in the moment, they eliminate future pains that you would otherwise have had. Ultimately speaking, what is or isn't bad for you is still just a matter of what is or isn't painful for you.

3. The Argument from Hedonism
With HD* in hand, we can now run an argument for FD2 of the Against Fearing Death argument.

The Argument from Hedonism
(AH1) If you cease to be conscious when you die, then being dead doesn't result in more pain than you would otherwise have had
(AH2) Something is bad for you if and only if it results in more pain than you would otherwise have had
(FD2) So, if you cease to be conscious when you die, then being dead isn't bad for you

76

Premise AH1 is trivial. Pain is a conscious state, so *if* you aren't conscious while you're dead, then you don't have any pain while you're dead. And the second premise is just our modified hedonist principle, HD*. Accordingly, one might try to resist the argument by attacking HD*. I'll consider three sorts of attacks.

First, one might point to people who suffer from congenital analgesia, a rare condition which involves an inability to experience pain. While this may at first seem like a good thing, it's easy to see on reflection why this is actually very bad for those who have it. They might, for instance, inadvertently place their hand in a fire and not realize it before their hand is irreparably damaged. But (the idea goes) HD* seems to entail that this condition can't be bad for those who have it, nor for that matter can anything bad ever befall them, since nothing can be painful for them.

In response, I deny that HD* entails any such thing. Remember that 'pain' isn't restricted to unpleasant physical sensations. It also includes the sort of *emotional* distress that one would have from irreparably damaging one's hand, and those suffering from this condition are entirely capable of experiencing these sorts of psychological pains.

Second, one might object to HD* on the grounds that something can be entirely pleasurable and yet still be a bad thing to do. Consider the following case:

STOLEN CRUISE
Brendan is about to go on a week-long cruise. His girlfriend, Pieper, serves him undercooked chicken, in hopes that he'll get food poisoning and will let her go in his place. Pieper's plan succeeds, and she has a great time on the cruise. She comes back refreshed, relaxed, and feeling no remorse whatsoever.

What Pieper did is bad, and yet it didn't lead to her having any unpleasant sensations.

Is that a problem for HD*? No. One must be careful to distinguish between something being *bad for you* and something being *bad to do*. HD* is only about the former and has nothing to say about the latter. If giving Brendan food poisoning doesn't end up being unpleasant for Pieper, then it isn't bad *for Pieper* that Brendan got food poisoning. But that's not at all to deny that deliberately giving him food poisoning was a bad thing to do (which of course it was).

Now for the third objection to HD*. Here the idea is to grant that hedonism is basically right, but to insist upon further changes to its formulation. Specifically, one might suggest that something can be bad for you not just by giving you painful sensations but also by depriving you of pleasant sensations:

> (HD**) Something is bad for you if and only if it results in more pain *or less pleasure* than you would otherwise have had

In short, the idea is that what's bad for you is what—in one way or another—makes you worse off in terms of pleasure and pain. If HD** is right, then we won't be able to get the Argument from Hedonism off the ground. After all, it's true (for most people) that they would have had more pleasure had they not died when they did, in which case HD** entails that being dead *is* bad for them.

The problem with HD** is that it is open to counterexamples like the following:

UNREAD MAIL

Carly meets Evan, and they immediately fall in love. Because things are going so well with Evan, Carly stops checking her online dating app. They have a long and entirely happy life together. It so happens that Jami had sent Carly a message shortly after Carly met Evan. If she hadn't met Evan, she would have seen Jami's message, fallen in love with *her*, and she and Jami would have had a long and happy life together. As a matter of fact, she would have been a little tiny bit happier with Jami than with Evan.

Carly would have been a tiny bit better off if she hadn't met Evan. Does that mean that it was bad for her that she met Evan? Of course not. Yet HD** wrongly implies that it *is* bad for her that she met Evan. After all, she would have had more pleasure in her life had she not met him.

This gives us a compelling argument against HD**:

The Unread Mail Argument

(UM1) Carly would have had more pleasure had she not met Evan

(UM2) If Carly would have had more pleasure had she not met Evan, then: if HD** is true, then meeting Evan was bad for her

(UM3) Meeting Evan was not bad for her

(UM4) So, HD** is false

Thus, one shouldn't prefer HD** to my formulation of the principle of hedonism, HD*, and we have not found any good reason to reject HD*, the second premise of the Argument from Hedonism.

4. Against Post-Mortem Consciousness

We've just seen an argument for the conditional premise that *if* you cease to be conscious when you die, *then* being dead is not bad for you. But why think that you do cease to be conscious when you die? In other words, why accept premise FD1 of the Against Fearing Death argument?

Some readers likely already accept it: when you die, you cease to exist and your consciousness is snuffed out completely. After all, your brain stops working and that's the source of all conscious experience. Others, however, may need some convincing. They may think that, after death, we continue to have conscious experiences in some sort of afterlife, perhaps in heaven or hell. Or they may be agnostic: we can't know what happens after we die, and we just have to wait and see.

I say we don't have to wait and see. We can settle the matter right now. Start by noticing that, right where you are, there is a living, breathing, flesh-and-blood human animal. For simplicity, I'll refer to it as 'Animal'. Here, then, is the argument that you will permanently cease to be conscious once you die:

Against Post-Mortem Consciousness

(PC1) If Animal ceases to be conscious when you die *and* you are Animal, then you cease to be conscious when you die

(PC2) Animal ceases to be conscious when you die

(PC3) You are Animal

(FD1) So, you cease to be conscious when you die

First, I'll explain the idea behind PC1 and PC2, which are both straightforward. Then I'll argue for PC3, which admittedly is more controversial.

PC1 is extremely plausible once you wrap your mind around what it's saying. PC1 is not saying that you are Animal, nor is it saying that Animal ceases to be conscious when you die. Rather, it's saying that *if* both of these things are true, *then* you (yourself) cease to be conscious when you die. Why is that? Suppose that you are literally the same thing as Animal. In that case, you and Animal are one thing, not two; 'you' and 'Animal' are just two ways of referring to one and the same thing. If you and Animal truly are one and the same thing, then anything that's true about Animal is also true of you. It can't be that Snoop Dogg goes to heaven and Calvin Broadus doesn't, since Snoop Dogg *is* Calvin Broadus. ('Snoop Dogg' is Calvin Broadus's stage name.) There is only one individual there to go or not go to heaven. By the same reasoning, if Animal ceases to be conscious when you die, then—supposing you are Animal—you must also cease to be conscious when you die. That's PC1.

Now for PC2. Set aside for a moment whether *you* cease to be conscious when you die, and just focus on Animal. Why think that Animal isn't conscious after you die? When you die, Animal will still be here on Earth, as a dead animal, waiting to be buried or cremated. It will have no brain function whatsoever. We can poke and prod it, and it won't feel anything. Even if you think there might be a conscious afterlife, you certainly don't think that it's the rotting human animals in the cemetery (the corpses) that are having the conscious experiences. In other words, even if you think there will be or might be a conscious afterlife, you should still accept PC2: you shouldn't think that Animal itself will be conscious after you die.

5. The Too Many Thinkers Argument

If you think that you will (or might) go on to enjoy a conscious afterlife, what you'll probably want to say is that you and Animal part ways after death: Animal ceases to be conscious at that point, but you go on having conscious experiences in the afterlife. But, as I have already argued, you and Animal can part ways *only if* you and Animal are two different things. Accordingly, you'll have to deny PC3, which says that you and Animal are one and the same.

And yet there is a simple and powerful argument for this premise. You'll want to sit down for this. (Seriously, sit down. And sit by yourself—if you've got a cat in your lap, shoo it away.) Here is the argument:

The Too Many Thinkers Argument
(TT1) Animal is in your chair and is thinking
(TT2) You are the only thing in your chair that is thinking
(PC3) So you are Animal

Let's take the premises one at a time. If both TT1 and TT2 can be successfully defended, then I will in turn have defended PC3, the crucial premise of the argument that you will cease to be conscious when you die.

At least on the face of it, TT1 is incredibly plausible. Your head is part of Animal and so is your brain. And this brain of yours is a fully functioning brain. Of course, it won't be a fully functioning brain after you die. But that's irrelevant, because TT1 doesn't say that Animal will be thinking after you die. It says that that Animal is thinking right now. And that seems undeniable, given that it now has a fully functioning brain as a part.

You may be tempted to object that it's not Animal itself that's thinking. Animal, you'll say, is a mere vessel, and it's *you*—a distinct, perhaps ghostly "soul" that inhabits the animal—that's doing all the thinking. Here's why you should resist the temptation. Certainly, you'll admit that other animals, like squirrels or dogs, are capable of thinking. (If you *don't* admit that, you'd have to say that squirrels and dogs have no intelligence whatsoever; after all, something can't very well be intelligent if it doesn't think.) But once you admit that *these* animals have thoughts, it would be absurd to deny that *human* animals, with their far more advanced brains, have thoughts.

How about TT2? TT2 says that you are the only thinking thing in your chair. To see the idea behind this premise, just think about what would be involved in denying it. You'd have to say that something *other than you* is in your chair right now with you, and it's thinking. But that seems absurd.

You might try to lessen the absurdity by saying that, yes, you and Animal are two different things, both in your chair, both thinking, *but* you're thinking about different things. You're thinking about abstract philosophical matters, and it's thinking about bodily concerns like eating lunch or taking a nap. But that can't be right. It's got the same brain as you, which means that it's thinking exactly the same thoughts as you. For instance, if you're thinking to yourself right now, "I'm a *person*, not a mere animal," it's because your brain is in a certain specific state. But Animal's brain is in exactly that same state. After all, it's got the same brain as you! So, it must be thinking exactly the same thing: "I'm a *person*, not a mere animal." The same goes for absolutely anything you and Animal are thinking. And that's completely absurd: surely there aren't two different things in your chair, simultaneously thinking all the same thoughts.

TT1 and TT2 together entail PC3. What that means is that if you don't want to accept PC3, you must reject one of these two premises. But, as we just saw, the premises are hard to deny, and in any case PC3 is already highly plausible. So, you should accept PC3.

6. Irrational Fears

I have thus far argued that being dead is not bad for you. The first premise, FD1, was that you cease to be conscious when you die, and I argued for this premise on the grounds that the human animal that's where you are ceases to be conscious when you die, which in turn means that *you* cease to be conscious when you die (since you are that animal). The second premise, FD2, was that death is bad for you only if you continue to be conscious after you die; after all, the only things that are bad for you, ultimately speaking, are pains and things that lead to pain.

But the claim that being dead is not bad for you (FD3) is merely a subconclusion of the argument. The ultimate conclusion (FD5) is that you shouldn't fear death, and for that we need one more premise.

The final premise of the Against Fearing Death argument, FD4, says that if being dead isn't bad for you, then you shouldn't fear death. To see why we should accept that, we need to think more generally about what makes a fear rational or irrational. Suppose a tarantula crawls onto your hand. Really, it's not all that dangerous. It's pretty unlikely to bite you, and even if it did it actually wouldn't be any more painful or harmful than an ordinary bee sting. But even knowing how harmless they are, you might still be utterly terrified of a tarantula crawling onto you. And that would be irrational. Why? Because that amount of fear is disproportionate to the likelihood of something bad happening to you and how bad it would be if it did.

Still, it *could* bite you, so it's rational to be a little bit afraid of the tarantula, just like it's rational to be a little bit afraid of honeybees. But there are other things that it is irrational to fear to *any* degree. Take ablutophobia, the fear of bathing. Ablutophobia is completely irrational because bathing is not bad for you, not even a little bit. Or take lepidopterophobia, the fear of butterflies. This is irrational too, and it's irrational because having an encounter with a butterfly is not in any way bad for you. Or take podophobia, the fear of seeing feet (including one's own). What makes all of these irrational fears so irrational is precisely that the object of the fear isn't in any way bad for the person who fears it. You shouldn't fear things that aren't bad for you. So, if indeed being dead isn't bad for you, you shouldn't fear it at all, just as FD4 says.

One might object that it's *unnatural* to fear all these other things, whereas it's completely natural to fear death. Fair enough. I'm not denying that fearing death is natural. I'm denying that fearing death is *rational*. Just because it comes naturally to us to act or react in a certain way, that doesn't mean it's rational. (Google 'cognitive biases', and you'll see what I mean.) And in any case, it just isn't true that all of those other fears are unnatural. It's entirely normal for people to experience excessive fear of spiders and other creepy crawlies. And we can all recognize, on reflection, that this degree of fear is excessive and irrational, despite being our natural reaction.

Thus, I conclude that death isn't bad for you and you shouldn't fear it. This is a surprising result, but not necessarily a bad one. After all, fearfulness is emotionally painful, and if this argument helps you do without that pain, that's good for you!

Reflection Questions

1. Can you think of any counterexamples to the hedonist principle HD* from section 2? Could such an example give us reason to prefer HD** from section 3?

2. Do the hedonist principles discussed in sections 2 and 3 imply that being born into this world was bad for you? Why or why not? If they do, can they be modified to avoid this implication?

3. Are you convinced by the Against Post-Mortem Consciousness argument in sections 4-5? In particular, are you convinced by the argument that you and Animal are one and the same thing?

4. In the final section, I suggested that it can never be rational to fear something that is not bad for you. Is that true? Can it be rational to fear something because it's bad for *others*? Should we fear death because (and only because) of how our deaths will affect other people?

Sources

The argument advanced here originates with the ancient Greek philosopher Epicurus, in his "Letter to Menoeceus." See Fred Feldman's *Confrontations with the Reaper* for a more in-depth discussion of philosophical questions about death, and in particular chapter 8 of his book for a defense of the idea that death is bad because it deprives one of good things. The Too Many Thinkers argument in section 5 is drawn from Eric Olson's "An Argument for Animalism." Here are some additional resources:

- Jorge Luis Borges: The Immortal
- Ben Bradley: Existential Terror
- Dorothy Grover: Posthumous Harm
- Lori Gruen: Death as a Social Harm
- A.A. Long and D.N. Sedley: *The Hellenistic Philosophers vol 1* (sec 24)
- Shelley Kagan: Death (Open Yale courses)
- Thomas Nagel: Death
- Richard Rowland: Hedonism and the Experience Machine
- Lynne Rudder Baker: Death and the Afterlife
- Travis Timmerman: The Symmetry Argument Against the Badness of Death (youtube.com)

CHAPTER 5
No Freedom

Views and arguments advanced in this chapter are not necessarily endorsed by the author of the textbook, nor are they original to the author, nor are they meant to be consistent with arguments advanced in other chapters. Different chapters represent different philosophical perspectives.

1. Introduction

Do we ever do anything of our own free will? You might think it's obvious that we do. It may seem obvious that your decision to read this chapter isn't unfree in the way that, say, an action performed under hypnosis is. You thought about whether to start reading the chapter, you made the decision to read it, and then you did that very thing that you decided to do. What more could be required for your action to count as free?

In what follows, I will argue that more is needed for freedom and, moreover, *nothing* anyone ever does has what it takes to count as free. I admit that this is a radical thesis, with radical implications. For instance, our very practice of holding people morally responsible for their actions presupposes that those actions were performed freely. (You wouldn't blame someone for kicking you when they're under the control of a hypnotist.) Accordingly, my thesis that no one acts freely evidently implies that no one should be held responsible for anything they do. But just because it's a radical thesis with radical implications, that doesn't mean it isn't true.

I'll present two arguments for my thesis that no one ever acts freely. The first turns on the idea that everything we do is a result of our desires, which are not under our control (sections 3-5). The second turns on the idea that everything we do is the inevitable result of things that happened long before we were even born (sections 6-9). Those who wish to stand by the intuitive idea that we do at least some things freely must find some flaw in each of the arguments.

2. Freedom Unmotivated

Before turning to my arguments that we never act freely, let me address—and attempt to undermine—the powerful intuition that we do often act freely. As indicated above, we tend to think we act freely because many of our actions seem to have all of the marks of freedom: we examine our options, we decide what to do, and we do what we decided to do. To better assess this line of reasoning, let's frame it as an explicit argument in defense of free action:

The Argument for Freedom

(FR1) Sometimes you perform an action after deciding to perform that action

(FR2) If one performs an action after deciding to perform it, then one performs that action freely

(FR3) So some of your actions are performed freely

Premise FR1 is certainly true: we do make decisions, and often our actions line up with our decisions. And premise FR2 has its merits as well. You decided to read this chapter right now, and here you are reading this chapter. That seems like a free action, and FR2 correctly predicts that it's a free action. But FR2 doesn't imply that *all* actions are free. To see this, consider the following case (inspired by a scene from the movie *Now You See Me*):

HYPNOTIC ACTION

Tia is on the run from the law and knows the cops are hot on her trail. She is also a master hypnotist. As she passes Jordan on the street, she hypnotizes him and plants an irresistible post-hypnotic suggestion: whenever he hears someone shout *Freeze!* he will fall into a hypnotic trance and tackle the person who said it. Just then, Kabir the cop arrives on the scene, sees Tia, shouts *Freeze!*, and Jordan tackles him.

Jordan never *decided* to tackle Kabir. He just fell into a trance, and when he emerged from the trance he found himself on top of Kabir pinning him to the ground. Certainly, Jordan's action isn't free: he didn't freely tackle Kabir. FR2 doesn't say that this action is free, and rightly so. Good job, FR2!

On closer inspection, though, it's clear that FR2 cannot be correct. Consider a variant of HYPNOTIC ACTION, in which the hypnotist is not only in control of the person's actions but also their decisions.

HYPNOTIC DECISION
Tia is on the run from the law and knows the cops are hot on her trail. She is also a master hypnotist. As she passes Colton on the street, she hypnotizes him and plants an irresistible post-hypnotic suggestion: whenever he hears someone shout *Freeze!* he will grow very angry with the person, decide to tackle them, and then tackle them. Just then, Kabir the cop arrives on the scene, sees Tia, and shouts *Freeze!* As a result of the hypnotic suggestion, Colton gets angry at Kabir, consciously decides to tackle him, and then tackles him.

Clearly, tackling Kabir isn't something Colton did of his own free will. True, it may seem to him, from the inside, as if he was free to do otherwise. He may even experience regret, feeling that he could have and should have controlled his temper and made a better decision. But, whether he realizes it or not, Tia's hypnotic hold over him is so powerful that he couldn't have decided otherwise. His will was not free nor was the action that sprung from it.

It's true that the HYPNOTIC DECISION case is unrealistic. But that doesn't stop it from being a counterexample to premise FR2. FR2 says that someone acted freely so long as they did what they decided to do, and Colton is a clear example of someone who isn't acting freely despite doing exactly what they decided to do. Since FR2 is false, our ordinary reason for thinking that we sometimes act freely is undermined. (For a discussion of how unrealistic cases can be relevant for assessing philosophical claims, see section 7 of the Introduction to this textbook.)

3. The Desire Argument Against Free Action
Colton's action in HYPNOTIC DECISION isn't free. But why not? The natural answer is that, although he made a choice and did what he wanted to do, his *desires* weren't under his control: he wasn't in control of the overwhelming desire to tackle Kabir. What this

suggests is that freedom requires more than just making choices and doing what you desire to do. It requires that your desires be under your control as well. And this is the insight that drives the first of my two arguments against free action. The argument can be stated as follows:

The Desire Argument
(DS1) What you choose to do is always determined by your desires
(DS2) You can't control your desires
(DS3) So, what you choose to do is always determined by something you can't control
(DS4) If what you choose to do is always determined by something you can't control, then you never act freely
(DS5) So, you never act freely

By 'desire', I mean any kind of wanting, including passionately yearning for something, but also less dramatic things, like wanting to buy some new socks. Let us examine the idea behind each of the premises, and then I'll turn to two ways that one might try to resist the argument.

Here is the idea behind DS1. You made a choice about what to have for lunch yesterday, and you chose to have Taco Bell rather than Panda Express. Why? Presumably, it's because you had a stronger desire for Mexican food than for Chinese. Or perhaps you decided to stay home and make a salad for lunch. Why? Because your desire to save money or for a healthy lunch was stronger than your desire for some delicious fast food.

Let me clarify what DS1 *is not* saying. DS1 doesn't say that you always act on *every* desire you have. Obviously, you don't act on all of your desires. In the case just mentioned, you stay home and make a salad *despite* having a strong desire for Taco Bell— which perhaps haunts you with every bite of lettuce. What DS1 is saying, rather, is that the choices you make are always a function of the various things you want and how badly you want them.

Think of desires like soldiers on a battlefield. Your desire for Taco Bell is fighting for you to choose Taco Bell for lunch. Your somewhat weaker desire for Panda Express is fighting, somewhat less effectively, for you to choose Panda Express. Meanwhile, your desire to save money has formed an alliance with your desires to eat healthy, to stay home, and to finish the produce in your fridge before it goes bad, all fighting for you to make a salad. As it turns out, this alliance was strong enough to overpower your desires for Taco Bell and Panda Express. DS1 says that you always act on whichever desire (or alliance of desires) is strongest, not that you always act on every desire that you have.

To see the idea behind DS2, notice that we do not choose our desires. Perhaps you're pre-med because you like helping people. But it's not as if, at some point, you *chose to* like helping people. At some point you realized that this is your passion, and at some point you chose to pursue that passion, but at no point did you choose to be passionate about it. Nor did you at any point choose to like Mexican food better than Chinese food, or dogs better than cats. We don't choose our likes and passions and desires; they come to us unbidden. (Returning to the battlefield metaphor, you don't get to decide which soldiers are on the battlefield or which ones have the best gear.) So, it would seem that which desires we end up with is not the sort of thing that's under our control.

The final premise, DS4, is motivated by our intuitions about HYPNOTIC DECISION. Even though Colton did choose to tackle Kabir (no one is denying that people make choices!), he didn't *freely* choose to do so, and the best explanation for this is that his desire to tackle Kabir was not under his control. In other words, because his choices were being controlled by something (his desire) which was not itself under his control, his action is unfree. Generalizing from that: an action can't be free if it's controlled by something that's not under your control. And that's exactly what DS4 is saying.

Some will be tempted to reject DS4, insisting that even if your choices are determined by desires that are outside your control, they're still *your* choices and *your* desires, and that's enough to make them free. But HYPNOTIC DECISION shows why that's a misguided response. It's plain to see that Colton wasn't acting freely when he tackled Kabir. And yet it's true that *he* chose to tackle Kabir, as a result of *his* desire to tackle Kabir. So, the mere fact that one's actions are the product of one's own desires and one's own choices is not enough to make those actions free.

Now that we have seen why the premises of the argument are at least initially plausible, let me address two important objections. According to the first, DS1 should be rejected because one's strongest desires do not always win out. According to the second, DS2 should be rejected because there are ways of controlling one's desires.

4. The Argument from Undesired Actions
A natural reaction to DS1 is to attempt to find cases in which one manages to overcome one's strongest desires. Suppose your alarm goes off early in the morning, waking you up for your 8am class. Your bed is so cozy; your hangover, so vicious. There is no part of you that wants to get out of bed. And yet, somehow, you drag yourself out of bed and get to class. Is this not a counterexample to DS1?

It isn't. The argument underlying this objection would have to go something like this:

The Argument from Undesired Action
(UA1) Your desire to stay in bed was stronger than your desire to get out of bed
(UA2) If your desire to stay in bed was stronger than your desire to get out of bed, then what you choose to do is not always determined by your desires
(UA3) So, what you choose to do is not always determined by your desires

UA1 may well be true. It may well be that you have no desire at all to get out of bed. But UA2 is false. What's true is that the desire to stay in bed isn't overpowered by a desire to get out of bed. But you have other desires that overpower it, for instance the desire to get a good grade in the class. If not for *that* desire, you wouldn't have gotten out of bed. So, in the end, this is just another case of your actions being determined by your desires.

Other putative counterexamples to DS1 fail for similar reasons. Maybe after reading my argument, just to (try to!) prove me wrong, you'll make yourself a banana and toothpaste omelet for lunch, and eat the whole thing despite how disgusting it tastes. Does that show that your actions aren't determined by your

91

desires? No, it just shows that your desire to do something absurd and unpredictable is stronger than your desire to eat something tasty. Or maybe you'll flip a coin to decide where to go for lunch: Panda Express if it's heads, Taco Bell if it's tails. It comes up heads and you go to Panda Express despite feeling more like Taco Bell. Does that show that something other than your desires is determining what you choose to do? No. All it shows is that your desire to honor the coin flip was stronger than your desire to eat what sounds tastiest.

One might still be worried about DS1. Suppose you're at a job interview and your arm suddenly and randomly twitches, causing you to spill a glass of water all over your interviewer. You surely had no desire motivating you to do that. Doesn't that show that what you do isn't always determined by your desires? Indeed, it does. But that's no problem for DS1. DS1 doesn't say that what you *do* is always determined by your desires. It says that what you *choose to do* is always determined by your desires. Since you didn't *choose* to spill the water—it's just something you did by accident—this is no counterexample to DS1.

5. The Argument from Desire-Defeating Actions

DS2 says that you cannot control your desires, which I motivated by pointing out that you don't choose your desires. One might object that, just because you don't *choose* your desires, that doesn't mean that you have no *control* over them. I didn't choose to have dark hair, but I do have control over whether I have dark hair. I can always dye it or shave my head. Likewise, even if I didn't choose my desires, I can take steps to change them.

An example. Suppose that, for ethical reasons, I decide to become a vegetarian. Yet I have such an overwhelming desire for meat that I can't stop myself from eating it. What's a wannabe vegetarian to do? Here's one thing I can do. I can force myself to sit through hours of horrific and disturbing videos of farm animals being slaughtered. In time, I will have conditioned myself to be nauseated by meat and will lose the desire for it altogether. Or suppose that I have become addicted to some drug, and I want to kick the addiction. I can check myself into rehab until the desire for the drug subsides. In other words, even though I never initially chose to desire meat or drugs so strongly, I can change those desires by taking actions that lead me to have the desires I'd prefer to have.

Let's call these actions that enable one to overcome one's desires "desire-defeating actions." One could try to argue against DS2 on the grounds that we are able to control our desires by performing desire-defeating actions:

The Argument from Desire-Defeating Action
(DD1) Your desires can be changed by performing desire-defeating actions

(DD2) If your desires can be changed by performing desire-defeating actions, then you can control your desires

(DD3) So, you can control your desires

I find this argument unconvincing, and here's why. In order to decide to perform a desire-defeating action, you have to *want* to perform it. If I had no desire to watch the videos to help curb my craving for meat, I wouldn't have. More generally, whether you *do* end up choosing to perform a desire-defeating action is determined by whether you have a *strong enough desire* to perform that desire-defeating action.

To see why that's a problem for the Argument from Desire-Defeating Action, forget about free will for a moment, and let's just think about the connection between ability and control. Suppose I'm taking a ferry across the river, and I want to get to the other side quickly. There are two ferries—one of which is much faster than the other—and there's an attendant directing people onto the ferries. He puts some people on the fast ferry and some on the slow ferry, and no one has any say over which ferry he puts them on. Yes, it's true is that I am able to get to the other side quickly if I get on the fast ferry. But it's not up to me which ferry I take. That's determined by the attendant, who I can't control and who has complete control over which ferry I take. Since I have no control over whether I get on the fast ferry, I have no control over whether I get to the other side quickly.

An exactly parallel point holds for desire-defeating actions. It's true that my desires can be changed by performing desire-defeating actions. (In other words, DD1 is true.) But it's not up to me whether I perform the desire-defeating action. That's determined by the strength of my desire to perform a desire-defeating action, which is something I don't control and which has complete control over whether I perform it. Since I have no control over whether I perform desire-defeating actions, I have no control over the desires I'm trying to change. So DD2 is false, and the Argument from Desire-Defeating Action fails.

6. Determinism

That completes our discussion of my first argument against free action. My second argument against free action involves the thesis of determinism, and argues from the truth of determinism to the conclusion that no actions are free. I present the Argument from Determinism in section 7, I address some challenges to determinism in section 8, and I address some attempts to show that free action is compatible with determinism in section 9.

But I'm getting ahead of myself: what is *determinism*? Roughly put, the idea is that everything that's happening now and that will happen in the future was already guaranteed to happen by things that happened in the distant past. Determinism can be stated more rigorously using the notion of *physical necessitation*. To say that one state of the universe physically necessitates some other state is to say that it is logically impossible for the one to occur without the other occurring, given what the laws of nature are. Determinism can then be formulated as the thesis that all present and future states of the universe are physically necessitated by states of the universe in the distant past (that is, before any of us were born).

To get a better sense of what determinism is saying, let's look at an analogy. Consider the counting rhyme *One Potato Two Potato*, which can be used as a way of randomly selecting some person or thing:

One potato **two** potato
Three potato **four**
Five potato **six** potato
Seven potato **more**

Here's how it works. You line some people up—let's say, Blake, Garrett, and Jason, in that order—and you start the rhyme by pointing at Blake as you say "One." Then each time you reach a word in bold, you advance to the next person. So, you move to Garrett on 'two', Jason on 'three', back to Blake on 'four', and so on until you reach 'more'. And whichever person you're pointing at on 'more' is the person you've randomly selected (it's Garrett).

But wait: the procedure isn't really random, is it? Run through it again (without moving the people around), and once again you end on Garrett. Do it a third time. Again, it's Garrett. What you're seeing is that the order of people and the rules of One Potato Two Potato together necessitate a unique outcome.

Determinism is making an analogous claim: past states of the universe and the laws of nature together necessitate a unique future. Just as with the counting rhyme, there is only one way for things to unfold given how things were at the outset and given the rules (the laws) that dictate how one state of the universe gives rise to the next. It won't always be obvious in advance how things will unfold (just like with the counting rhyme). Even so, given how things were in the distant past and given the laws governing how earlier states give rise to later states, there is only one way for things to end up. Or so says determinism.

Before moving on to discuss how determinism is supposed to rule out free action, let me make two points of clarification about what determinism is *not* saying. First, there is a sense in which according to determinism, everything that happens is "fated" to happen. It was already settled, long before you were born, that you would do the things you have done and would experience the things you have experienced. But when people say that something was fated to happen, they often mean that, if it hadn't happened in the way it did, it would somehow have happened some other way. For instance, that if you and your boyfriend hadn't randomly met in some late-night diner, the universe would have conspired for you to meet in some other way (because you were "fated" to be together). Determinism says nothing of the sort. What determinism says is that things couldn't have happened in any other way than the exact way they did happen, given the laws of nature and the way things were in the distant past.

Here's the second point of clarification. You may be wondering: *which* fact about the distant past is supposed to explain why (for instance) you chose to wear a red shirt today rather than a blue shirt? But determinism isn't making the absurd claim that we can pinpoint one specific thing that happened hundreds of years ago that fully explains why you decided to wear this shirt. Rather, the idea is that the entire state of the universe hundreds of years ago, with all of its mind-boggling complexity, physically necessitated the state of the universe this morning, which included you putting on that shirt.

The following analogy may be helpful. Imagine a pool table with billiard balls scattered all around it. And imagine that, like me, you're a terrible pool player and your go-to strategy is just to hit the cue ball as hard as you can towards the biggest cluster of balls and hope that in all the chaos something ends up going in. Suppose your wish comes true: the cue ball hits the seven ball and the eleven ball, and the seven ball knocks the nine ball towards the pocket and the eleven ball knocks the two ball out of the way just in time for the nine ball to go in. Given how the balls were arranged on the pool table just before your shot, together with how hard you hit the ball, the nine ball was bound to go in (as long as there was no outside interference). But there is no one ball that was responsible for the nine ball going in. It isn't just that the nine ball was placed here, or just that the eleven ball was placed there, or just that you were aiming the cue ball in that exact direction. It was all of these things taken together that guaranteed that the nine ball would go in, and any changes in any one of them would have changed the final outcome.

Likewise, determinism isn't saying that there's some one fact in the distant past we can identify that's responsible for some decision you made today. Rather, the idea is that the universe is like a gigantic pool table with atoms crashing around in seemingly chaotic but actually lawfully guided ways, and that those laws guarantee that whole earlier states of the universe will give way to specific later states of the universe.

7. The Argument from Determinism

Perhaps you can already see how determinism is going to cause trouble for free action. But let's make the argument explicit:

The Argument from Determinism
(DT1) Determinism is true

(DT2) If determinism is true, then you are never able to do otherwise

(DT3) If you are never able to do otherwise, then none of your actions are free

(DT4) So, none of your actions are free

In the previous section, I explained what determinism is. But I haven't yet given you any reason to think it's true. So why accept DT1? Here's one reason. Suppose that you are taking a physics exam, which poses a question about a game of pool. The cue ball has just been struck and is headed towards the eight ball. You're given complete information about the state of the pool table immediately following the shot: the masses and positions of the various balls, the velocity of the cue ball and the direction it's traveling, the dimensions of the table, the positions and size of the pockets, and so on. The question is whether the eight ball will go in the pocket.

This is a fair question. With some effort, you can use the laws of physics and information about the balls and the table to calculate whether the shot is successful. But the question is fair, it would seem, only if determinism is true. For if the laws of physics together with the initial state of the table don't determine whether the ball will go in—if things could go either way, as far as physics is concerned—then there would be no way to tell, even in principle, whether the eight ball will go in.

DT2 says that if determinism is true, then "you are never able to do otherwise." What that means is that, for any given thing that you've done, you couldn't have done anything other than that very thing. Suppose that yesterday you were choosing between Taco Bell and Panda Express, and you ended up going to Taco Bell. It might seem like you *could* have gone to Panda Express; you just didn't go there. In other words, it might seem as if you were, in that moment, able to do something other than what you in fact did. What DT2 is saying is that, if determinism is true, then that's not so. In that moment, you couldn't have done anything other than go to Taco Bell.

97

Why accept DT2? The idea is that, if determinism is true, then all of your actions are consequences of things that you are powerless to change—the laws of nature and the distant past—which in turn means that the actions themselves are things you are powerless to change.

How about DT3? Here, the idea is that acting freely requires having multiple courses of action available to you and being able to choose among them. Yet if those courses of action you didn't take weren't really available you—if in truth you couldn't have done anything other than what you in fact did—then your action wasn't free after all.

Any one of these premises can be resisted. So, let's consider each of them in turn.

8. On Rejecting Determinism

As its name suggests, the Argument from Determinism is premised on the assumption that determinism is true. Here I'll consider two things that one might say in order to challenge that assumption: first that decisions and other mental events are exempt from determination by the laws of nature and the distant past, and second that there is genuine randomness in the universe.

I can imagine someone insisting that determinism is true only when restricted to its proper domain: the physical world. What's true is that physical states of the universe in the distant past physically necessitate all present and future *physical* states of the universe. But, the idea goes, they don't physically necessitate present and future *nonphysical* states of the universe, like decisions and other mental states.

It's hardly obvious that mental states aren't physical states (aren't they just brain states?), but, for the sake of the argument, let's just grant that mental states are nonphysical. Still, this is not enough to block the Argument from Determinism. For the envisaged objector agrees that determinism still applies to all physical events, which includes everything that happens in and to our physical bodies. However, if everything that our bodies do is determined, then, by the same reasoning given above, our bodies are never able to do otherwise than what they in fact do. In that case, nothing we do with our bodies is done freely. But *everything* we do (other than thinking) is something we do with

98

our bodies. So, we still get the result that virtually nothing anyone does is done freely, including everyday actions like going to Taco Bell for lunch or going for a morning run.

A different way of challenging DT1 is to insist that even the physical world isn't governed by deterministic laws, because there is genuine randomness in the universe. Indeed, the view that the physical universe is nondeterministic arguably draws support from one of our best confirmed physical theories, quantum mechanics, which is standardly interpreted as saying that some things happen just as a matter of chance and that the laws of nature to some extent leave open what will happen next. But if there is genuine randomness in the physical universe (not just the apparent randomness you get with One Potato Two Potato), then determinism is false: the laws of nature don't guarantee that a specific future will result from past physical states of the universe.

Perhaps one could challenge quantum mechanics, though that seems unwise, especially for those of us who don't have a Ph.D. in physics. More modestly, one could challenge the standard, indeterministic *interpretation* of quantum mechanics (the "Copenhagen" interpretation), and argue for one of the alternative, deterministic interpretations (like the "many-worlds" interpretation). But I'm not going to do either of those things. In fact, let's just grant the point. Suppose that there is genuine randomness in the universe. Suppose DT1 is false. Still, it's a shallow victory, since it's hard to see how randomness is supposed to vindicate free action.

To see why, let's suppose it was a matter of chance that you decided to read this chapter right now. Let's say there was a 30% chance that you'd decide to read the chapter, a 25% chance you'd decide to go for a walk, and a 45% chance that you'd decide to take a nap, and that for no further reason than that—just as a random fluke—you ended up deciding to read rather than nap or walk. That doesn't sound like freedom to me! Think of it this way. If you were to rewind time to the moment just before you decided to read this chapter, over and over again a hundred times, then you'd do the reading about 30 times, nap about 45 times, and go for a walk about 25 times. It's completely random that, in this actual timeline, you decided to read. But if it was a random occurrence, then it wasn't in any sense up to you or under your control whether to read or nap or walk. And actions that aren't up to you or under your control aren't free.

What this suggests is that, surprisingly, our actions are unfree *whether or not* they're determined. We can use this insight to fortify the Argument from Determinism, doing away with the assumption that determinism is in fact true:

The Doomed Regardless Argument
(DM1) If an action is determined to happen, then you couldn't have done otherwise
(DM2) If you couldn't have done otherwise, then the action is not free
(DM3) So, if an action is determined to happen, then it is not free
(DM4) If an action happens randomly, then it is not free
(DM5) Every action you perform is either determined to happen or happens randomly
(DM6) So, none of your actions are free

We have already seen the motivation behind most of the premises, so I can be brief. The idea behind DM1 is that if an action is determined, then you have no control over the factors that are controlling your action (namely, the laws and distant past). The idea behind DM2 is that freedom requires a genuine ability to choose among different courses of action. The idea behind DM4 is that, if it was just a random matter of chance that you did what you did, then it was not up to you whether you did it. DM5 says that all actions are either random ones or determined ones, and indeed it is hard to see what middle ground there could be. If something is undetermined then nothing guarantees that it happens, in which case it must be a matter of chance that it happened. DM6 follows from these four premises: since there are only the two categories of actions, and actions belonging to either category are unfree, no actions are free.

9. Compatibilism
What we have seen is that it is no use trying to resist the Argument from Determinism by rejecting determinism, since I can always

shift to the Doomed Regardless Argument. Indeed, what we have just seen is that free action might *require* determinism, since undetermined random actions can never be free. Thus, one might be tempted by a different strategy, a *compatibilist* strategy, which grants the truth of determinism (DT1) but insists that free action is actually entirely compatible with determinism.

Don't get too excited. A compatibilist still has to find some premise to deny in the Argument from Determinism (as well as the Doomed Regardless Argument). Here again is the argument:

The Argument from Determinism
(DT1) Determinism is true
(DT2) If determinism is true, then you are never able to do otherwise
(DT3) If you are never able to do otherwise, then none of your actions are free
(DT4) So, none of your actions are free

The compatibilist does not deny DT1. So, she has to reject either DT2 or DT3. Let's consider the prospects of each of these options.

9.1 The Consequence Argument
The idea behind DT2 was that, if determinism is true, then all of your actions are consequences of things that you are powerless to change—the laws of nature and the distant past—which in turn means that the actions themselves are things you are powerless to change. Let's break down this line of reasoning.

The Consequence Argument
(CQ1) If determinism is true, then what you do is always a consequence of the laws of nature and the distant past
(CQ2) You have no control over the laws of nature or the distant past
(CQ3) So, if determinism is true, then what you do is always a consequence of things over which you have no control

> (CQ4) If what you do is always a consequence of things over which you have no control, then you are never able to do otherwise
>
> (DT2) So, if determinism is true, you are never able to do otherwise

The idea behind CQ1 is that, given determinism, *everything* that is happening and will happen is physically necessitated by events in the distant past, and what your body and brain do is no exception. Notice that CQ1 is not saying that determinism *is* true. Nor is it saying that what you do is always a consequence of the laws of nature and the distant past. Rather, it's drawing a conceptual connection between two things: *if* everything is determined by the laws and the distant past *then* everything you do is determined by the laws and the distant past. By analogy, suppose that Kristina just got carded at the bar. Even if you think that Kristina is over 21 and is old enough order a drink, you could still agree that *if* Kristina is under 21 *then* she isn't old enough to order a drink. Likewise, even if you reject determinism, you could (and should) still accept CQ1.

CQ2 is certainly true as well: try as you might, you can't change the physical laws and you can't change what happened before you were born. Perhaps you could if you had a time machine but, alas, you don't.

To see why CQ4 is true, imagine that I've got you by the wrists, and I'm hitting you with your own fists and taunting you: "Stop hitting yourself! Stop hitting yourself!" Why is that so upsetting? Because I have overpowered you, and you can't stop hitting yourself. You can't do otherwise. And why is that? Because you have no control over that which is determining what you're doing (namely, me). Generalizing: if you never have control over the things that determine what you do, then you could never have done otherwise than what you in fact did.

9.2 Freedom without Options

The case for DT2 seems airtight: clearly, you can never do otherwise if everything you do is a consequence of things that lie outside your control. That means that compatibilists will have to deny DT3. But how could anyone deny DT3? How could an action be free if you had no choice but to perform that action?

To see how this is possible, the compatibilist might invoke a hypnosis case of her own.

HYPNOTIC BACKUP

Tia the master hypnotist is on the run from the law and hires Clay to tackle any cop who turns up. Concerned that Clay might betray her, Tia gives Clay an irresistible post-hypnotic suggestion to tackle any cop he sees, but which will kick in only if she triggers it by shouting *Abracadabra!* When Kabir the cop arrives on the scene, Tia keeps a watchful eye on Clay to see if he's going to back out. But Clay comes through: he decides to tackle Kabir all on his own, without Tia having to trigger the post-hypnotic suggestion that would have forced him to tackle Kabir.

Here is how this case is supposed to help the compatibilist. Notice that Clay could not have done otherwise. He's either going to decide on his own to tackle Kabir, or he's going to decide not to in which case Tia will trigger the irresistible post-hypnotic suggestion forcing him to tackle Kabir. Either way he tackles Kabir. But the mere fact that he couldn't have done otherwise doesn't stop us from holding him responsible for what he did. That fact by itself doesn't convince us that tackling Kabir is something he didn't do freely. After all, as it happens neither his decision nor his action was the result of hypnosis (although the tackling *would* have been the result of hypnosis had he shown signs of backing out). What this suggests is that the mere inability to do otherwise isn't *by itself* reason to think that an action is unfree. Accordingly, the compatibilist might say, we have no good reason to accept DT3.

Even I have to admit that this is a clever objection. But ultimately the argument can be revised so as to sidestep this case. To see how, let me first try to diagnose our reaction to HYPNOTIC BACKUP. When we think about the tackling, we are inclined to hold Clay responsible and think that being prevented from doing otherwise didn't prevent him from acting freely. Why are we so inclined? Because we think it was at least up to him whether to *decide* to tackle Kabir. Since he could have decided not to tackle Kabir, and since he did decide to tackle Kabir, we are open to thinking of the tackling as something he did freely.

But if determinism is true, then not only your actions but also your (and Clay's) *decisions* are determined. With this in mind, we can revise the Argument from Determinism as follows:

The Argument from Determined Decision
(DT1) Determinism is true
(DT2*) If determinism is true, then you are never able to
   decide to do otherwise
(DT3*) If you are never able to *decide* to do otherwise, then
   none of your actions are free
(DT4) So, none of your actions are free

DT2* is just as plausible as DT2: if determinism is true then everything about you, including what goes on in your brain, is determined by factors outside your control. And DT3* is no longer threatened by HYPNOTIC BACKUP. As I said, HYPNOTIC BACKUP gives us reason to reject DT3 only insofar as we were thinking that Clay could have decided not to tackle Kabir. In order to challenge DT3*, we'd need to change the case so that Clay couldn't even have decided not to tackle Kabir. But when we revise the case in that way, our sense that he may still have been acting freely vanishes altogether.

10. Freedom and Responsibility
I have provided two arguments against the seemingly obvious claim that people sometimes act freely. The first turned on the assumption that our actions are determined by our desires, and the second turned on the assumption that our actions are determined by the laws of nature together with events that long preceded our births. Either way, our actions are determined by something over which we have no control, which, I have argued, suffices to show that no one ever acts freely.

At this point, you may be wondering whether it really even matters whether our actions are free. Of course it does! If nothing we do is under our control and no one ever does anything freely, then no one is ever morally responsible for what they do (just as no one is responsible for things they do when they are in a hypnotic trance). Nor does anyone genuinely deserve praise or blame for anything they do. Accepting the arguments of this chapter requires drastically rethinking our assessments of people and their actions.

If no one is responsible or blameworthy for the things that they do, does it mean that no one should ever be punished for wrongdoing? Not necessarily. What's true is that people should not be punished *because* they deserve it or *because* they're to blame for what they've done. But it still makes good sense to punish people—and to threaten would-be criminals with punishment— to the extent that this has a positive effect on their behavior. In a world without free will, punishment must be seen as "forward-looking" as opposed to "backward-looking." We should punish people because punishment (and the threat thereof) has certain desirable consequences, not because it "sets things right" by addressing some past wrongdoing.

Reflection Questions

1. Premise DS1 of the Desire Argument says that what you choose to do is always determined by your desires. But isn't what you choose to do also at least *partly* determined by your beliefs? For instance, whether your desire for Taco Bell causes you to go to Taco Bell depends in part on whether you believe that Taco Bell is open for business. Can this observation about the influence of beliefs be used to challenge to Desire Argument?

2. Can the Argument from Undesired Actions be defended against the sorts of objections I raise in section 4? Are there better examples of undesired actions, which escape my objections?

3. Premise DM5 of the Doomed Regardless Argument (section 8) says that every action is either determined to happen or random. Is there really no middle ground?

4. At the end of section 9, I said that the HYPNOTIC BACKUP case cannot be revised to serve as a counterexample to DT3* of the Argument from Determined Decisions. Is that true?

Sources
Both the Desire Argument and the Argument from Determinism can be found in Baron d'Holbach's "Of the System of Man's Free Agency." The Consequence Argument in section 9.1 is drawn from Peter van Inwagen's *Essay on Free Will*, and the hypnotic backup case in section 9.2 is a variation on an example from Harry Frankfurt's "Alternate Possibilities and Moral Responsibility." For discussion of whether quantum mechanics is at odds with determinism, see Tim Maudlin's "Distilling Metaphysics from Quantum Physics." Here are some additional resources:

- Maria Alvarez: Actions, Thought Experiments, and the Principle of Alternative Possibilities
- A. J. Ayer: Freedom and Necessity
- Gregg Caruso: The Dark Side of Free Will (youtube.com)
- Clarence Darrow: Crime and Criminals (Address to the Prisoners in the Chicago Jail)
- John Martin Fischer, Robert Kane, Manuel Vargas, and Derk Pereboom: *Four Views on Free Will*
- Meghan Griffith: *Free Will: The Basics*
- R.E. Hobart: Free Will as Involving Determination and Inconceivable Without It
- David Hume: Of Liberty and Necessity
- Kristin M. Mickelson: The Manipulation Argument
- Adina Roskies: Neuroscientific Challenges to Free Will and Responsibility
- Peter van Inwagen: The Powers of Rational Beings
- Susan Wolf: Sanity and the Metaphysics of Responsibility

CHAPTER 6
You Know Nothing

Views and arguments advanced in this chapter are not necessarily endorsed by the author of the textbook, nor are they original to the author, nor are they meant to be consistent with arguments advanced in other chapters. Different chapters represent different philosophical perspectives.

You probably think you know all sorts of things about the world. You know when your earliest class starts tomorrow. You know that it will be colder on average in February than in August, and that the sun will rise and set tomorrow. You know who the president is, you know where your family lives, you know how you celebrated your last birthday, you know some trivia—like the capital of Alaska—and you know some immediately obvious things, like that you're reading a book right now.

I will argue that you don't know any of these things. My aim will be to show that you don't know anything about the world, by which I mean the external physical world. I won't try to argue that you don't know anything about your own internal states—like thoughts and feelings—nor will I try to argue that you don't know anything about nonphysical things like numbers, for instance that 1+1=2. (The title of the chapter admittedly overstates things a bit.) I'll begin by arguing that you don't know what the world will be like in the future, not even one moment from now (sections 1-4). Then I'll argue that you don't even know what the world is like *presently*, not even what's happening right in front of you (sections 5-9).

1. Skepticism about the Future
My first skeptical argument begins with the observation that *if* we know anything about the world, it would have to be in one of two ways. The first way is by *direct observation*. This is just what it sounds like: using your sense organs to obtain information that's immediately available to you. That would be how you know that you're holding a book (or a laptop) in your hands right now, that

you're wearing a bracelet, that the room smells like grandma for some reason, and so on.

But not everything we take ourselves to know about the world can be known on the basis of direct observation. Here's an example. You wake up in the morning, look out the window, and see that everything is wet: the trees are dripping, the lawn is soaked, there are puddles in the street, and so on. You conclude that it rained overnight. But you didn't directly observe it raining. Rather, you *infer* that it rained from things that you've directly observed in the past. In the past, you've observed this sort of watery result being caused by rain falling from the sky. So, you draw the seemingly plausible inference that that's how it happened this time.

This sort of reasoning is what's called an *induction*: reasoning from the fact that certain things you've directly observed are always or usually a certain way to the conclusion that certain things you haven't directly observed are that way too. Inductive reasoning isn't foolproof. It's possible that a plane dropped all that water to put out a fire, and that's why everything is soaked. But the mere fact that induction can sometimes lead us astray doesn't (by itself) show that it's irrational to rely on it.

Our beliefs about how the world will be in the future are likewise based on induction. You expect the sun to set in the west tomorrow. Why? Because every time you've observed the sun set, it has set in the west. Or maybe you're some kind of nerd and you believe the sun will set in the west tomorrow on the basis of laws of planetary motion. But why think those same laws of planetary motion will be in effect tomorrow? Presumably, it's because they've always been in effect in the past.

Now that we have a handle on what induction is, let's get to the argument. The argument is going to turn on the status of a certain principle, which I'll call the *Future Like Past* principle, or FLP for short:

(FLP) Future states of the world will be like past states of the world

The argument, in short, is that we can't know anything about the future because we're not justified in believing FLP, that is, we have no good reason to believe that FLP is true.

Using your belief that the sun will set in the west tomorrow as an illustration, the argument runs as follows:

Against Knowing the Future
(KF1) If you are not justified in believing that FLP is true, then your belief that the sun will set in the west tomorrow is unjustified

(KF2) You are not justified in believing that FLP is true

(KF3) So, your belief that the sun will set in the west tomorrow is unjustified

(KF4) If your belief that the sun will set in the west tomorrow is unjustified, then you don't know that the sun will set in the west tomorrow

(KF5) So, you don't know that the sun will set in the west tomorrow

I'll explain the rationale behind KF1 and KF2 in the following two sections. (Though you may find it worthwhile to pause for a moment right now and ask yourself: what reason *do* you have for believing FLP?) As for KF4, the idea is that being justified in believing something—having good reason for believing it—is a bare minimum requirement for counting as knowing it. For instance, if you think that there are sparrows in Australia, but this is just a guess and you don't actually have any evidence that there are, then you obviously don't *know* that there are sparrows in Australia, even if you happen to have guessed right.

2. What It Takes to Know the Future
Premise KF1 says that your belief that the sun will rise tomorrow is justified *only if* you have good reason to think that that FLP is true. Here's the argument for that premise:

The Faulty Foundation Argument
(FF1) Your belief that the sun will set in the west tomorrow is based on FLP

(FF2) If a belief is based on something that you aren't justified in believing, then that belief itself is unjustified

(KF1) So, if you are not justified in believing that FLP is true, then your belief that the sun will set in the west tomorrow is unjustified

To see the idea behind FF1, let's again ask: why do you believe that the sun will set in the west tomorrow? You infer it from the fact that in the past it has always set in the west. But, implicitly, the inference relies on FLP. In other words, you're at least implicitly running through a line of reasoning something like this:

In the past the sun has always set in the west
Future states of the world will be like past states of the world
So, tomorrow the sun will set in the west

Likewise for your belief that eating that whole McDonalds extra value meal is going to make you sleepy.

In the past eating an entire extra value meal always made me sleepy
Future states of the world will be like past states of the world
So, eating this entire extra value meal will make me sleepy

Implicitly or explicitly, you arrive at all your beliefs about future states of the world in this way.

I don't mean to suggest that we treat FLP as a hard and fast rule. No one thinks that the future will be like the past *in every respect*. We wouldn't use it to infer that there will never be flying cars or a cure for cancer. The principle we actually rely on in our reasoning is more nuanced, perhaps something like this:

(FLP*) Future states of the world will be like past states of the world *except in respects in which we can expect them to differ*

110

These complications needn't concern us here. All I need for the argument for FF1 is that we always rely on *some* principle like this in our reasoning about the future, and that much seems indisputable. You can feel free to replace FLP with FLP*—or whichever other inductive principle you prefer—in the arguments below.

How about FF2? The idea there is that a justified belief can't be built on a faulty foundation: if your reasons for believing something are no good, then that belief itself is no good. To help see this, consider the following case:

POWER POSE
Jared is getting ready for a job interview, and thinks it will help his chances if he spends five minutes "power posing" in front of the mirror. When his fiancée Ashley asks him why he thinks that will help, Jared tells her that scientists have shown that power posing releases performance-enhancing hormones into your bloodstream. Skeptical, Ashley does some Googling and informs Jared that the power-posing study has been completely discredited and is now widely regarded as "pseudo-science."

When Jared finds out that the study has been discredited, that renders his belief that power posing releases performance-enhancing hormones unjustified. But if *that* belief is unjustified, then any belief based on it is going to be unjustified as well. It would obviously be irrational for Jared to go on believing that power posing will help him in the interview once he admits that he has no good reason to believe that power posing releases performance-enhancing hormones. That's the idea behind FF2.

3. Why Believe the Future Will Be Like the Past?

What we have just seen is that your belief about tomorrow's sunset is justified *only if* you're justified in believing FLP, the Future Like Past principle. That means that, if I can establish that you're *not* justified in believing FLP, it follows that your beliefs about tomorrow's sunset aren't justified either. So, let's turn now to KF2, which says that you indeed aren't justified in believing FLP.

111

The idea behind KF2 is that there are only two possible ways for a belief in FLP to be justified, and it isn't justified in either of those ways. Here is the argument:

FLP is Unjustified
(UJ1) If your belief in FLP is justified, then it is either justified by direct observation or by inductive reasoning
(UJ2) Your belief in FLP isn't justified by direct observation
(UJ3) Your belief in FLP isn't justified by inductive reasoning
(KF2) So, your belief in FLP is unjustified

I'll quickly explain why we should accept UJ1 and UJ2, and then in section 4 we'll turn to UJ3.

Why accept UJ1? You might worry that direct observation and inductive reasoning aren't the *only* possible sources of justification. For instance, your beliefs about your own mental life—that you're having certain thoughts and feelings right now—aren't based on any inference (inductive or otherwise) and also aren't based on direct observation (using your sense organs). Rather, they seem to have some further source of justification, as do beliefs about nonphysical things like numbers (for instance, that 3+4=7).

I don't deny that there are other possible sources of justification, for instance introspection or mathematical intuitions. Still, it is hard to see what other than direct observation and induction could justify the beliefs I am targeting here, namely *beliefs about the external physical world*. Introspection and mathematical intuitions can tell you about internal states like thoughts and feelings and nonphysical things like numbers, but they don't by themselves tell us anything about the external physical world. (Of course, they can tell you something about the external world when *combined* with direct observation. For instance, if you saw three slices of pizza, and then you see two of them get eaten, mathematical intuition, together with these direct observations, can tell you that there's one slice left.) And since FLP is a claim about the external physical world—it tells us that future physical states of the external world resemble past physical states

112

of the external world—a belief in FLP would have to be justified by direct observation or inductive inference. Just as UJ1 says.

To see the idea behind UJ2, notice that FLP is a claim about similarity. It's claiming that two things (the past and the future) are similar to one another. Plausibly, in order for direct observation to justify you in believing that two things are similar, you have to be able to directly observe both of them. But you *can't* directly observe the future. (Maybe you could if you had a time machine but, drat, you don't.) So, you can't be justified in believing that the future will be like the past on the basis of direct observation. That's UJ2.

4. No Inductive Argument for FLP

All that remains to be done is to defend UJ3. If I can show that it's true—that FLP can't be justified by inductive inference—then we have a well-motivated argument that your belief in FLP isn't justified, and an argument from there to the conclusion that you don't know that the sun will set in the west tomorrow. The idea behind UJ3 is that any inductive justification for FLP would be circular, and circularity is bad. Unpacking that a bit:

> **The Anti-Circularity Argument**
> (AC1) All inductive reasoning about the future assumes the truth of FLP
> (AC2) If all inductive reasoning about the future assumes the truth of FLP, then any inductive reasoning about FLP is circular
> (AC3) No belief can be justified by circular reasoning
> (UJ3) So, FLP isn't justified by inductive reasoning

Let's take it one premise at a time.

The case for AC1 is the same as the case for premise FF1 of the Faulty Foundation Argument. All inductive reasoning about what's going to happen in the future either explicitly or at least implicitly relies on FLP. In the past the sun has set in the west, and future states of the world will be like past states of the world, so in the future it'll set in the west. The laws of planetary motion have always been this way in the past, and future states of the world will be like past states of the world, so in the future they'll be like this. In the past, beer before liquor makes you sicker, and future states of the world will be like past states of the world, so... you get the idea. All of these lines of reasoning rely on FLP. That's what AC1 says.

AC2 involves the notion of *circularity*. A circular line of reasoning is one whose conclusion also appears as a premise of that reasoning. To see the idea behind AC2, suppose it's true that inductive reasoning about future states of the world always assumes the truth of FLP. Well, FLP itself is about future states of the world: it says that future states are going to be like past states. So, it follows that inductive reasoning about FLP assumes the truth of FLP. In other words, FLP will be both a premise and the conclusion of that line of reasoning, thus qualifying as circular.

To illustrate, the inductive defense of induction might look something like this:

> In the past, each day resembled the day that preceded it
> Future states of the world will be like past states of the world
> So, future days will resemble days in the past

The conclusion of this line of reasoning, "Future days will resemble days in the past," is just another way of saying "Future states of the world will be like past states of the world," which is the second premise of the reasoning. That means that you've got one and the same claim showing up both as a premise and as the conclusion of the reasoning. That fits our definition of circularity.

As for AC3, it's easy to see that circular reasoning is terrible reasoning. As an illustration, consider the following case, involving a Magic 8-Ball toy (which randomly displays answers like Yes, No, and Maybe when you shake it up):

MAGIC 8-BALL
Madhu shakes up his Magic 8-Ball, asks whether Smitha has a crush on him, and it issues its verdict: *yes*. Madhu's excitement lasts only for a moment, as he suddenly realizes that he has no reason to believe that the 8-ball can be trusted. So, he decides to check. He shakes up the 8-Ball, asks it whether it can be trusted, and it issues its verdict: *yes*. "That

settles it," Madhu thinks to himself, "the 8-ball can be trusted, and Smitha does have a crush on me!"

Obviously, Madhu's reasoning here is deeply problematic. The first time he shakes up the toy, he reasons from *it said she has a crush on me* to *she does have a crush on me*, implicitly relying on the assumption that the 8-Ball can be trusted—which he has no good reason to assume. The second time he shakes it up, he reasons from *it said it can be trusted* to *it indeed can be trusted*, again relying on the assumption that he can trust what it says. The first time was bad enough, since the assumption was unfounded. The second time is even worse, and the natural diagnosis of why that line of reasoning is so bad is that it's circular: *the 8-ball can be trusted* appears both as the conclusion and as a premise of Madhu's reasoning. Surely you can't be justified in believing anything on the basis of reasoning like that. And that's just what AC3 is saying.

This concludes my argument that you don't know that the sun will set in the west tomorrow. But the example of tomorrow's sunset was chosen more or less at random. I could have chosen virtually any belief you have about the future and used the same reasoning to show that it is justified only if your belief in FLP is justified. Accordingly, if KF2 is true—and I have just argued at length that it *is* true—then all of your beliefs about how things will be in the future are unjustified. You don't know what's going to happen one year from now, one hour from now, or even one second from now.

5. The Dreaming Argument
We just saw that you don't know anything at all about what the world is going to be like in the future. Now I want to turn to an even more radical conclusion, namely that you don't know anything about what's going on in the world at this very moment, not even what is going on right in front of your eyes. My argument will focus on one particular thing you take yourself to know about the world—that you're sitting down reading—but it will be obvious how the argument generalizes to all your other beliefs about the world: the color of the chair you're sitting in, the number of people in the room with you, and so on.

My argument involves a certain hypothesis, which I'll call *the dreaming hypothesis,* or TDH for short:

(TDH) You are currently lying down in bed dreaming about sitting down reading a philosophy textbook

With TDH in mind, here is how I'll argue that you don't know that you're sitting down reading:

The Dreaming Argument
(DR1) If you have no way of knowing that TDH is false, then you don't know that you're sitting down reading
(DR2) You have no way of knowing that TDH is false
(DR3) So you don't know that you're sitting down reading

Notice that TDH is not itself a premise of the argument. Accordingly, I don't have to try to convince you that TDH is true, or even that it's probably true. Indeed, I don't need to give you any reason whatsoever for thinking it's true, and it's fine with me if you think that it's incredibly unlikely that it's true. All I need to show concerning TDH is that you have no way of knowing it's false. And that I can do.

Let's turn, then, to the defense of the premises. In section 6, I'll present some arguments for DR1. Then, in section 7, I'll present an argument for DR2. Finally, in sections 8-9, I'll conclude the discussion of the dreaming argument by addressing a likely objection to DR2, namely that you can tell you're not dreaming by performing some sort of test, like pinching yourself.

6. Why You Have to Rule Out the Dreaming Hypothesis
DR1 says that you must be able to rule out the dreaming hypothesis in order to know that you're sitting down reading. Why is that? Why can't you claim to know that you're sitting down reading, while at the same time admitting that you have no way to rule out crazy ideas like TDH? I'll give two reasons.

The first reason for accepting DR1 involves thinking about everyday ways of challenging someone's claim to know something. If we see a large bird in the sky and you say that it's a hawk, I might ask how you know it's not an eagle or a falcon.

Perhaps you are able to rule out these competing hypotheses. For instance, perhaps you can tell it's not an eagle by its tailfeathers or by its beak. If, however, you *aren't* able to rule out these competing hypotheses, then you can't truly claim to know that it's a hawk.

This suggests the following argument for DR1:

The Competing Hypotheses Argument
(CH1) One knows a certain thing only if one has some way of knowing that all competing hypotheses are false
(CH2) TDH is a hypothesis that competes with your belief that you're sitting down reading
(DR1) So, if you have no way of knowing that TDH is false, then you don't know that you're sitting down reading

CH1 reflects a general lesson that can be extracted from the hawk example: in order to truly know what's going on in a given situation, you have to be able to rule out competing hypotheses about what's going on in that situation. That's why the observation that you can't rule out the hypothesis that the bird we saw is an eagle constitutes a genuine challenge to your claim to know that the bird is a hawk.

CH2 is straightforward: when you have all of these experiences as of sitting down and reading, and you assume that you indeed are sitting down reading, a competing explanation of what's going on is that you're in bed having an incredibly vivid dream in which you're sitting down reading. I'm not saying this is an especially plausible hypothesis, just that it's a competing hypothesis.

Now for the second reason to accept DR1. Suppose you really did know that you were sitting down reading right now. In that case, you *would* have a way of definitively ruling out TDH. After all, if you genuinely knew that you were sitting, then you'd be able to infer that you aren't lying down—since you can't simultaneously be sitting and lying down—and thus that you aren't lying down dreaming. Knowing you're sitting down would therefore give you a way of knowing that TDH is false, so if you truly have *no* way of knowing that TDH is false then you must not

117

know that you're sitting down reading. Which is exactly what DR1 says.

We can develop this idea more explicitly using the notion of a *deduction*. A deduction is a certain type of reasoning, where the conclusion of the reasoning is logically guaranteed by the premises. In other words, you would be contradicting yourself if you accepted all the premises and yet denied the conclusion. As an illustration, if you reason from *the coin either landed heads or tails* and *it did not land heads* to the conclusion *it landed tails*, that's a deduction. You deduced that it landed tails from those other two beliefs. Using this notion of deduction, we can run the following argument:

The Argument from Deduction

(DE1) If you know you're sitting down reading, then you can deduce that TDH is false from things you know

(DE2) If you can deduce something from things you know, then you have a way of knowing that thing

(DE3) So, if you know you're sitting down reading, then you have a way of knowing that TDH is false

DE1 says that there's a certain kind of deduction you'd be able to perform if you really did know that you were sitting down reading. Specifically, you'd be able to perform the following deduction:

(i) I'm sitting down reading

(ii) If I'm sitting down reading, then I'm sitting

(iii) If I'm sitting, then I'm not lying down

(iv) If I'm not lying down, then I'm not lying down dreaming

(v) If I'm not lying down dreaming, then TDH is false

(vi) So, TDH is false

This is a way of deducing that TDH is false. Steps (ii), (iii), (iv), and (v) of the reasoning are easily known conceptual truths. For instance, you know (iii) just by observing that it follows from the definition of *sitting* that if you're sitting you're not lying down. So, *if* you know the first step as well—that you're sitting down reading—then what we have here is a way of deducing that TDH is false from things you know. That's what DE1 says.

The idea behind DE2 is straightforward. Suppose I tell you that I flipped a normal coin and that it didn't come up heads. You tell me that it came up tails. How did you know?? Answer: by deducing it from things you know: that it was either heads or tails, and that it wasn't heads. Of course, if you ran through that same deduction, but you didn't actually know that it wasn't heads—you were merely guessing it wasn't heads, let's say—we wouldn't say that you *knew* it was tails. But when you deduce something from things you actually do know, then you know the thing you deduced as well. That's what DE2 is saying.

DE1 and DE2 are both true, and they together entail DE3. But notice that DE3 says *exactly the same thing* as DR1:

(DE3) If you know you're sitting down reading, then you have a way of knowing that TDH is false

(DR1) If you have no way of knowing that TDH is false, then you don't know that you're sitting down reading

To see that these say the same thing, notice that "if A is true then B is true" is just another way of saying "if B isn't true, then A isn't true." These are simply two different ways of saying that you don't get A without B. (An example: "if Farid is from Paris then he is from France" is exactly equivalent to saying "if Farid isn't from France then he isn't from Paris.") And since DR1 and DE3 say exactly the same thing, the Argument from Deduction serves as an argument for DR1.

7. Why You Can't Rule Out the Dreaming Hypothesis

Having shown that you *have* to be able to rule out TDH in order to know that you're sitting down reading, I turn now to the second premise, DR2, which says that you *can't* rule out TDH. Simply put, the argument is that you haven't got any evidence against TDH, and you can't know that a claim is false if you haven't got any evidence against it.

119

The No Evidence Argument
(NE1) If you have no evidence against something, then you have no way of knowing it's false
(NE2) You have no evidence against TDH
(DR2) So, you have no way of knowing that TDH is false

NE1 is eminently plausible. I might tell you that J. K. Rowling is the best-selling author of all time. You may have your doubts. You may choose not to believe me. But you can't *know* that what I said is false unless you have at least some evidence that she isn't the best-selling author of all time.

The idea behind NE2 is that TDH is compatible with all your evidence. After all, what evidence do you have that you're sitting down reading? Your evidence is that it *looks* to you like your legs are bent in a sitting position atop a chair (or couch), that it *feels* like you're holding a book (or tablet or laptop), and so on. But that's all entirely compatible with TDH. Indeed, this is exactly how things would look and feel to you if you were merely dreaming that you were sitting down reading. So, the fact that it looks and feels like you're sitting down reading is hardly evidence that you aren't merely dreaming that you're sitting down reading. In other words, it's not evidence that TDH is false.

You might suspect at this point that my own argument can be turned against me. After all, you might insist, we don't have any evidence *for* TDH either. So, it would seem that we can run a parallel argument for the conclusion that we can't know that TDH is *true*:

The Flipped Evidence Argument
(FE1) If you have no evidence for something, then you have no way of knowing it's true
(FE2) You have no evidence for TDH
(FE3) So, you have no way of knowing that TDH is true

But this argument doesn't worry me at all. It's not that I have some objection to one of the premises. Indeed, I agree with both of the premises, and I happily accept the conclusion of the argument. As I already explained above (in section 5), my argument doesn't require establishing that TDH is true, or even that TDH is probably true. All I need to establish is that you can't know it's false. And I have now done so, using the No Evidence Argument.

Still, you might wonder how I can accept both arguments. After all, don't their conclusions contradict one another? Not at all: DR2 and FE3 are entirely compatible. It *would* be contradictory to say that TDH both is and isn't true, or that you both can and can't know that TDH is true. But that's not what you get when you combine DR2 and FE3. Instead, what you get is a perfectly consistent claim with which I am in complete agreement: that we have no way of knowing, one way or the other, whether TDH is true or false.

8. Can You Tell You're Not Dreaming?

I can imagine someone objecting that there *is* a way to know you're not dreaming: dreams are different from waking life in all sorts of ways, and you can know whether you're dreaming by checking for those differences. For instance, you might point out that your present experiences are incredibly vivid and coherent, whereas dreams tend to be blurry nonsense. You might then claim that this undermines DR2: you can know that TDH is false by attending to the vividness of your experiences. And you might insist that NE2 of the No Evidence Argument is false as well, because the vividness of your experience counts as evidence against TDH.

The easiest way to see why this objection won't work is to slightly modify TDH as follows:

(TDH+) You are currently lying down in bed dreaming about sitting down reading a philosophy textbook, and it's the most incredibly vivid dream you've ever had

You can't know that TDH+ is false just by attending to the vividness of your experiences. Nor can the vividness be evidence against TDH+. Having vivid experiences is entirely compatible with TDH+; indeed, it's exactly what TDH+ predicts your experiences will be like. What this shows is that I can sidestep this objection from vividness by simply replacing TDH with TDH+ in all the arguments.

Exactly the same point applies to other ways you might try to check whether you're dreaming. For instance, you might point out that you're a complete novice at philosophy, and that these are brilliant philosophical arguments that you never knew about before. But, you might insist, you can't dream about an idea you've never heard before.

First of all, don't sell yourself short: if Paul McCartney can compose the song *Yesterday* in a dream, then you can come up with the Dreaming Argument in a dream. (It's not *that* brilliant, really.) Second, we can once again sidestep this concern by simply modifying TDH. For instance, we can modify it to say that you're a brilliant philosophy professor, dreaming that you're a student reading a philosophy textbook for the first time. Or that you're dreaming about reading philosophical arguments that only *seem* brilliant but actually they're complete gibberish.

(There's an old joke about a guy who dreamed that he came up with a single objection that could refute every philosophical position. One by one, he approached every great philosopher in history, all of whom presented their arguments but then admitted defeat upon hearing the objection. He woke up in a daze, scribbled the objection on a piece of paper so he wouldn't forget it, and went back to sleep. When he awoke the next morning, he grabbed the piece of paper excitedly, and found that what he had scribbled down was: "that's what *you* say!")

9. No Useful Tests for Dreaming

It should be fairly clear that, for any test you come up with for checking whether you're dreaming, I'll be able to modify TDH to get around the test. Even better, though, if I can nip this sort of response in the bud by giving a more direct argument that no test can ever enable you to know whether you're dreaming. Not pinching yourself and checking if you feel it, not flipping light switches and checking if the lighting changes, not—as a student of mine once argued in a term paper—peeing and checking if you still feel like you have to pee. (If you do, he argued, then you must have only dreamt that you peed.)

Let's call a way of testing whether you're dreaming a "dreaming test." A *reliable* dreaming test is one that tells you you're dreaming only when you really are dreaming, and that tells you you're awake only when you really are awake. Here's the argument:

The No Useful Tests Argument
(NU1) If you don't know that a dreaming test is reliable, then you can't know whether you're dreaming by using it
(NU2) You can never know that a dreaming test is reliable
(NU3) So, you can never know whether you're dreaming by using a dreaming test

NU1 says that, in order to know whether you're dreaming by using a certain dreaming test, you have to know that the test actually *works*. Suppose I ask you how you know you're awake and you say, "because I spun a top and it fell over instead of spinning forever." Then I ask you how you know that's a good test for whether you're dreaming and you say, "oh, I have no idea if it works, I just saw it in a movie once." If you don't already somehow know that tops always spin forever in dreams and never spin forever in reality—that is, unless you know that the spinning top test is a reliable dreaming test—then you can't know you're awake by using that test.

What about NU2? Why can't you ever know that a dreaming test is reliable? Here's why. Knowing a test is reliable is a matter of knowing that it's worked in the past: those times you were dreaming, the test correctly said you were dreaming, and those times you were awake, it correctly said you were awake. So, for instance, to assure yourself that the pinching test is reliable, you might reason as follows: "Yesterday, I pinched myself while I was awake at the gym and I felt it. Last night, I pinched myself while I was dreaming and I didn't feel anything. This morning, right after I woke up, I pinched myself again and I felt it."

But wait a minute. That line of reasoning presupposes that you really were awake on the first and third occasion. For all you know, maybe you merely *dreamed* that you woke up this morning. Maybe you are still dreaming, and the supposed awakening was merely a dream within a dream coming to an end. Perhaps for the last fifteen years you've been lying in bed in a coma, moving in and out of dreams in which you feel pinches and dreams-within-dreams in which you can't feel them. You have no way of ruling that out. And if you can't rule that out, then you can't know that your rationale for thinking the pinching test is reliable is any good. And if you can't know that your rationale for thinking the pinching test is reliable is any good, then you can't know that the pinching test is reliable. And the same goes for all other dreaming tests. Just like NU2 says.

10. Conclusion

I've argued that you know nothing about the external world, either how it will be in the future or even how it is right now. You can't know anything about future because all of your beliefs about the future are based on an assumption that you have no good reason to accept: that future states of the world will be like past states of the world. And you can't know anything about the present because you have no way to rule out the possibility that all of your present experiences are part of an unusually vivid dream.

Reflection Questions

1. The argument in section 3 turns on the claim that induction and direct observation are the only ways of knowing about the world. Is that true? When a detective solves a crime unlike any crime she's ever seen before, is she using resources other than induction and direct observation? If so, how might that help with resisting the argument?

2. At the end of section 4, I say that the argument extends to all of your beliefs about the future. Is that true? Can it be used to undermine the belief that 1+1 will still be equal to 2 tomorrow? If not, why not?

3. Are you convinced by the Competing Hypotheses argument in section 6? If you think that not all competing hypotheses need to be ruled out, how would you distinguish between those that do and those that don't?

4. Do you have any evidence that the dreaming hypothesis is false? If so, what is it? If the evidence takes the form of a

dreaming test, how would you respond to the No Useful Tests argument in section 9?

5. Can you think of a way of modifying some of the arguments from this chapter to produce an argument that we can't know anything about the *past*?

6. I argued that no one knows anything about the world. Are my arguments self-defeating? Can they also be used to show that *I don't know* that no one knows anything about the world? If so, is that a problem? If not, why not?

Sources
The Against Knowing the Future Argument—more commonly known as the problem of induction—can be found in David Hume's *Enquiry Concerning Human Understanding*. The Magic 8-Ball example is drawn from Richard Fumerton's *Metaepistemology*. The Dreaming Argument is drawn from René Descartes's *Meditations on First Philosophy*, and also has roots in Zhuangzi's "Discussion on Making All Things Equal." See Fred Dretske's "Is Knowledge Closed Under Known Entailment?" for discussion of the Argument from Deduction. The joke about the philosopher's dream in section 8 is from Raymond Smullyan's *5000 BC and Other Philosophical Fantasies*. Here are some additional resources:

- Daniel Greco: Hume's Skepticism (wi-phi.com)
- Michael Huemer: The Problem of Memory Knowledge
- Ned Markosian: Do You Know That You Are Not a Brain in a Vat?
- Jennifer Nagel: *Knowledge: A Very Short Introduction*
- Jennifer Nagel: Three Responses to Skepticism (wi-phi.com)
- Susanna Rinard: Reasoning One's Way Out of Skepticism
- Wesley Salmon: An Encounter with David Hume
- Gail Stine: Skepticism, Relevant Alternatives, and Deductive Closure
- Jonathan Stoltz: *Illuminating the Mind: An Introduction to Buddhist Epistemology*
- Ruth Weintraub: Skepticism about Induction
- Catherine Wilson: *Descartes's Meditations: An Introduction* (ch.2)

CHAPTER 7
Against Prisons and Taxes

Views and arguments advanced in this chapter are not necessarily endorsed by the author of the textbook, nor are they original to the author, nor are they meant to be consistent with arguments advanced in other chapters. Different chapters represent different philosophical perspectives.

Governments sometimes do things that are morally questionable, for instance instituting drug laws that disproportionately punish low income and minority groups, or distributing tax dollars to controversial organizations. What I aim to show here is that even some of the most basic and seemingly uncontroversial functions of government are morally questionable. Specifically, I will argue that it is morally wrong for governments to tax or imprison their citizens *at all*.

In section 1, I advance my argument against taxation and incarceration, which turns on the idea that there is no relevant difference between taxation and extortion, or between imprisoning and kidnapping. In section 2, I consider and dismiss a number of attempts to justify taxes and prisons. In sections 3-4, I criticize the most promising attempt to resist the argument, according to which we consent to this treatment by entering into a "social contract" with the government. Finally, in section 5, I show how my argument can be adapted to establish that there should be no restrictions on immigration.

1. Taxation and Extortion
Maybe it seems obvious to you that the government has every right to imprison and tax its citizens. To begin to see why it's not so obvious, notice how morally problematic it would be for an ordinary citizen to do more or less the same thing.

> ### VIGILANTE
> Jasmine discovers that some con men have set up a fake charity and are conning some people in her neighborhood. She captures them at gunpoint, takes them to her basement, and plans to keep them there for a year as punishment.

Quickly realizing how expensive it is to take care of them, Jasmine goes to her neighbors and demands $50 from each of them, at gunpoint. She explains that half the money will go towards taking care of her prisoners and that the rest will go towards a community gym to help keep troubled kids off the street. Those who do not comply are locked up in her basement with her other prisoners.

I'm going to go out on a limb here and say that what Jasmine is doing is wrong. When she demands money from her neighbors at gunpoint, that's called *extortion*. When she locks her neighbors in her basement, that's called *kidnapping*. It is wrong to kidnap people, and it is wrong to extort people, even when it's for a good cause.

My argument against taxation and imprisonment is going to turn on the idea that there's no *morally relevant difference* between what Jasmine does and what the government does. Let me begin by saying something about what that means. Suppose I walk into my house, raid my fridge, sit down on my couch, and flip on my TV. There's nothing wrong with that. Now suppose that I walk into *your* house (without permission), raid your fridge, sit down on your couch, and start watching your TV. That isn't morally okay.

Why is it morally okay in the one case but not in the other? Here's the obvious difference: my house belongs to me, and your house doesn't belong to me. In other words, the fact that my house and fridge belong to me and yours don't is a difference between the actions that explains the moral difference between them, why the one is morally okay and the other isn't. This difference in ownership is an example of what I'm calling a morally relevant difference. More precisely, a morally relevant difference between two things is a difference between them that can explain why they differ morally. In other words, it's a difference that *makes* a difference to the morality of a situation.

Not just any difference will count as a morally relevant difference. To see this, suppose I'm in my car and I run over a jogger, and compare this to a case in which I run over a cockroach. The cases differ in multiple ways. In the one case, the thing I ran over was jogging and in the other case the thing I ran over was crawling. But *that's* not what explains the moral difference between the two actions, why I did something immoral in the one case but not the other. Rather, the morally relevant difference is that in the first case it's a person I ran over and in the second case it's a cockroach. What this shows is that just because you've identified *a* difference between two cases, it still may not be a morally relevant difference. Indeed, it may be that two cases differ in all sorts of ways, and yet *none* of the differences are morally relevant.

Now that I have explained the notion of a morally relevant difference, we are ready to see the argument:

Against Taxation and Imprisonment
(TX1) If there is no morally relevant difference between two actions A and B, and A is wrong, then B is wrong
(TX2) It is wrong for Jasmine to extort and kidnap her neighbors
(TX3) There is no morally relevant difference between Jasmine extorting and kidnapping her neighbors and the government taxing and imprisoning its citizens
(TX4) So, it is wrong for the government to tax and imprison its citizens

The idea behind TX1 is that, whenever there is some moral difference between two cases, there must always be some further difference between them to explain why they differ morally. Absent some such difference, it would be arbitrary to say that the one action is wrong and the other isn't—just as it would be arbitrary for me to bump some students with an 86% up to a B+ but not others. As for TX2, my hope is that it will strike you as obvious. I'm not sure what more I could say to convince you that extortion and kidnapping are wrong.

TX3, by contrast, probably doesn't strike you as obvious. Maybe you've already thought of multiple differences between what Jasmine does and what the government does that could potentially explain why what she does is wrong but what the government does isn't. The following three sections will be devoted to defending the argument by addressing such putative differences.

2. Morally Relevant Differences

In this section, I'll consider six putative morally relevant differences between what Jasmine does and what the government does, and I'll show that they do not undermine the argument—either because they are not morally relevant after all, or because we can adjust the VIGILANTE case to make the differences go away.

First, one might suggest that the morally relevant difference is that what Jasmine does is illegal, whereas what the government does is not illegal. I admit that it's not illegal when the government does it. And since it's the government that makes the laws, it's no surprise that it permits itself to tax and imprison people. Yet plenty of immoral things aren't illegal, for instance cheating on your boyfriend or on a midterm exam. And plenty of illegal things aren't immoral, for instance underage drinking, or driving without a seatbelt. So, it's far from clear why this difference in *legal* permissibility would be a *morally* relevant difference.

Second, one might observe that, unlike Jasmine, the government doesn't come to your door and demand money at gunpoint when taxes are due. That's true. Though let's not forget that they will eventually come to your door with guns to take you to prison if you keep ignoring their polite reminders. With that in mind, let's revise the Jasmine case to tighten the analogy:

> **BUREAUCRATIC VIGILANTE**
> Jasmine sends an email to all of her neighbors, informing them that they must each send her $50 by April 15; that if they don't, they'll automatically be granted an extension, but will be charged a small late fee; and that if they still don't pay, she will lock them in her basement. Some don't pay even by the extended deadline, and she shows up at their door, escorts them to her home at gunpoint, and locks them in her basement.

By revising the story so that Jasmine doesn't take their money at gunpoint—but instead leads them to her basement at gunpoint when they consistently fail to pay—we have eliminated the alleged morally relevant difference between the two cases. We no longer have an objection to TX3. Of course, now that we have changed the details of the case, we need to make sure that TX2—which says that Jasmine is doing something wrong—is still plausible. But surely it is, even when we modify the procedure by which she extorts and kidnaps her neighbors.

Third, one might point out that government officials have been *elected* to serve as representatives of our interests, whereas Jasmine was not elected. This may indeed be a morally relevant difference, but we can again revise the case so as to circumvent it.

ELECTED VIGILANTE
Jasmine plans to start taking prisoners and demanding $50 at gunpoint from each of her neighbors to pay for the prisoners and a gym. Zhiwen thinks it would be better to demand $75, with the additional $25 going towards hiring a nurse to provide free medical care to anyone in the neighborhood. Jasmine and Zhiwen let their neighbors vote on which of them should get to set the policies for kidnapping and extortion. Many don't vote but, of those who do, the majority prefer Jasmine. Zhiwen accepts the results of the election, and Jasmine begins kidnapping and extorting her neighbors.

It still seems as if Jasmine is doing something wrong. So TX2 remains true. And since Jasmine is elected in this revised case, the proposed objection to TX3 fails. Nor should it be any surprise that holding an election doesn't make a difference. Suppose I order pizza for the whole class, and when it arrives we vote on who pays the bill. The majority of the students vote that you should pay, and so I point a gun at you and demand that you pay. That would be wrong, even though we voted on it.

Fourth, one might insist that it's okay for the government to imprison criminals because it's public knowledge what the laws are and what the penalties are for violating them, whereas Jasmine just starts kidnapping and extorting people out of nowhere. There's an easy fix here as well. We simply build it into the story that, before she starts kidnapping people and demanding money at gunpoint, she puts up a large, laminated poster in the center of town, labeled 'Jasmine's Rules', and once everyone has had a chance to read it, she begins locking up violators in her basement and demanding money from her neighbors on threat of imprisonment.

Fifth, one might insist that taxation and imprisonment are morally justified because we would all be so much worse off without them. That's almost certainly true, but it's irrelevant. Jasmine's kidnapping and extortion are also making things better in her neighborhood. There are fewer con men, and the gym really is helping keep troubled kids off the street. So, this isn't even a difference between the cases, let alone a morally relevant one.

Furthermore, just because something would make the world a better place, that doesn't necessarily mean it's morally permissible for someone to bring it about. To see this, consider the following case:

> SAINT AND SINNER
> A saint and a sinner both need a kidney transplant, but there is only one kidney available. The saint refuses it and insists that it be given to the sinner. The doctor, knowing that the world will be better off if the saint survives than if the sinner survives, forcibly anesthetizes the saint and gives her the kidney against her wishes and without her consent. The saint (who would otherwise have died) goes on to live a long life and does many saintly things.

Surely you'll agree that it was morally impermissible for the doctor to force the kidney upon the saint, even though the doctor's actions made the world a better place on the whole. Likewise, even if the world would be a worse place without someone locking up criminals and forcing the rest of us to help pay for it, that doesn't mean it's morally okay for anyone to actually do it.

Sixth, one might insist that the country *belongs* to the government, whereas the neighborhood does not belong to Jasmine, and that this is why the government but not Jasmine is allowed to do these things. But I see no more reason to think that the country literally belongs to the government than that some street corner literally belongs to the drug dealers that have claimed it. It's true that the government *acts* like they own the place, and that they have enough power to cow people into letting

131

them do what they want. But there's no good reason to think that some patch of the surface of the Earth is literally owned by the government. It's just not plausible that the country and the neighborhood differ in this way.

Furthermore, even supposing that government owns the country, we can once again revise the case so as to circumvent the putative morally relevant difference:

LANDLORD

Jasmine owns an apartment complex and discovers that some of her tenants have been conning some of the other tenants. She locks the con men in the basement of the complex, and plans to keep them there for a year as punishment. Jasmine then demands an additional $50 from each of her other tenants, to cover the expense of caring of her prisoners. Tenants who do not comply are locked in the basement with the other prisoners.

It still seems as if Jasmine is doing something wrong. So TX2 remains true. And since Jasmine *does* own the apartment complex in this case, the envisaged morally relevant difference has disappeared, and the present objection to TX3 fails.

3. The Social Contract

What we have just seen is that, while there are plenty of differences between what Jasmine does in VIGILANTE and what the government does in taxing and imprisoning its citizens, many of those differences don't have what it takes to undermine TX3 of the argument. I turn now to a somewhat more promising proposal, but we will see that it ultimately fails as well.

Here, the idea is that we have entered into a sort of contract with the government. They provide us with things like roads, fire departments, national parks, and protection from criminals and hostile governments. In return, we agree to pay taxes and obey the laws of the land. And contracts can make a moral difference. It would be wrong for me to let myself into your home... unless you are subletting it to me, since in that case we have a contract permitting me to enter. Accordingly, this could potentially be the morally relevant difference we've been looking for.

Have we entered into such a contract with our government? Unlike a typical contract, you never explicitly agreed to this arrangement, either verbally or in writing. But that doesn't *necessarily* mean you haven't consented to the arrangement. After all, there is such a thing as tacit (or implicit) consent, where one consents through one's conduct, without any stated agreement. How does that sort of thing happen?

It can happen in all sorts of ways. I'll mention three. First, one can sometimes tacitly consent to something by accepting certain kinds of benefits. When you get into a taxi and give the driver an address, you thereby consent to paying the fare when you arrive. When you order food at a restaurant, you thereby consent to paying the bill; when the bill arrives, you don't get to say "hey wait, I never said I was going to *pay* for any of this!" Second, you can tacitly consent to something by sticking around. If I make it clear that anyone who is still at my party after midnight has to help clean up, and you stay past midnight, you've consented to helping clean up. That's so even if you never explicitly said you were willing to help. Third, it's possible to tacitly consent to something by passively going along with it without objection. For instance, if your professor says "I'm planning to move the exam to 9am, is that a problem?" and no one says anything, you've all tacitly consented to the exam being moved to 9am.

Every one of these potential sources of tacit consent is present in our relationship with the government. First, we accept all sorts of services that the government provides. We use the roads and public parks, for instance, and benefit from the (relative) lack of crime provided by police departments. Second, we choose to stick around in the country, knowing full well that we'll be expected to follow the laws and pay some taxes. Third, we passively accept the laws and taxes without objection. We may gripe about them, but we don't explicitly refuse to obey the laws or pay our taxes.

4. No Social Contract
We have just seen reason to think that we have entered into an unspoken contract with the government. We also saw that the existence of a contract can make a moral difference, as in the case of subletting. Is this, finally, the morally relevant difference we need in order to resist TX3? No, it's not.

133

To see why not, notice that we haven't actually identified a *difference* between our relationship with the government and Jasmine's relationship with her neighbors. First, even if they didn't ask for it, they too are enjoying the benefits of having fewer con men and other criminals running around. Second, they too choose to stay in the neighborhood even though they know that Jasmine is going to demand money from them. Who could blame them? They've lived their whole lives in that neighborhood. That's where their family and friends are. That's where their job is. They couldn't afford to up and move to a new neighborhood even if they wanted to. Third, they don't vocally object to what Jasmine is doing. After all, it's unlikely to make any difference, and she's clearly a very dangerous person.

What this all shows, I think, is that—despite receiving benefits, sticking around, and being passive—her neighbors have not consented to living by Jasmine's rules. But then, by parity of reason, we haven't tacitly consented to living by the government's rules *simply* by virtue of receiving benefits, sticking around, and being passive. (Similar remarks apply to sexual consent. Just because someone comes home with you after being taken out for dinner, doesn't try to leave, and doesn't vocally object to your advances, that doesn't mean that they have consented to having sex with you.) And if we haven't thereby tacitly consented to living by the government's rules, then there's no good reason to think we have entered into any "social contract" with the government.

We are, however, still left with the question of why these behaviors don't constitute tacit consent in the case of Jasmine and the government and yet do constitute tacit consent in the other cases: getting into a taxi, sticking around the party, and not objecting to the time change. The answer is that there are certain further conditions that have to be met in order for these types of behaviors to constitute tacit consent. I'll mention two.

The first condition is that there has to be a reasonable way of opting out of the arrangement. In those other cases, there *is* a reasonable way of opting out: you could just pass on the taxi and walk home, leave the party before midnight, or speak up and say that the time change doesn't work for you. By contrast, there's no reasonable way to opt out of the services the government provides. For instance, you can't get anywhere without using their roads. Additionally, you'd have to leave the country to stop benefitting from the protection that the government provides, and most people can't afford to leave the country even if they wanted to. And even if they could afford to leave, it would require completely uprooting their lives. And even if they were willing to do that, where would they go? There's virtually nowhere on the planet for them to go that doesn't have taxes and prisons. There is no reasonable way to opt out.

The second condition that has to be met in order for those behaviors to constitute tacit consent is that explicit refusal to opt in has to be recognized. Suppose you go to a restaurant and they bring you food and charge you for it even though you explicitly said you didn't want any. Or suppose that the professor was clearly going to move the exam to 9am even if you and others did object to the time change. In that case, you haven't tacitly consented, because explicit refusal to opt in is not recognized. The same is true of our arrangement with the government. Here is what happens when people try to live "off the grid" and explicitly refuse to pay taxes: government agents show up with guns and take them to prison. Explicit refusal to opt in is not recognized.

We can turn these observations into an argument that we have not tacitly consented to paying taxes and following the laws.

No Consent
(NC1) Someone tacitly consents to an arrangement only if (i) there is a reasonable way to opt out and (ii) explicit refusal to opt in is recognized
(NC2) There is no reasonable way to opt out of paying taxes and following laws, and explicit refusal to opt in is not recognized
(NC3) So, we have not tacitly consented to paying taxes and following laws

Since we have not tacitly consented to following the laws or being subjected to taxation and imprisonment, there is no good reason to think that we have entered into an unspoken contract with the government. But that was supposed to be the morally relevant difference between what Jasmine does and what the government does. Thus, we are back where we started, with no morally relevant difference to wield against TX3 of the Against Taxation and Imprisonment argument.

5. Immigration
We have seen that governmental practices of taxation and imprisonment are immoral. It would be wrong for an ordinary citizen to do these sorts of things—even for a good cause—and the government isn't different from an ordinary citizen in any way that makes for a moral difference between the two. This same style of argument can be put to work to undermine other governmental practices as well. Let's look at just one example: immigration.

Once again, we'll start with a Jasmine case, and argue from there to a conclusion about immigration policy. Here is the case:

UNWANTED VISITORS
Jasmine and her friends arrive at their neighborhood park for their weekly soccer game, only to find a group from another neighborhood already using the park for a game of their own. Guns drawn, she directs them into her van, drives them back to their own neighborhood, and threatens to lock them in her basement if they ever return without first getting her permission. Some do ask for her permission, and most of the time she refuses. Some return without her permission, and she locks them in her basement.

And here is the argument:

The Argument for Open Borders
(OB1) If there is no morally relevant difference between two actions A and B, and A is wrong, then B is wrong
(OB2) It is wrong for Jasmine to restrict access to the park
(OB3) There is no morally relevant difference between Jasmine restricting access to the park and the government restricting access to the country
(OB4) So, it is wrong for the government to restrict access to the country

136

OB1 is the same as TX1, so no further defense is needed. OB2, I hope, is obvious. So, as before, the crucial question is whether we should accept the third premise. Is there a morally relevant difference between Jasmine closing off the park and the government closing off its borders?

The difference can't be that the park doesn't belong to her, since (as argued in section 2) it's equally true that this portion of the Earth's surface doesn't belong to the government. Nor is the difference that people who come into the country without permission reap the benefits of tax dollars without paying any taxes themselves. For the same is true in Jasmine's case. The visitors are enjoying the benefits of a crime-free park, and the lack of crime is subsidized by Jasmine's extorted neighbors. Indeed, it's precisely because it's crime-free that the visitors have come to her park rather than using the one in their own neighborhood.

6. What Can the Government Do?

We have seen that ordinary governmental practices of taxing citizens, imprisoning criminals, and restricting immigration are all morally problematic. Is there *anything* the government can do that isn't wrong? The reasoning I've been using above suggests the following answer: it is morally acceptable for a government to do a certain thing only if it would be morally acceptable for Jasmine to do the same sort of thing.

With that in mind, here is one thing the government is permitted to do: use weapons and threat of violence to prevent imminent threats from foreign countries. This passes the "Jasmine Test" since it also wouldn't be wrong for Jasmine to use guns and threat of imprisonment to deter someone who is actively trying to kill her neighbors. I am skeptical, however, that the Jasmine Test can be used to justify much else that the government does. For instance, it wouldn't be okay for Jasmine to extort her neighbors in order to buy and stockpile weapons in preparation for a purely hypothetical future threat to her neighborhood. Accordingly, the Jasmine Test can't be used to justify governmental practices of taxing people in order to build up the military in preparation for hypothetical attacks from other countries.

Let me close by once again emphasizing that the conclusion of this chapter is not that the world would be better off without taxes and prisons. It almost certainly wouldn't be. The point, rather, is that these practices are immoral. Sometimes, as in the SAINT AND SINNER case, there is something that could make the world a better place, but no one is morally permitted to do it.

Reflection Questions
1. I claimed in section 2 that the government doesn't own the country. But how does anyone come to own anything? Try to think of a plausible general account of how people come to own things, and see what it implies about whether the government owns the country.

2. Is it possible to justify taxation on the grounds that much of the wealth that people enjoy is wealth that they are not really entitled to, for instance because they acquired it in some unjust way?

3. At the end of the chapter, we used the "Jasmine Test" to show that some functions of the government could still be legitimate. What does this test say about other governmental functions that we haven't considered here? Is this the right test for evaluating whether governmental practices are right or wrong?

Sources
The arguments against political authority and the social contract are drawn from Michael Huemer's *The Problem of Political Authority*, chapters 1-2. For classic defenses of the social contract theory, see Thomas Hobbes's *Leviathan*, John Locke's *Second Treatise of Government*, and Jean-Jacques Rousseau's *The Social Contract*. For a more contemporary defense of a social contract theory, see John Rawls's *A Theory of Justice*. I learned the SAINT AND SINNER example from David Boonin. Here some additional resources:

*   Luvell Anderson: The Original Position (youtube.com)
*   David Boonin: *The Problem of Punishment*
*   Steven M. Cahn: *Political Philosophy: The Essential Texts*

- Margaret Gilbert: *A Theory of Political Obligation: Membership, Commitment and the Bonds of Society*
- Jean Hampton: The Moral Education Theory of Punishment
- Jean Hampton: *Political Philosophy*
- Michael Huemer: Is Taxation Theft?
- Cynthia Stark: Hypothetical Consent and Justification
- Christopher Heath Wellman and A. John Simmons: *Is There a Duty to Obey the Law? For and Against*

CHAPTER 8
The Ethics of Abortion

Views and arguments advanced in this chapter are not necessarily endorsed by the author of the textbook, nor are they original to the author, nor are they meant to be consistent with arguments advanced in other chapters. Different chapters represent different philosophical perspectives.

1. Preliminaries

My ultimate aim in this chapter is to argue that abortion is immoral, at least in typical cases. But my broader aim is to show that those looking to defend the immorality of abortion need to be discerning. Not every argument against abortion is a good argument. With this end in mind, I begin by considering a number of common arguments—including an argument that proceeds from the assumption that the embryo has a right to life—and showing that they all fall short. Finally, I advance a more promising argument against abortion, which turns on the idea that killing an embryo is immoral because the embryo is thereby deprived of a future full of valuable experiences, projects, and activities.

Some preliminary points before we proceed. We should begin by noting that one can think that abortion is immoral in some cases but not others. For instance, one might think it's permissible to abort a pregnancy after six weeks but not after six months. Or one might think it's immoral to abort a healthy pregnancy but permissible to abort a pregnancy that is likely to kill the mother. To help anchor our discussion, it will be useful to focus on a specific case.

UNWANTED PREGNANCY
Taylor just discovered that she is pregnant with Emm, a six-week-old embryo. The pregnancy resulted from consensual, casual sex. Taylor didn't want to get pregnant, and her partner wore a condom, but they were aware that condoms sometimes break, which is what happened in this case. Both Taylor and Emm are healthy, and carrying out the pregnancy will not pose any threat to Taylor's life. Even so, Taylor knows

that going through with the pregnancy will be a huge burden—physically, emotionally, and financially. So, Taylor decides to have an abortion, killing Emm.

Take a moment to Google *embryo at eight weeks* to get an accurate picture of what Emm would look like. Why "eight weeks" if Emm is six weeks old? Because doctors count the number of weeks you have been pregnant starting from your last period, which is two weeks prior to ovulation and, so, two weeks prior to conception. That means that someone who is "eight weeks pregnant" is carrying an embryo that was conceived six weeks ago.

I focus on the case of Emm because it is both a typical case—a good deal of abortions occur within the first eight weeks and about half involve failed contraception—as well as being a case that parties to the debates typically disagree about. So, if we can resolve the question of whether it was immoral to kill Emm, we will have made significant progress on the morality of abortion.

I will use the usual labels of "pro-life" and "pro-choice" to characterize the different sides of the debate. A *pro-lifer* holds that it was immoral to abort Emm when she was six weeks old. A *pro-choicer* holds that it was morally permissible to abort Emm when she was six weeks old. But one must be cautious not to read too much into these labels. As I use the labels here, they're specifically about Emm. One cannot infer that someone thinks that aborting a life-threatening pregnancy is immoral just because they are pro-life (in my sense), nor that someone thinks it is permissible to abort a planned pregnancy just because they are pro-choice (in my sense).

Additionally, I want to separate the question of whether abortion is immoral from the question of whether abortion should be illegal. One can think that abortion is immoral without thinking that it should be against the law, just as one can think that adultery is immoral without thinking that it should be against the law. So, one should not assume that those who are pro-life (in my sense) think that anyone should be legally prohibited from having an abortion. One can think, as I do, that abortion is immoral while also supporting the legal right to choose. More on this in section 12.

141

Finally, notice that very minor transgressions are sometimes immoral, for instance shoplifting a pack of gum. Even pro-choicers may agree that aborting Emm is at least *somewhat* immoral, perhaps to a relatively minor degree. To sharpen the debate between pro-lifers and pro-choicers, then, I'll focus on the question of whether aborting Emm is *seriously* immoral, by which I mean: approximately as immoral as killing a typical human adult.

2. Identifying Wrong-Making Features

A useful strategy for trying to make headway on the ethics of abortion is to try to identify some feature that embryos have or lack that seems relevant to the permissibility of abortion. The pro-lifer, for instance, tries to find some feature to fill in for X in this argument schema:

Emm is (or has) X
So, it's seriously immoral to kill Emm

For instance, she may point to the fact that Emm *is alive*, or that she *has human DNA*, or that she *has a beating heart*.

The pro-choicer, by contrast, tries to find some feature to fill in for Y in this argument schema:

Emm isn't Y
So, it isn't seriously immoral to kill Emm

For instance, she may point to the fact that Emm *isn't rational*, or that she *isn't self-sufficient*, or that she *isn't wanted*.

We'll need to evaluate each of these ways of developing the argument separately. But first notice that the argument schemas above aren't yet complete. What's needed is some moral principle that can take us from the observation that Emm has or lacks a certain property to the conclusion that it is or isn't seriously immoral to abort her. What's needed is a principle that tells us that being or having X makes killing wrong, or that lacking Y makes killing permissible. In other words, the complete schema for the pro-life arguments will look like this:

The X-Schema
(X1) Emm is (or has) X

(X2) It's always seriously immoral to kill something that is
    (or has) X

(X3) So it's seriously immoral to kill Emm

The complete schema for the pro-choice arguments will look like this:

The Y-Schema
(Y1) Emm isn't Y

(Y2) It's seriously immoral to kill something only if it is Y

(Y3) So it's not seriously immoral to kill Emm

Let us see, then, which (if any) of the various features that Emm has or lacks can yield a satisfying argument for or against the permissibility of killing Emm.

3. Some Bad Pro-Choice Arguments
We'll begin by examining some ways of generating pro-choice arguments from the Y-schema, starting with the observation that Emm isn't rational. In other words, she isn't capable of conscious self-reflection or using reason and logic. The argument would go like this:

The Argument from Rationality
(YR1) Emm isn't rational

(YR2) It's seriously immoral to kill something only if it is
    rational

(YR3) So it's not seriously immoral to kill Emm

YR1 is clearly true: Emm is a very simple creature indeed. But, just as clearly, YR2 is false. After all, a healthy newborn infant also lacks rationality in this sense. So YR2 entails that it isn't seriously immoral to kill such an infant. But obviously it is. So YR2 is false, and the argument fails.

Other instances of the Y-schema fail for the same reason. You might think that it isn't seriously immoral to kill Emm because Emm isn't self-sufficient: she is entirely dependent on Taylor and wouldn't be able to survive on her own. This yields the following argument:

The Argument from Self-Sufficiency
(YS1) Emm isn't self-sufficient
(YS2) It's seriously immoral to kill something only if it is self-sufficient
(YS3) So it's not seriously immoral to kill Emm

But YS2 is open to the same counterexample as YR2: healthy newborn infants also aren't self-sufficient, and yet it clearly is seriously immoral to kill them. The same goes for some elderly and severely disabled people. YS2 is false.

Nor is the fact that Taylor doesn't want to have a child sufficient to show that it isn't seriously immoral to kill Emm. Here's what that argument would look like:

The Argument from Being Unwanted
(YU1) Emm isn't wanted
(YU2) It's seriously immoral to kill something only if it is wanted
(YU3) So it's not seriously immoral to kill Emm

This one fares a *little* better than the previous arguments. YU2 doesn't entail that it's okay to kill just any healthy newborn infant. But consider a healthy newborn infant who isn't wanted by her parents, and let's suppose no one else even knows about her. In that case, no one in the whole world wants her. YU2 entails that it wouldn't be seriously immoral to kill that infant. But it would be seriously immoral. Counterexample. (YU2 also has the absurd consequence that it wouldn't be seriously immoral to kill an extremely annoying, friendless adult who everyone hates having around.)

What pro-choicers need is some wrong-making feature that licenses killing Emm without also licensing killing healthy newborn infants. Accordingly, they need to find some difference between Emm and an infant, and exploit that in their defense of aborting Emm. One difference that immediately springs to mind is that, unlike an infant, Emm is physically attached to someone (namely, Taylor). Putting that to work in the argument:

The Argument from Attachment
(YA1) Emm is attached to another human
(YA2) It's seriously immoral to kill something only if it isn't attached to any other human
(YA3) So it's not seriously immoral to kill Emm

YA2 says that it can't ever be seriously immoral to kill something when it's attached to another human. To get a counterexample to that, we need an example of something that it *is* seriously immoral to kill and that *is* physically attached to some human. Healthy newborn infants—even unwanted ones—aren't physically attached to other humans, so they are no counterexample to YA2. Well… except for the ones being carried around in a baby wrap. That's a way of attaching an infant to your body. So YA2 implies (absurdly) that it is okay to kill infants in baby wraps.

You might object that I've been unfair here. The obvious difference between Emm and the infant in the baby wrap is that there's a *body part* connecting Emm to Taylor, namely an umbilical cord. They are, let's say, "bodily-attached." The idea then would be to revise the Argument from Attachment as follows:

The Argument from Bodily Attachment
(YA1*) Emm is bodily-attached to another human
(YA2*) It's seriously immoral to kill something only if it isn't bodily-attached to any other human
(YA3) So it's not seriously immoral to kill Emm

The infant in the wrap isn't a counterexample to YA2*, since that's the wrong kind of attachment. But one needn't look far for other counterexamples. Take a healthy newborn who has just entered the world and whose cord still hasn't been cut. Certainly, it would be seriously immoral to kill that newborn. Or take conjoined twins. Since they're attached to one another, YA2* says that it isn't seriously immoral to kill one of them. But clearly that would be seriously immoral.

Finally, the pro-choicer might try a different tactic, pointing to the fact that Emm is not *conscious*. That's true: Emm won't become conscious until five months into the pregnancy at the earliest. Moreover, this avoids all the counterexamples we have seen thus far. After all, even healthy, unwanted conjoined twins in baby wraps are conscious. So, we get what might seem to be a more promising argument:

The Argument from Consciousness
(YC1) Emm is not conscious
(YC2) It's seriously immoral to kill something only if it's conscious
(YC3) So it's not seriously immoral to kill Emm

Alas, there are counterexamples to YC2 as well. Normal human adults in deep, dreamless sleep or who are heavily sedated aren't conscious. But it *is* seriously immoral to kill such people. So YC2 is false.

We have examined a number of pro-choice arguments and found them all to be inadequate. Let us turn now to some of the usual pro-life arguments and see whether they fare any better. (Spoiler: they don't.)

4. Some Bad Pro-Life Arguments
Arguments from the pro-life position can be constructed by identifying some features that Emm has, and filling it in for X in the X-Schema (from section 2). Let's begin with the proposal that killing Emm is seriously immoral because Emm is alive:

The Argument from Life
(XL1) Emm is alive
(XL2) It's always seriously immoral to kill something that's alive
(XL3) So it's seriously immoral to kill Emm

This perhaps captures the common pro-life slogan, "life begins at conception," which is meant to serve as a reason to think that aborting an embryo like Emm is seriously immoral. Is this a good argument?

No doubt XL1 is true: Emm is a living organism. But what about XL2? To show that it's false, one would only need to identify a case in which it's permissible to kill a living thing. Pro-choicers might be tempted to reach for cases in which it's morally okay to kill a person, like the death penalty or physician-assisted suicide. But, in fact, we can see that XL2 is false without even touching such controversial cases. The fact that it's not seriously immoral to kill a living blade of grass is already enough to show that XL2 is (hopelessly) mistaken. Thus, the pro-choicer can resist the Argument from Life without having to take a controversial stance on the death penalty or euthanasia. She doesn't even have to deny that life begins at conception. She can grant that it does, but then deny XL2.

The pro-lifer might instead point to the fact that Emm has human DNA:

The Argument from Human DNA
(XD1) Emm has human DNA
(XD2) It's always seriously immoral to kill something that has human DNA
(XD3) So it's seriously immoral to kill Emm

XD2 is immune to the previous counterexample: blades of grass don't have human DNA. Human skin cells do, though, as do human cancer cells. So, if XD2 is true, then it's seriously immoral to kill those things. But it obviously isn't seriously immoral to kill human skin cells or cancer cells. So, XD2 is false.

Next, one might point to the fact that Emm has a beating heart. This suggests another line of argument:

The Argument from Hearts
(XH1) Emm has a beating heart
(XH2) It's always seriously immoral to kill something that has a beating heart
(XH3) So it's seriously immoral to kill Emm

XH1 is true: like most six-week-old embryos, Emm does have a beating heart. And XH2 avoids the previous counterexamples.

Neither blades of grass nor human cells have beating hearts, so XH2 won't wrongly entail that it is seriously immoral to kill them. But you know what does have a beating heart? A worm! XH2 therefore implies that it is seriously immoral to kill worms. And surely that's not seriously immoral. So, XH2 is false.

Finally, let's consider the suggestion that it's seriously immoral to kill Emm because she has the *potential* to become a person:

The Argument from Potentiality
(XP1) Emm is a potential person
(XP2) It's always seriously immoral to kill a potential person
(XP3) So it's seriously immoral to kill Emm

XP1 is true. It's a healthy pregnancy and, if brought to term, Emm will be a full-fledged person. Additionally, since neither worms nor skin cells nor blades of grass have the potential to become people, XP2 is immune to all the previous counterexamples. Indeed, it is hard to think of any uncontroversial counterexample to XP2.

Still, it is unclear why we should accept XP2. Even supposing that it's always seriously immoral to kill a person because (say) they have a right to life, it's hardly obvious that something that merely has the *potential* to become a person has those same rights. I have the potential to become a US president, but that doesn't mean that I *now* have all the rights of a president (the right to pardon criminals, veto legislation, etc.). Likewise, there is no reason to think that Emm has all the rights of a person *simply* by virtue of potentially becoming a person. Furthermore, as we are about to see (in sections 5-7), even if Emm *does* have same moral right to life as an adult human, that may not be enough to establish that it's immoral to kill her.

None of these arguments for the immorality of abortion is successful, and no one—pro-lifers included—should be convinced by them. One must look elsewhere for a satisfying argument against abortion.

5. The Right to Life Argument

Let's turn now to a somewhat different pro-life argument. Here the idea is that it's seriously immoral to kill Emm because she's a person with a right to life. We can frame the argument like this:

The Right to Life Argument
(RL1) Emm has a right to life
(RL2) If Emm has a right to life, then it is seriously immoral to deprive Emm of Taylor's womb
(RL3) So, it's seriously immoral to deprive Emm of Taylor's womb

Since abortion deprives Emm of Taylor's womb, it follows trivially from RL3 that aborting Emm is seriously immoral.

What's nice about the appeal to a right to life is that it avoids the problems that plagued the arguments from sections 3-4. Worms, skin cells, and blades of grass clearly don't have a right to life, while infants, conjoined twins, and heavily sedated people do all have a right to life. Plus, at least on the face of it, it seems obvious why something's having a right to life makes it wrong to kill that thing, while it is somewhat obscure why merely having a beating heart or a certain kind of DNA makes it wrong to kill something.

Still, there are two major problems with the argument. The first (which I won't pursue here) is that pro-choicers are likely just to reject RL1 out of hand. "Sure," they'll say, "Emm *potentially* has a right to life, but why think she has one already?" More would need to be said in defense of RL1 if the argument is to have any hope of persuading pro-choicers.

The second problem is that even if the pro-lifer is correct that Emm has a right to life—and even if she can somehow convince the pro-choicer of this—the argument *still* doesn't work. Or so I shall argue. And if I'm right about this, then the pro-lifer must again look elsewhere for a viable argument against abortion.

6. The Violinist Argument

To see the problem, let's take a closer look at RL2 and at why we are supposed to accept that premise in the first place. If we were to unpack the reasoning behind that premise, it would presumably go something like this:

The Requirements of Life Argument
(RQ1) If something (or someone) has a right to life, and it needs a certain something in order to survive, then it has a right to that thing
(RQ2) Emm needs Taylor's womb in order to survive
(RQ3) So, if Emm has a right to life, then Emm has a right to Taylor's womb
(RQ4) If Emm has a right to Taylor's womb, then it is seriously immoral to deprive Emm of Taylor's womb
(RL2) So, if Emm has a right to life, then it is seriously immoral to deprive Emm of Taylor's womb

RQ1, at least at first glance, seems fairly plausible: having a right to life would seem to entail having a right to such basic necessities of life. RQ2 is uncontroversial. For a six-week old embryo like Emm, remaining in the womb is a basic necessity of life. RQ4 is plausible as well: if Emm not only needs Taylor's womb but, moreover, has the *right* to use it, then killing her by depriving her of it is plausibly seriously immoral.

Surprisingly, though, RQ1 is demonstrably false. To see why, consider the following two cases:

THE VIOLINIST
During his morning jog, Riley is kidnapped and drugged. When he comes to, he finds himself lying in a hospital bed, connected by some blood-filled tubes to a woman in a separate bed. His kidnappers explain that the woman, Maurissa, is a world-famous violinist. She was found unconscious, and they are trying to save her life. Maurissa is in need of a complete blood transfusion—already underway, using Riley's blood—which will take nine months. Riley is told that if he unplugs himself from Maurissa before the transfusion is complete, she will die immediately. When the kidnappers leave the room, Riley sees his chance to escape. With a heavy heart, he unplugs himself and sneaks away, and Maurissa dies as expected.

THE ROCK

You have become completely obsessed with People Magazine's 2016 Sexiest Man of the Year, Dwayne "The Rock" Johnson. So obsessed, in fact, that the thought of living without him makes you physically ill. Deathly ill. At this point, the only thing that can save your life is the touch of The Rock's cool hand on your fevered brow. The Rock is notified, and told that you will die if he does not come visit you in the next few days. But The Rock is a busy man and he sends his regrets. You die, as expected.

No doubt, it would have been morally praiseworthy of Riley to remain plugged into Maurissa, or for The Rock to drop what he was doing and come visit you in your sickbed. And place his cool hand on your fevered brow. But do you have a *right* to The Rock's hand? Suppose you managed to get ahold of his hand and, as he tried to pull it away, you said, "Give that back! It is my right to have this hand on my forehead!" Surely that's not true. As much as you may need it, you are not in any position to demand the hand. Nor, however much she may need it, does Maurissa have a right to the blood in Riley's veins. Were she to awaken, she could plead with him, but she isn't in any position to demand that he stay plugged in.

These cases are therefore counterexamples to RQ1. You have a right to life and The Rock is depriving you of something that (strange but true) you need in order to survive, but you do not have a right to that thing. Maurissa has a right to life, and Riley is depriving her of something she needs in order to survive (his blood), but Riley does not have a right to that thing. We can make the latter argument against RQ1 explicit, as follows:

The Violinist Argument

(VA1) Maurissa has a right to life and needs Riley's blood in order to survive

(VA2) Maurissa does not have a right to Riley's blood

(VA3) So, someone who has a right to life does not thereby have a right to all the things they need in order to survive

One might point out that there are disanalogies between these cases and UNWANTED PREGNANCY. Riley's predicament, for instance, arose without his consent, whereas Taylor's resulted from consensual sex. We'll see momentarily how that might be relevant. But, analogous or not, THE VIOLINIST and THE ROCK are enough to show that RQ1 is false, and without RQ1 we are left without any argument for RL2, a crucial premise of The Right to Life Argument.

7. Risk, Consent, and the Right to the Womb

What we have just seen is that the right to life does not guarantee a right to everything one needs in order to survive. One cannot argue directly from Emm's having a right to life to Emm's having a right to use Taylor's womb. But if one can find some *other* way of establishing that Emm has a right to use Taylor's womb, then perhaps one can argue directly from there to the conclusion that Taylor's abortion was seriously immoral.

Why else might one think that Emm has a right to Taylor's womb? One might suggest that Emm has this right because Taylor, in one way or another, *consented* to Emm using her womb. If I offer to let you use my spare sleeping bag, I can't then demand it back from you when we reach the campsite. When I consent to you using it, you acquire a right to it. Or suppose Riley had volunteered to be plugged into Maurissa, knowing that prematurely unplugging himself would kill her. In that case, he consented to her using his blood, and she thereby acquired a right to it.

So, if the pro-lifer can establish that Taylor consented to Emm using her womb, then we can arguably use that to establish that Emm has a right to use her womb. That said, Taylor didn't exactly volunteer to have Emm in her womb. Quite the opposite: she took deliberate steps to avoid it by having protected sex. So what reason could there be to think that Taylor consented to Emm using her womb? One might suggest that Taylor consents to it by freely choosing to have sex, which is something she knew might lead to pregnancy (even with the precaution of a condom). Even though she didn't want to get pregnant, she knew the risk she was taking.

Putting the pieces together, the argument that Emm has a right to Taylor's womb, and that the abortion was therefore seriously immoral, would go something like this:

The Known Risk Argument
(KR1) Taylor freely chose to have sex and knew that this could lead to Emm using her womb
(KR2) Whenever someone freely does something and knows that it could lead to certain consequences, one consents to those consequences
(KR3) So, Taylor consented to Emm using her womb
(KR4) If Taylor consented to Emm using her womb, then Emm has a right to Taylor's womb
(KR5) If Emm has a right to Taylor's womb, then it is seriously immoral to deprive Emm of Taylor's womb
(KR6) So, it is seriously immoral to deprive Emm of Taylor's womb

You might worry a bit about KR4. Just because Taylor at one point consented to Emm being in her womb, perhaps she can later withdraw consent, thereby depriving Emm of the right to her womb. (Clearly, one can withdraw consent in other cases, for instance after initially consenting to sex.) But whatever one thinks of KR4, there is an even more glaring problem with the argument.

The problem is that KR2 is a ludicrous theory of consent. To see this, consider the following case:

OPEN WINDOW
Astrid lives in a dangerous neighborhood with lots of hooligans. She has bars on her windows and keeps the windows closed and latched as an extra precaution. One hot summer day, she opens the windows to get some cool air, trusting that the bars will keep the hooligans out (though knowing that they are not 100% reliable). Unfortunately, the bars are defective. Some hooligans pull them off, climb through the window, plant themselves on her couch, and start playing her PlayStation.

Astrid freely chose to open the windows and knew this could lead to hooligans entering her house. Certainly they don't have any right to be in there and certainly she did not consent to them being in there just by opening her barred windows. But KR2 absurdly implies that she did consent to them being in there.

Consent requires something more robust than simply taking actions that open one up to the risk of some consequences. Accordingly, there would seem to be no way of getting anything like the present argument for KR3 off the ground. It would be a different story if Taylor had "invited" Emm into her womb, for instance if she hadn't used protection and had been *trying* to get pregnant. Perhaps in that case an argument from consent could be made to work. But it seems hopeless in cases like Taylor's, where the pregnancy is the unwanted consequence of protected sex.

8. The Future Like Ours Argument

Not all pro-life arguments are created equal, and we have seen that a number of common arguments are fatally flawed, including the Right to Life argument. Let us turn now, finally, to what I take to be a successful argument for the pro-life position.

This superior argument turns on the idea that, if the pregnancy were carried to term, Emm would have had a future filled with valuable experiences, including valuable activities, relationships, projects, achievements, and pleasant sensations. She has a future like ours, or "FLO" for short. That doesn't necessarily mean *exactly* like ours, but like ours in that it's filled with valuable experiences.

Aborting Emm deprives her of FLO and this, I contend, is what makes the abortion seriously immoral:

The Simple FLO Argument
(SF1) It is seriously immoral to kill something (or someone) if killing it deprives it of a future like ours
(SF2) Killing Emm deprives Emm of a future like ours
(SF3) So, it is seriously immoral to kill Emm

I call this "The Simple FLO Argument" because, as we'll see in section 11, we will need to complicate it a bit in order to handle a certain range of objections. But for the moment, it will be useful to focus on this somewhat oversimplified version of the argument.

SF1 is initially quite plausible. To see this, ask yourself why it is wrong to murder a normal, healthy human adult. Why is killing someone one of the worst things (if not *the* worst thing) you can do to a person? The natural answer is that it's because one thereby deprives them of all the things that make life so valuable. That's why it seems even more horrific to kill an infant, for one thereby deprives them of a *whole life's* worth of valuable things. SF1 seems to put its finger on precisely the thing that makes these other killings seriously immoral.

How about SF2? Even supposing that her life gets off to a rocky start—as a result of being put up for adoption or being raised by an overworked single mom—Emm still would have had a full lifetime of achievements, friendships, and other such valuable experiences.

You might wonder how I know that Emm would have had FLO, and won't for instance be born with some terrible birth defect and die before she's a year old. The short answer is that it's my example: I can fill in details however I like, and I'm *telling* you that she would have had a happy, fulfilling life had she not been aborted. Of course, for any actual pregnancy, we can never be 100% sure that the embryo has FLO, even if medical tests suggest that it's a healthy pregnancy. Still—with some exceptions, which we'll discuss in section 11—you can usually be reasonably confident that the embryo will have FLO. That, together with SF1, tells us that you can be reasonably confident you'd be doing something seriously immoral by aborting the pregnancy. And if you can be reasonably confident that an action is seriously immoral, you shouldn't do it—even if there's some small chance that what you're doing isn't actually immoral.

(I'm reminded of a scene in a movie you've never heard of called *Adam's Apples*. One character shoots another in the head. Not only does the gunshot victim survive, the bullet also obliterates his brain tumor and saves his life. This could in principle happen in real life too. But that doesn't mean it's okay for you to go around shooting people in the head. Why not? Because, even though there's some small chance you'll actually be helping them, you can be reasonably confident that in fact you'd be killing them and doing something seriously immoral.)

For these reasons, it's no use challenging SF2, and critics of the argument should focus instead on SF1. Let's turn, then, to four objections one might raise against SF1: three that won't work at all (section 9) and one that does work but that can be avoided by revising the argument (section 10).

9. Bad Objections to the FLO Argument

First, one might think that the following sort of case is a problem for SF1:

HOPEFUL GONER

Guillermo has accidentally ingested a deadly poison and is in horrible, debilitating pain. He thinks he'll get better, but he's wrong: the poison is quickly spreading through his body and will kill him within a few hours. Nadja, who finds Guillermo terribly annoying and would like to see him dead as soon as possible, is attempting to inject Guillermo with a substance that will kill him instantly and painlessly. Guillermo resists and pleads for Nadja to stop. But Nadja gives Guillermo the injection, despite his protests, and Guillermo dies mere hours before the poison would have killed him anyway.

What Nadja did seems to be seriously immoral, and yet she didn't deprive Guillermo of FLO. Guillermo's future would have contained only a few hours of horrible pain and no valuable experiences.

Here is why this is not a problem for SF1. SF1 says that depriving someone of FLO always makes it seriously immoral to kill them. In other words, depriving someone of FLO is *sufficient* for a killing to be seriously immoral. SF1 doesn't say that depriving someone of FLO is the only way for a killing to be seriously immoral. That is, it doesn't say that depriving someone of FLO is *necessary* for a killing to be seriously immoral. Since SF1 leaves it open that there are other ways for a killing to be seriously immoral—perhaps by failing to respect the victim's desire to stay alive—HOPEFUL GONER is no counterexample to SF1.

Second, one might object that SF1 absurdly implies that ordinary contraception is seriously immoral. After all, the idea goes, when one uses condoms or spermicide, one is depriving millions of sperm cells of FLO. The argument would go like this:

The Contraception Argument
(CC1) Killing sperm deprives them of a future like ours
(CC2) If killing sperm deprives them of a future like ours,
      then: if SF1 is true, then it is seriously immoral to kill
      sperm
(CC3) It isn't seriously immoral to kill sperm
(CC4) So, SF1 is false

The problem with this argument is CC1. *No* sperm cell has FLO, not even a sperm cell that successfully fertilizes an egg. It is not as if the sperm cell enters the egg and then grows into an embryo. Rather, it enters the egg, releases a tiny amount of genetic material, and then the sperm cell dissolves and ceases to exist altogether, never to have any valuable experiences. (How about the egg? It's an interesting question whether it has FLO, but it is not a question we need to answer. After all, SF1 only prohibits *killing* things with FLO, and using a spermicide-coated condom doesn't kill the egg.)

Even if sperm cells don't have FLO, what *is* true is that the spermicide prevents a being with FLO from coming into existence. Is that enough to cause trouble for SF1? The argument would have to go like this:

The Revised Contraception Argument
(CC1*) Killing sperm prevents the creation of a being with
      FLO
(CC2*) If killing sperm prevents the creation of a being with
      FLO, then: if SF1 is true, then it is seriously immoral
      to kill sperm
(CC3) It isn't seriously immoral to kill sperm
(CC4) So, SF1 is false

We have merely moved the bump in the rug, for now the problem is the second premise, CC2*. SF1 doesn't say that it's seriously immoral to prevent things with FLO from coming into existence. It only says that it's immoral to take an already-existing thing with FLO and deprive it of FLO by killing it. So CC2* misrepresents what is implied by SF1.

Let's look at one more unsuccessful objection to SF1. Recall that SF1 was motivated by the idea that it provides the best explanation of what makes seriously immoral killings—like killing a normal human adult—seriously immoral. One way of challenging SF1, then, is to reject the proposed explanation of the serious immorality of killing an adult. But one would then need to provide some alternative explanation of why it is seriously immoral to kill an adult.

Here's an initially attractive proposal: what makes it seriously immoral to kill normal human adults is that they *desire* a future full of valuable experiences. If that's right, then all that is supported by the proper explanation of the immorality of killing is the weaker premise SF1*:

(SF1*) It is seriously immoral to kill something (or someone) if killing it deprives it of a future like ours *that it desires*

But unlike SF1, SF1* does *not* imply that it is seriously immoral to kill Emm. Emm is a very simple creature, which does not even have a brain, let alone desires. Killing her does deprive her of FLO, but it does not deprive her of anything she desires.

The problem with this line of reasoning is that the proposed alternative explanation of the wrongness of killing human adults is deeply flawed. Consider a heavily sedated adult, who (like Emm) has no desires, or any other conscious mental states for that matter. Or consider an overwhelmed teenager experiencing his first heartbreak: he genuinely doesn't want to go on living, but these feelings will pass in a week or so. It is seriously immoral to kill these people, and the original future-like-ours account has no trouble explaining why: because they have FLO. By contrast, the competing account that we are now considering fails to explain why it is seriously immoral to kill them. After all, they do not desire a future like ours. The desire account of what makes killing wrong that underwrites SF1* is therefore inferior to the FLO-

account that underwrites SF1. Accordingly, we should reject SF1*
and stick with SF1.

10. FLO-Overriding Factors

There is, however, a more serious style of objection to SF1, one
that will require us to revise the argument. Suppose that someone
is trying to kill you and you can save your own life only by killing
them first. One can imagine having qualms about killing them,
but certainly it's not seriously immoral to do so. Or take the
following case.

> ### CRUEL GAME
> M'Baku is preparing to detonate an atomic bomb in the heart
> of a densely populated city. He has kidnapped two innocent
> people, Okoye and Shuri, and he commands Okoye to kill
> Shuri. If she complies, he will release Okoye and won't
> detonate the bomb. If she refuses, he will release both of them
> and detonate the bomb, killing hundreds of thousands of
> people. Okoye tries to find a way to stop the detonation
> without killing Shuri, but M'Baku has thought of everything.
> So, with a heavy heart, Okoye kills Shuri.

Given the circumstances, what Okoye did isn't seriously immoral,
despite the fact that Shuri has FLO. Unlike HOPEFUL GONER, this
is a genuine counterexample to SF1. So, the Simple FLO Argument
must go.

What cases like CRUEL GAME demonstrate is that, in certain
situations, there are factors in play that can justify killing normal
adults—even innocent adults—who have FLO. Let's call these
FLO-overriding factors, which I'll define as follows: a killing
involves a FLO-overriding factor if and only if that killing
involves the sort of factors that could justify killing a normal
human adult with FLO. So, a FLO-overriding factor is a special
kind of mitigating factor.

Here is one example of a FLO-overriding factor: that killing a
person is necessary for preventing the deaths of hundreds of
thousands of people. That's a FLO-overriding factor because, as
reflection on CRUEL GAME reveals, it's the sort of factor that can
justify killing Shuri, a normal human adult with FLO. But the

159

following would not be a FLO-overriding factor: that a person is incredibly annoying. If I want to kill someone with FLO, the fact that they are incredibly annoying is not reason enough to kill them. Being incredibly annoying is not the sort of factor that could justify killing a normal human adult.

Using the notion of a FLO-overriding factor, we can patch up the Simple FLO Argument as follows:

The Modified FLO Argument
(MF1) It is seriously immoral to kill something (or someone) if killing it deprives it of a future like ours *and* the killing does not involve any FLO-overriding factors
(MF2) Killing Emm deprives Emm of a future like ours
(MF3) Killing Emm does not involve any FLO-overriding factors
(MF4) So, it is seriously immoral to kill Emm

MF1 has all of the plausibility of SF1, without being open to counterexamples like CRUEL GAME. And MF2 is the same as SF2. But now that we have included an additional condition for a killing to be classified as seriously immoral, we need to include an additional premise, MF3, affirming that killing Emm meets that condition.

To evaluate MF3, we have to consider various candidate FLO-overriding factors that might be present in the case of Emm. To check whether a factor is FLO-overriding, remember, we have to check whether it's the sort of factor whose presence could justify killing a normal human adult. So let's look at some possible candidates.

One might point to the fact that seven more months of pregnancy places a major burden on Taylor—financially, physically, and emotionally. That's true. But is it a FLO-overriding factor? To answer that, we need to ask whether such burdens would justify killing a normal human adult. And certainly they wouldn't. Some parents who would rather not continue to care for their broke, freeloading adult son can't just kill him, regardless of the financial, physical, or emotional toll it takes on their life. This is not to say that that case is entirely analogous to the case of Emm. It's not. But it does demonstrate that such burdens do not meet the conditions for being FLO-overriding factors.

Relatedly, one might point to the way in which keeping the pregnancy would have seriously disrupted Taylor's life plans, perhaps forcing her to quit her job or drop out of school. But this too is no FLO-overriding factor. To see this, consider the following case.

RUNNER-UP
Krystal has struggled for years to make it as an actress, and finally gets her big audition. If she gets the role, it will catapult her into fame and fortune. As it turns out, Jacqueline gets the role. But Krystal is the runner-up and is told that if anything should happen to Jacqueline, the role will go to her. So, Krystal discreetly kills Jacqueline and gets the role.

Having Jacqueline around was severely disruptive to Krystal's life plans and was depriving her of significant opportunities. Still, that was not enough to justify killing Jacqueline, even supposing that Jacqueline's presence completely derails and ruins Krystal's life. So the disruption to Taylor's life plans, substantial as it is, is no FLO-overriding factor and no reason to reject MF3.

11. Making Exceptions

I have argued that, in typical cases, aborting an unwanted but healthy embryo early on in the pregnancy is seriously immoral. I also argued that a pro-lifer must be discerning: some pro-life arguments are utterly unconvincing, including those that turn on the idea that life begins at conception, that the embryo has a right to life, or that the mother is responsible for the pregnancy by choosing to have sex in the first place.

What about less typical cases of abortion? Can pro-lifers allow that, in certain cases, abortion isn't seriously immoral? Yes, but they must do so in a principled way. We have only been able to find one good argument for the immorality of abortion. Those who oppose abortion in typical cases on the strength of my FLO argument—let's call them "FLO-lifers"—will have to check which exceptions the FLO-account *permits* them to make. Let's see, then, what the FLO-account says about three potential exceptions:

161

unhealthy embryos, life-threatening pregnancies, and pregnancies resulting from rape.

Can the FLO-lifer make an exception for an unhealthy embryo? That depends entirely on how unhealthy the embryo is and, in particular, whether it has FLO. An embryo that is certain to die in the womb or to die within a year after being born does not have FLO, and the FLO-lifer can allow abortion in such cases compatibly with the FLO-account. What it won't allow is the abortion of an embryo that is known to have some serious disability, like blindness or Down syndrome. Such embryos certainly do have FLO. Perhaps they don't have a future *exactly* like ours, but it's still a future full of valuable experiences.

Can the FLO-lifer make an exception if it is known that keeping the pregnancy will kill the mother? Certainly she can make an exception if the unborn child will die as well, for in that case the child has no FLO. But suppose the mother is expected to die during childbirth, while the baby can be saved. In that case, the embryo does have FLO. So, by MF1, the abortion is permissible only if the threat to the mother's life is a FLO-overriding factor, the sort of factor that would justify killing a normal human adult.

And, indeed, there is reason to think it is FLO-overriding. Consider the following case:

QUICKSAND
Ahmed is drowning in quicksand. He has gotten ahold of Omar's pantleg, and is frantically trying to pull himself out. But in doing so he is pulling Omar into the quicksand. Ahmed is in such a panicked state that he doesn't realize what he is doing, and Omar's pleas fall on deaf ears. Unless Omar stops him by pushing him under, Ahmed will pull him in and scramble out over Omar's subsumed body, killing him. So, with a heavy heart, and in order to save his own life, Omar kills Ahmed by pushing him under.

What Omar had to do may be horrifying, but it is not seriously immoral. The fact that Ahmed's continued existence is a threat to Omar's life justified him in killing Ahmed. Accordingly, the fact that a certain embryo's continued existence is a threat to the mother's life is a FLO-overriding factor, and the FLO-lifer can consistently grant that abortion is permissible in such cases.

Can a FLO-lifer grant that abortion is permissible in the case of a healthy pregnancy that results from rape? In such cases, the embryo does have FLO, so the FLO-lifer can and should make this concession so long as such cases involve a FLO-overriding factor. What might that FLO-overriding factor be? Here is a plausible candidate: that the embryo's dependence on the mother was the result of violent actions that she was not able to control. To see that this counts as a FLO-overriding factor, recall THE VIOLINIST from section 6. As praiseworthy as it may have been for Riley to stay plugged in, it does strike me as permissible for Riley to unplug himself, thereby killing Maurissa (a normal human adult). And one plausible explanation of why it was permissible for Riley to kill her is that her dependence on him was the result of violent actions (by the kidnappers) that he was not able to control.

What we have just seen is that the best argument against abortion cannot be used to show that aborting pregnancies resulting from rape or pregnancies that threaten the life of the mother are seriously immoral. Pro-lifers who do not want to make an exception even in these special cases must look elsewhere for an argument to support this position. And it is hard to see what such an argument would look like, since the obvious candidates— for instance that such embryos have a right to life or are potential people—were shown above to be deeply flawed.

12. Making Laws

I have argued that abortion is seriously immoral, at least in cases like UNWANTED PREGNANCY. But it would be a mistake to think that this settles the question of whether it should be *legal*. For, as we saw in section 1, there are plenty of things we take to be immoral that no one thinks should be illegal, for instance cheating on your boyfriend.

My own view is that, despite being seriously immoral, abortion should be legal in cases like UNWANTED PREGNANCY. It is one thing to think that, in deciding to abort a healthy pregnancy, Taylor did something seriously immoral. It is quite another to think that it would have been permissible for government officials (or anyone else for that matter) to *force* her to remain pregnant, or to punish her for terminating the pregnancy. The government would arguably have a role to play if Taylor were violating Emm's rights by terminating the pregnancy. But, as we saw in sections 6-7, aborting the pregnancy *doesn't* violate Emm's rights—including Emm's right to life—since Emm never had a right to use Taylor's womb in the first place. The reason that it was seriously immoral to abort Emm is because Emm had FLO, not because it violated Emm's right to life.

It may be illuminating to compare UNWANTED PREGNANCY with the following variation on THE ROCK:

ROCK FORCED
The only thing that can save your life is the touch of The Rock's cool hand on your fevered brow. As it happens, The Rock is passing through the hospital where you lay dying. You ask for his help and he refuses. You grab his hand, but he pulls it away.

Even if The Rock's refusal is morally monstrous in this case—and I would agree that it is—surely it should not be illegal. He shouldn't be legally required to assist you, and the police should not have the authority to forcibly prevent him from withdrawing his hand. It's his hand, and since you have no right to it, he should not be legally required to share it with you.

Similarly, even if you think Taylor was *morally* required to keep the pregnancy—because you think Emm was a person, with a right to life, with a valuable future ahead of her, and with interests that aren't outweighed by Taylor's own interests in wanting to terminate the pregnancy—you shouldn't think she should be legally required the keep the pregnancy. One can (and should) be pro-life without supporting forced birth.

Reflection Questions
1. Can you find a way to rescue the rights-based arguments in sections 5-7 from my objections? For instance, can you find a more promising way to argue that the embryo has a right to the womb?

164

2. Can the case of THE VIOLINIST from section 6 be used to resist MF3 of the Modified FLO Argument in section 10?

3. In section 9, I considered a competing account of what makes killing wrong. Can that account be defended against my objections?

4. We saw that the Modified FLO-argument cannot be used to show that abortion is immoral in the case of rape or life-threatening pregnancies. Can you think of an argument that does cover these cases, and that does not fall victim to the objections raised in sections 4-7?

5. Consider the key idea behind the FLO-arguments: that the embryo would have had a future full of valuable experiences had it not been killed. What does this assume about personal identity? Is the Psychological Descendant Account (discussed in chapter 3) compatible with the idea that fully-grown people used to be embryos? Is your preferred response to the Too Many Thinkers Argument (discussed in chapter 4) compatible with the idea that we used to be embryos?

Sources
The Violinist argument and the critique of the Right to Life argument are drawn from Judith Jarvis Thomson's "A Defense of Abortion." The FLO-argument is drawn from Don Marquis's "Why Abortion is Immoral," as are many of the criticisms of bad pro-life and pro-choice arguments discussed in sections 3 and 4. Here are some additional resources:

- David Boonin: *Beyond Roe: Why Abortion Should Be Legal Even if the Fetus is a Person*
- David Boonin: *A Defense of Abortion*
- Sidney Callahan: "Abortion and the Sexual Agenda: A Case for Pro-Life Feminism"
- Ann E. Cudd: "Enforced Pregnancy, Rape, and the Image of a Woman"
- Jane English: "Abortion and the Concept of a Person"

- Elizabeth Harman: "Creation Ethics: The Moral Status of Early Fetuses and the Ethics of Abortion"
- Elizabeth Harman: "The Potentiality Problem"
- Elizabeth Harman: "What Amy Coney Barrett Doesn't Understand About Abortion"
- George W. Harris: "Fathers and Fetuses"
- Margaret Olivia Little: "Abortion, Intimacy, and the Duty to Gestate"
- Alastair Norcross: "Killing, Abortion, and Contraception: A Reply to Marquis"
- Michael Tooley: "Abortion and Infanticide"
- Mary Anne Warren: "On the Moral and Legal Status of Abortion"

CHAPTER 9

Eating Animals

Views and arguments advanced in this chapter are not necessarily endorsed by the author of the textbook, nor are they original to the author, nor are they meant to be consistent with arguments advanced in other chapters. Different chapters represent different philosophical perspectives.

1. Introduction

In what follows, I will defend the view that, in most cases, buying and eating meat is morally impermissible. First, I will argue that there is no good reason to think that eating meat *is* morally permissible. In particular, I address three common reasons for thinking that it's not wrong to eat meat: that it is natural to eat meat, that it is necessary to eat meat, and that people have always eaten meat. Second, I argue directly for the immorality of buying and eating meat, by developing an analogy in which puppies are subjected to much the same treatment as farm animals (sections 5-6). I then defend my argument from analogy against various objections (sections 7-8).

In defending the claim that it is morally impermissible for you to eat meat, I will be making some assumptions about you. First, I am assuming that you know that the meat you eat is the flesh of slaughtered animals. A friend of mine once had the following conversation with her children at the dinner table:

> Them [eating chicken]: "Mom, where does chicken come from?"
> Her: "Well… it comes from chickens. You're eating a chicken."
> Them: "C'mon, mom!! Seriously, where does chicken come from?"

Perhaps you didn't know. Now you know.

Second, I am assuming that the meat you eat was killed in order to be eaten. Perhaps you eat only dead animals you find in the road. In that case, go for it; my arguments do not apply to you.

Third, I am assuming that you do not live in some faraway land, where you have to eat meat because there is no way to get your hands on tofu, broccoli, oatmeal, avocados, almonds, beans, pumpkin seeds, hummus, lentils, quinoa, tempeh, peanut butter, veggie burgers, or other such alternative sources of protein. I am assuming that you are not stranded on a deserted island with nothing to eat but wild boar. Perhaps I'm wrong. If you are currently stranded on a deserted island, go ahead and eat the boar.

More generally, just because you can imagine *some* possible situation in which it's morally okay to do a certain thing, that doesn't mean it's morally okay to do that thing in *ordinary* situations. If a hiker gets caught in a blizzard and will freeze to death if he doesn't break into someone's empty cabin for the night, it's morally okay for him to break in. That obviously doesn't mean that it's morally okay for you, right now, to break into a random person's home. If the Nazis are at the good Samaritan's door, it's morally okay for her to lie to them to save the Jews hiding in her attic. That obviously doesn't mean that it's morally okay for you, right now, to lie to whomever you want, whenever you want. And just because it's okay for *certain* people to eat *certain* types of meat in *certain* situations, that doesn't mean that it's okay for you—in the situation you currently find yourself in— to eat whatever meat you want whenever you want.

2. The Argument from Precedent
In the United States, we consume somewhere around ten billion farm animals per year. Eating lots of animals involves killing lots of conscious creatures, creatures that are capable of experiencing pain, discomfort, fear, and distress. Is there some good reason to think that eating meat is morally permissible, despite all the killing and suffering that is involved in getting the meat off of those animals and onto our plates? Sure, meat is delicious, and bacon is especially delicious. But the pleasure you get from eating bacon doesn't make eating meat *morally* acceptable, any more than the pleasure a sadist gets from kicking puppies makes kicking puppies morally acceptable. So let us see if we can do better.

The first argument we'll consider for the moral permissibility of meat-eating is that there is such a strong precedent for eating meat. People have eaten meat all throughout human history. By eating meat, we aren't doing anything different from what our ancestors have done.

The argument evidently runs as follows:

The Argument from Precedent
(PR1) There have been people who eat meat throughout human history
(PR2) If there have been people doing a certain thing throughout human history, then it is morally permissible for you to do it
(PR3) So, it is morally permissible for you to eat meat

PR1 is indisputable. But PR2 is obviously false. People have murdered other people throughout human history as well. If PR2 were true, then that would mean that it's morally acceptable for *you* to murder people. But, of course, it isn't morally acceptable for you to murder people.

You may object that while it's true that there have always been murderers, it's not true that *most* people have been murderers throughout human history. This suggests a way of reinstating the Argument from Precedent, without the overly strong premise PR2:

The Argument from Majority Precedent
(PR1*) Most people have eaten meat throughout human history
(PR2*) If most people have done a certain thing throughout human history, then it is morally permissible for you to do it
(PR3) So, it is morally permissible for you to eat meat

Since it isn't true that most people throughout human history have been murderers, PR2* (unlike PR2) doesn't have the absurd consequence that you are permitted to murder people. But other counterexamples are easy to find. For instance, there has been a widespread practice of people beating their children throughout human history. That certainly does not mean that it is morally okay for people now (or even back then) to beat their children.

Perhaps you doubt that child abuse was so prevalent through human history. But let me ask you this: in order to figure out whether it's morally acceptable now for people to beat their children, do you first have to sort out how common it's been in human history? Of course not. You already know it's wrong, regardless of how many people have done in the past. Humans have a long history of all sorts of immoral practices: slavery, torture, persecution, and discrimination. What's right or wrong has nothing to do with what sorts of practices our ancestors did or didn't approve of, or how many of them engaged in those practices. There is no reason to accept anything like PR2 or PR2*.

I should emphasize that my objection to these arguments from precedent does not rest on the assumption that killing animals for meat is morally *equivalent* to these other objectionable practices. Everything I have said is compatible with thinking that child abuse is far worse than slaughtering animals. Maybe it is, maybe it isn't. My point is just that, as with these other practices, the long history of meat-eating doesn't by itself give us *any* reason to think that meat-eating is morally acceptable.

3. The Argument from Naturalness

Let's turn to a second possible defense of meat-eating. Here, the idea is that eating meat is *natural*. This could mean a couple of different things, so we'll need to look at different ways of clarifying this appeal to naturalness.

First, the idea might be that it's part of the natural order of things for animals to eat other animals. Owls eat mice. Wolves eat deer. We eat chickens and pigs and cows. This is just part of nature.

The argument evidently runs as follows:

The Natural Order Argument
(NO1) Other animals eat meat
(NO2) If other animals do something, then it's morally permissible for you to do it
(NO3) So, it's morally permissible for you to eat meat

There is no denying NO1. But just like PR2 above, NO2 is open to endless counterexamples. Other animals engage in cannibalism, kill innocent humans, force themselves sexually upon unwilling partners, and in some cases chew off the heads of their partners during intercourse. Needless to say, these are not things that it would be morally acceptable for *you* to do. And yet, if NO2 is true, then it follows straightaway that it is morally acceptable for you to do these things. So, NO2 must be false. Yet without NO2, it is unclear how to get from the indisputable truth of NO1 to any interesting conclusion about the moral acceptability of eating meat.

(Does this mean that it's immoral for cheetahs to eat gazelles? Of course not. Because they're incapable of moral thinking, and thus incapable of recognizing actions as moral or immoral, cheetahs aren't morally accountable for their actions. But since we *are* capable of recognizing actions as moral or immoral, we can be held morally accountable when we perform those same actions.)

A theme is emerging. Defenses of meat-eating cite some uncontroversial fact about eating meat, for instance that humans or nonhuman animals regularly eat meat. A conclusion is then drawn about the moral permissibility of eating meat. To get from the uncontroversial premise to the moral conclusion, however, we need to assume that we have identified some right-making feature: that, in general, the fact that our ancestors or nonhuman animals have done something makes it okay for us to do it. And that underlying assumption, on closer inspection, turns out to be grossly implausible.

Let's see how this same problem arises for a second way of developing the idea that eating meat is natural. Here the idea is that we have a natural capacity for eating meat. Other animals have mouths and guts and taste buds that are adapted for a vegetarian diet. Not us. We have just the right kinds of teeth and digestive systems for getting nutrition from meat, and we naturally enjoy eating it. Therefore, the idea goes, it's morally permissible for us to eat meat.

What is the argument here? It seems to be the following:

The Natural Capacity Argument
(CP1) You are naturally capable of eating meat
(CP2) If you are naturally capable of doing a certain thing,
        then it is morally permissible for you to do that thing
(CP3) So, it is morally permissible for you to eat meat

CP1 is of course true. But CP2 is obviously false. There are plenty of things that you are naturally capable of doing that are not morally permissible: lying, stealing, enslaving other human beings, torturing puppies, and so on. Just because nature has endowed you with the ability to do something—and even if you find that doing that thing comes naturally to you—that hardly entails that it's morally okay for you to do it. Indeed, morality is often a matter of *overcoming* our natural impulses.

4. The Argument from Necessity

Perhaps the most common defense of the moral permissibility of meat-eating is that eating meat is *necessary*. Necessary for what, though? Obviously it isn't necessary for survival. You probably know some vegetarians, and you can check their pulse for yourself.

Maybe the idea is that, even if you can survive without eating meat, you can't be *healthy* without eating meat. For instance, it is sometimes suggested that you can't get the necessary amounts of *protein* without eating meat. If that's right, then perhaps the following argument can be used to establish the permissibility of eating meat:

The Necessity of Protein Argument

(NP1) Eating meat is necessary for getting enough protein
(NP2) If doing something is necessary for getting enough
protein, then it is morally permissible for you to do it
(NP3) So, it is morally permissible for you to eat meat

We already saw, however, that NP1 is false. I listed a number of alternative sources of protein in section 1 (broccoli, peanut butter, etc.), and it is well known that getting your protein from these sources is healthier than getting it from meat. There is no truth to claim that eating meat is necessary for getting enough protein. Indeed, a number of top athletes—some of the healthiest people on the planet—are vegetarians, including tennis pro Venus Williams, Olympic medalist Carl Lewis, and UFC fighters Nate Diaz and Colleen Schneider. So it undoubtedly is possible to have a healthy diet without meat.

Moreover, even if meat-eating *were* necessary for getting optimal amounts of protein, there would still be a question of whether meat-eating is permissible. Suppose you are a prisoner of war, and—while you are in absolutely no danger of dying— you are not as healthy as you could be because your captors aren't giving you enough protein. Would it then be morally permissible for you to steal your fellow prisoners' rations? Of course not. Morality doesn't permit doing whatever it takes to get the FDA-recommended amount of protein. So NP2 is demonstrably false as well.

5. Meet Your Meat

Thus far, all we have seen is that standard arguments in defense of meat-eating all fail. In other words, we have no good positive reason to think that meat-eating *is* morally acceptable. That's not yet to say that eating meat is morally *un*acceptable. But I do want to draw this stronger conclusion. So let me turn now to an argument that eating meat is immoral.

Once again, though, I want to narrow the scope of my argument somewhat. I will not try to argue that eating meat is immoral in all cases, or even that it is immoral in all cases in which alternative sources of protein are readily available. Rather, I want to restrict my argument to cases in which the animals being eaten endured a great deal of suffering before ending up on your plate. If you frequent the pricier "pasture raised" portion of the meat aisle, there is some possibility that these animals were raised on a small family farm and treated kindly, that they spent their days goofing around with the children of the household, curled up at night with their animal families in a warm barn, and were treated to a painless death. I won't try to argue that it is immoral to eat such animals.

Most of the meat consumed in the United States, however, comes from concentrated animal feeding operations (CAFOs), also known as "factory farms." This includes pretty much all the chicken, beef, and pork products you're buying if you're not making a concerted effort to seek out humanely raised meat. Animals in CAFOs spend much of their lives in cages or otherwise cramped conditions. They are regularly mutilated: chickens have portions of their beaks sliced off, cattle are dehorned and castrated, and pigs are castrated and have their tails cut off, typically without anesthesia. The slaughter, as you can imagine, is no picnic either. Animals typically aren't slaughtered on site, but are instead transported—often long distances, in all kinds of weather—to slaughterhouses, and the slaughter is (let us say) an imperfect process, given the sheer number of scared and squirming animals coming through the slaughterhouse each day.

Needless to say, this is not cruelty for cruelty's sake. Conditions in the farming industry have made it all but impossible to turn a profit from a small, idyllic farm, and farmers are forced to scale up in order to make ends meet. Confining the animals to small spaces is necessary for keeping costs low, and the mutilations help curb the distraught animals' tendency and ability to attack and harm one another. Farmers are not *trying* to harm the animals. They care about their animals' well-being. Some even install "happy cow back scratchers" for their cattle. The suffering involved in CAFOs, by their lights, is a regrettable but unavoidable consequence of the industry. But this is their livelihood, and as long as you keep buying, they will keep supplying.

I should add that I am no expert on the meat industry, and it is difficult to find good information on the treatment of animals in CAFOs, due in part to "ag gag" laws and other efforts by agribusiness lobbyists to restrict access to these sites. One can find footage online of animals in CAFOs being treated horrifically, but of course animal welfare groups are going to highlight the most egregious cases of mistreatment they can find. One can also find footage of animals being treated humanely in CAFOs, but of course farmers are going to put their best foot forward. So we can't expect videos from these sources to give us a *representative* look at the treatment of animals in CAFOs. My advice (as a non-expert) for getting at least some reliable sense of the present-day realities of animal farming is to track down and browse some online "how-to" guides for beak trimming, dehorning, castrating, and tail-docking, as well as online catalogs selling farmers equipment for performing these mutilations.

6. Fred and His Puppies

I will assume in what follows that when you eat meat, you are buying meat that came from a CAFO—which, as I said above, is almost certainly the case if you are not making a special effort and financial sacrifice to buy only humanely raised meat. (If you *are* making this effort, the argument does not apply to you. But a revised version of the argument might. More on this in section 9.) I will argue that it is immoral for you to buy and eat that meat by presenting you with a fictional case involving the horrific treatment of puppies, and arguing that there is no morally relevant difference between what is done in this fictional case and what you are doing when you eat meat.

Here is the case:

COCOAMONE FARM

As a result of a head injury, Fred's brain stops naturally producing cocoamone, the hormone that enables humans to taste chocolate. Fred discovers that the only way to obtain useable cocoamone is to distill it from the brains of puppies. (The science behind this is very complicated and you wouldn't understand it.) So Fred buys twenty Labrador puppies from a local breeder. He slices off their tails, yanks out their canine teeth, and castrates the males, all without anesthesia. He keeps them locked in small cages in his spare bedroom, slaughters them, grinds up their brains, and distills a month's supply of cocoamone. He sips some cocoamone and—*voilà*—it works! So he buys twenty more puppies for the next month's supply, mutilates them, and locks them up.

And here is the argument:

The Argument from Fred's Puppies

(FP1) If there is no morally relevant difference between two actions A and B, and A is immoral, then B is immoral

(FP2) What Fred does is immoral

(FP3) There is no morally relevant difference between what Fred does and you buying and eating factory-farmed meat

(FP4) So, it is immoral for you to buy and eat factory-farmed meat

The idea behind FP1 is that, whenever there is some moral difference between two actions—for instance that one is immoral and the other isn't—there must always be some *explanation* of why they differ morally. Absent some such explanation, it would be arbitrary to say that the one action is immoral and the other isn't.

FP2 should strike you as obvious. Some, despite finding it obvious, may still wring their hands, remembering that in some cultures dogs are routinely killed and eaten for food. If you are wringing your hands, you should remind yourself that there are also cultures in which they routinely mutilate the genitals of young girls. Next, you should re-read section 2 above and remind yourself that the fact that lots of people engage in some practice doesn't make it morally permissible, for them or for you. The fact that some people mutilate their own daughters' genitals, raise dogs for food, or (for that matter) confine, mutilate, and slaughter farm animals, does not by itself settle the question of whether any of these practices are morally acceptable. Finally, with all this in mind, I invite you to re-read COCOAMONE FARM with fresh eyes, ask yourself whether Fred's actions seem immoral, find your moral compass, and admit that FP2 is something that you agree with.

How about FP3? I don't expect this premise to strike you as obvious. Indeed, you've probably already thought of several differences between what Fred is doing and what you do when you buy and eat meat. So let us consider some of the putative differences.

7. Morally Relevant Differences

There are plenty of differences between the case of Fred and his puppies and the case of you and the farm animals whose flesh you are buying and eating. Labrador puppies are cute and cuddly, for instance, whereas chickens and pigs are ugly and smelly. That's a difference. But it isn't a *morally relevant* difference. How cute or ugly something or someone is doesn't make any difference to what we are morally permitted to do to them.

So, what might be a morally relevant difference between the cases, that is, a difference that could potentially make for a moral difference? I'll consider five possibilities: that puppies aren't bred to be consumed, that Fred's cruelty is unnecessary, that meat (unlike chocolate) has actual health benefits, that Fred (unlike you) is directly harming the animals, and that Fred giving up cocoamone would have an actual impact on the amount of animal suffering whereas you giving up meat would have no impact.

First, one might point to a difference in what puppies and livestock are bred for. Puppies, the idea goes, are bred to serve as human companions, whereas chickens and pigs are bred for human consumption. But there is reason to doubt that this is a morally relevant difference. If someone were breeding human children specifically so they could be put to work as slaves, enslaving those children would be just as immoral as enslaving any other child.

Furthermore, we can simply revise the COCOAMONE FARM case so that this difference disappears.

BRED FOR COCOAMONE

Fred goes to a breeder and buys some dogs, some male and some female. Recognizing that these dogs were bred to be human companions, he treats them well. But he breeds the dogs, intending to use their puppies for cocoamone. Once they have their puppies—which *weren't* bred for human companionship—he takes the puppies, locks them in cages, mutilates them, slaughters them, and distills their cocoamone.

By revising the case in this way, we eliminate the difference that was supposed to be morally relevant. Yet what Fred does to these puppies still seems wrong, even though they were bred for the sole purpose of being slaughtered for their cocoamone. So FP2 remains true—despite changing the details of what Fred does— and the proposed objection to FP3 fails.

Second, one might contend that, whereas the farm animals' suffering is unavoidable, Fred's cruel treatment of the puppies is entirely unnecessary. If all he needs is the cocoamone, why extract their teeth and cut off their tails and keep them in small cages?

Well, here's the thing. Fred lives in a small two-bedroom apartment, and it would be complete chaos if he gave those twenty dogs the run of the house. There's no reasonable alternative to keeping them in cages. Of course, being all cooped up like this makes them crazy and aggressive, and castrating them curbs their aggression, while removing their teeth and tails diminishes their ability to harm one another. Why not get a bigger apartment? And why no anesthesia? He can't afford it! Why not extract the cocoamone from their brains without slaughtering them? One does not simply "extract the cocoamone." It's not as if there's a little pouch in there filling up with the stuff. There's no way to get at it without grinding up the brain and straining it out. So, we have failed to identify a difference between the cases, let alone a morally relevant difference. In both cases, the suffering is an unavoidable consequence of the only feasible and financially sound way of obtaining the relevant resource (be it meat or cocoamone).

Third, one might contend that the morally relevant difference is that meat, but not cocoamone, makes a positive contribution to one's health. Not so fast. Cocoamone does make a positive contribution to Fred's *psychological* health. He loves the taste of chocolate, and the thought of never tasting it again is very depressing for him. Perhaps you'll object that meat doesn't merely make a positive contribution to one's health; meat (unlike cocoamone) is *necessary* for a healthy diet. But as we saw in section 4, that's just false. There is nothing, protein included, that's needed for survival or health and that can only be gotten from meat.

Fourth, one might say that Fred directly harms the puppies in Cocoamone Farm, whereas you do not directly harm any farm animals. The farm animals have already been confined, mutilated, and slaughtered by the time you buy and eat the meat. (Notice, by the way, that this is the opposite of the common refrain that it's okay to eat meat as long as you'd be willing to kill it yourself. Here, the idea is that it's okay precisely because you're *not* killing it yourself.)

In response: the absence of direct harm doesn't typically absolve someone of moral responsibility. If I hire a hitman to kill someone, intuitively what I have done is no less wrong than if I had committed the murder myself. In any case, we can revise the Fred story once more to eliminate the putative difference.

HIRED HELP
Too squeamish to mutilate and slaughter the dogs himself, Fred hires Nysha to do it for him. She buys twenty dogs, mutilates them, keeps them confined in small cages, slaughters them, and provides Fred with one vial of cocoamone each month. He pays her for her services.

Now, Fred is not directly harming the puppies. But his hands are not clean; it is immoral for him to hire Nysha to set up a cocoamone farm. So FP2 remains true even when we revise the story to incorporate something more analogous to the indirect harm of buying meat. The putative morally relevant difference between the cases disappears and can no longer serve as an objection to FP3.

8. The No Impact Objection
Let's consider one last attempt to identify a morally relevant difference between you and Fred. Here, the idea is that if Fred stops what he's doing—whether that's running a cocoamone farm himself or paying Nysha to do it for him—there will be a substantial decrease in the number of puppies confined, mutilated, and slaughtered for their cocoamone. That number will drop to zero. By contrast, if you stopped buying and eating meat, in all likelihood it would make no difference whatsoever to the number of farm animals confined, mutilated, and slaughtered for their meat.

Why think that your decision to stop buying meat will have no impact on animal suffering? The average meat-eater consumes the equivalent of twenty-five chickens per year. So suppose you give up meat for a whole year, and twenty-five chickens' worth of meat goes unpurchased as a result. It is not as if the barons of the meat industry are going to take notice and say: "Egad! Last year we sold eight billion chickens, and this year we only sold 7,999,999,975. We'd better confine, mutilate, and slaughter twenty-five fewer chickens next year." Demand is going to have to shrink by thousands of animals per year before anyone takes notice, and that's not something you yourself can make happen just by giving up meat.

This does look like it has what it takes to be a morally relevant difference. If one action actually has an impact on the amount of suffering in the world, and another has no impact whatsoever, then that very plausibly makes for a moral difference between the two actions.

That said, this ultimately is not a convincing objection to FP3. For once again, we can revise the case to make the difference disappear:

SECOND DESSERT
Fred decides not to start his own cocoamone farm, and has now gone months without tasting chocolate. Out to dinner, for old times' sake, he orders a chocolate mousse for dessert. To his surprise, he is able to taste the chocolate. Elated, he calls the waiter over to order a second mousse and asks if there's something special about it. The waiter explains that, yes, the mousse is infused with cocoamone from the brains of slaughtered, mutilated puppies that they keep caged up in the back. They go through twenty puppies a day, he says. Fred is horrified. But he does not cancel his order, and he enjoys a second cocoamone-infused mousse.

It's wrong for Fred to order a second mousse, now that he knows about the puppy suffering involved in making it. And yet canceling the order would have had no impact on the amount of puppy suffering. They slaughter all the puppies before dinner service even begins, and they'll slaughter twenty more tomorrow even if they end up with some leftover mousse tonight. So there is no morally relevant difference between what Fred does in SECOND DESSERT and what you do when buying and eating meat. The objection to FP3 has been defused.

How, though, can Fred's actions in SECOND DESSERT be immoral if they have no impact? The obvious answer is that he is part of a group whose actions collectively do make an impact, namely the restaurant's customers. The restaurant keeps slaughtering the puppies only because customers keep ordering the mousse. The customers are doing something immoral, and Fred's actions are immoral by virtue of contributing to the impact that the group as a whole has on puppy suffering. This is the same reason why it's wrong to throw your plastic bottles in the garbage rather than recycling them, even though the results will almost certainly be the same even without your small contribution. And this is the same reason why it's wrong to buy meat, even if your personal meat consumption doesn't by itself make a difference. (Of course, the meat that you and others purchase today is from animals that are already dead, so you're not contributing to the suffering of *those* animals. But you and others are affecting the next generation of farm animals, by incentivizing farmers to continue raising and mistreating them.)

I'll close by considering a variation on the no-impact objection. It is sometimes objected that even if *everyone* switched to a vegetarian diet, that wouldn't make any difference to the amount of animal suffering. After all, farming crops results in the deaths of countless mice and other field animals that get caught up in farm machinery. Cutting out meat would lead to less killing of livestock, but this would just be replaced with more crop farming and thus more mouse killing. Since we have to eat something, the idea goes, and since animals are going to be dying either way, we may as well eat meat.

I find this unconvincing for several reasons. First, one must take into account not just the quantity of the deaths but also the quality of the lives. The mice killed in crop farming live normal lives up until they are killed by the farming equipment, whereas livestock in CAFOs are subjected to a lifetime of confinement with mutilated bodies. Second, it's far from obvious that a worldwide switch to vegetarianism would result in any increase in the number of field animals killed. In the U.S., only about a quarter of farmed crops are directly consumed by humans, and more than half are grown and farmed to serve as animal feed. Replacing the latter with crops meant for human consumption would likely lead to an overall *decrease* in crop farming and mouse killings, as well as reducing the number of mice killed in laboratories while developing and testing antibiotics for farm animals. Third, there are feasible, nonlethal methods of driving mice from the fields before farming them, whereas there are no nonlethal methods of slaughtering animals for their meat.

9. Beyond Factory Farming

I have argued that eating meat cannot be justified on the grounds that people have been doing it for all of recorded history, or on the grounds that eating meat is necessary, or on the grounds that eating meat is "natural." I also argued that it is immoral for you to buy and eat meat produced in CAFOs, which is pretty much all the meat you've been buying assuming that you haven't been going out of your way to buy humanely raised meat. If I'm right about this, then my arguments are highly relevant to most people's eating habits. If you have been casually buying meat at supermarkets, restaurants, and fast food establishments, then you are doing something immoral and ought to change your dietary practices.

Is it *ever* morally permissible to eat meat or other animal products? The Argument from Fred's Puppies only establishes that eating meat from CAFOs is immoral, and not all meat comes from CAFOs. That said, the Argument from Fred's Puppies can be adapted to shed light on other sorts of cases.

First, consider eggs and dairy products like cheese and milk. Just like the meat you buy, pretty much all of the eggs and dairy that you buy comes from CAFOs. Dairy cows and egg-laying chickens endure the same sorts of confinement and mutilations as the cows and chickens raised for meat. In light of that, we can revise Fred's case to show that it is immoral to buy and consume eggs and dairy that come from CAFOs.

SWEATY PUPPIES

Fred's brain stops producing cocoamone, and the only way to obtain useable cocoamone is to distill it from the sweat of puppies. He asks his friends if he can collect sweat off of their puppies, but they think that's creepy and won't let him do it. So he buys twenty puppies, locks them in cages, mutilates them, collects their sweat, and distills a month's supply of cocoamone.

What Fred does is immoral. But there's no morally relevant difference between him caging and mutilating the puppies for their cocoamone, and you buying and consuming eggs and dairy from CAFOs. (See section 7 for a reminder about why Fred has no choice but to cage and mutilate the puppies.)

How about meat from humanely raised animals? Here, again, we can look to Fred for guidance.

PAINLESS DEATH
Fred's brain stops producing cocoamone, and the only way to obtain useable cocoamone is to distill it from the brains of puppies. So he buys twenty puppies, lets them run around free in his apartment, takes them for walks, buys them toys, and treats them well. Then, once they're a year old, he sneaks up on them one by one, swiftly decapitates them, grinds up their brains, and distills a month's supply of cocoamone.

Is Fred doing something immoral? I would say so, though I'll admit that what he does in PAINLESS DEATH isn't nearly as bad as what he does in the original COCOAMONE FARM case. If you agree that it's wrong for Fred to slaughter puppies for their cocoamone even if he otherwise treats them well, then you should agree that it's wrong for you to buy meat even from humanely-raised farm animals.

How about eggs and dairy from humanely raised animals? For instance, suppose that someone keeps chickens and cows as pets, treats them well, never slaughters them, and sells their milk and (unfertilized) eggs. Would it be wrong to buy and consume their milk and eggs? To find the answer, let's consider what would be the analogous case for Fred:

HAPPY PUPPY SWEAT
Fred's brain stops producing cocoamone, and the only way to obtain useable cocoamone is to distill it from the sweat of puppies. So he buys twenty puppies, lets them run around free in his apartment, takes them for walks, buys them toys, and treats them well. He collects their sweat—without killing them or harming them in any way—and distills a month's supply of cocoamone.

This case seems to combine all the best features of the previous two cases with none of their problematic features. Certainly Fred isn't doing anything immoral. So, by parity of reason, there's nothing immoral about buying eggs and dairy from humanely raised animals on a no-kill farm.

Finally, what about lab-grown meat? We currently have the technology to "grow" beef in a laboratory—just the meat, with no animal attached—without any living animals being harmed in the process. Someday soon, you may be able to buy this lab-grown meat in stores and restaurants. Would that be immoral? Once again, we can answer the question by imagining Fred getting his cocoamone in an analogous way:

COCOAMONE LAB
Fred's brain stops producing cocoamone. So he buys a hundred small clusters of brain cells that were painlessly extracted from living puppies without harming those puppies in any way. He keeps the cells alive in a chemical solution, and collects the cocoamone that they produce.

When we drastically change the details of the case in this way, it no longer seems like Fred is doing anything immoral. No animals have to die or suffer in order for him to get his cocoamone. Since there is no morally relevant difference between what Fred does in COCOAMONE LAB and buying lab-grown meat, and since Fred isn't doing anything immoral in COCOAMONE LAB, there's nothing immoral about buying and eating lab-grown meat.

What we've just seen is that the arguments of this chapter don't support the extreme view that it's *never* permissible to buy or consume meat or other animal products. But even though I haven't shown that eating meat is *always* immoral, I have shown that it's immoral to buy any of the meat (and most of the eggs and dairy) that's presently for sale in stores and restaurants.

Suppose you are convinced that you ought to stop buying and eating meat. But you can't bring yourself to cut out meat completely, perhaps because you love Taco Bell too much or because grandma will be crushed if you refuse to eat her Christmas roast. What's a wannabe vegetarian to do? What I would say is that morality comes in degrees. It's wrong to eat meat, but it's far worse to eat meat at every meal than to eat meat just on holidays and a Taco Bell Double Decker Taco now and again. So, my advice is to make a good faith effort to decrease your meat consumption, to once a day or once a week. In other words, you can become a "reducetarian." Then, when you're ready, you can transition to a 100% (or 99%) vegetarian diet.

Reflection Questions

1. Can the arguments from precedent or naturalness be defended against my objections? Or can you think of a superior line of argument in defense of eating meat?

2. Can you think of a plausible way of arguing against premise FP2, that what Fred does is immoral? Make sure that your argument in defense of slaughtering puppies won't double as a defense of slaughtering human infants.

3. Can you defend one of the putative morally relevant differences discussed in sections 7 and 8 against my objections? Or can you think of a morally relevant difference that was not discussed?

4. If not for the meat industry, the billions of animals raised and slaughtered annually for food would never have existed. Could this fact be used as the basis for an argument in defense of eating meat? Why or why not?

5. What should someone who accepts the Argument from Fred's Puppies think about freeganism, the practice of eating only meat that someone else has purchased or thrown in the dumpster and that would otherwise go to waste?

Sources
The discussion of the Arguments from Precedent, Naturalness, and Necessity draws heavily from Dan Lowe's "Common Arguments for the Moral Acceptability of Eating Meat." The Argument from Fred's Puppies and subsequent discussion is drawn from Alastair Norcross's "Puppies, Pigs, and People." The argument from killing mice in section 8 is drawn from Mike Archer's "Ordering the Vegetarian Meal? There's More Animal Blood on Your Hands," and the response to that argument is

drawn from the All Animals Australia blog's "Debunking 'Ordering the Vegetarian Meal?'" The statistics in section 8 about the proportion of crops grown to feed animals are drawn from Brad Plumer's "How Much of the World's Cropland is Actually Used to Grow Food?" Here are some additional resources:

- Elizabeth Anderson: Animal Rights and the Values of Nonhuman Life
- Animal Kill Clock (animalclock.org/)
- Andrew Chignell, Terence Cuneo, and Matthew C. Halteman: *Philosophy Comes to Dinner*
- Cora Diamond: Eating Meat and Eating People
- Tyler Doggett: Killing Animals for Food (wi-phi.com)
- Mylan Engel Jr.: Fishy Reasoning and the Ethics of Eating
- Lori Gruen: *Ethics and Animals: An Introduction*
- Elizabeth Harman: The Moral Significance of Animal Pain and Animal Death
- Michael Huemer: *Dialogues on Ethical Vegetarianism*
- Anja Jauernig: Speaking Up for Animals
- Christine Korsgaard: A Kantian Case for Animal Rights
- Loren Lomasky: Is it Wrong to Eat Animals?
- Jeff McMahan: The Meat Eaters
- Peter Singer: All Animals are Equal
- David Foster Wallace: Consider the Lobster

CHAPTER 10
What Makes Things Right

Views and arguments advanced in this chapter are not necessarily endorsed by the author of the textbook, nor are they original to the author, nor are they meant to be consistent with arguments advanced in other chapters. Different chapters represent different philosophical perspectives.

1. Utilitarianism

We're constantly confronted with questions about the right or wrong thing to do. Some arise in our daily lives: is it wrong to download pirated movies, run a red light at an empty intersection, tell on a friend who you know cheated on an exam? Some arise in political discussion: is it wrong for the government to ban assault rifles, or abortions? Some arise in stories and movies: is it wrong for the super-villain to kill off half the population so that the survivors can benefit from the abundance of resources?

We'd like to know which of these things are right and which are wrong. What would be even better is a perfectly general answer to the question of which things are right and wrong, an answer that identifies what makes right actions right and wrong actions wrong. My aim here is to answer that question. In particular, I will defend a *utilitarian* answer, according to which the rightness or wrongness of an action is entirely a function of how it contributes (positively or negatively) to people's well-being. Since a person's well-being is ultimately a matter of how happy they are, what this means is that an action's rightness or wrongness comes down to how much an action increases or decreases levels of happiness.

Here, then, is the utilitarian theory of morality that I plan to defend, which we'll call "act utilitarianism."

Act Utilitarianism

Performing a certain action is the right thing to do if and only if it will have a more positive effect on overall levels of happiness than any other available action

By 'happiness', I mean any sort of pleasurable mental state, including both physical and emotional pleasures. And I'm thinking of "levels of happiness" as including degrees of *un*happiness. Two situations in which everyone is unhappy may still differ in their level of happiness if they are unhappier in one than in the other.

In section 2, I'll explain why act utilitarianism is an appealing theory of morality. Then, in section 3, I'll consider an important objection to the view, namely that it implies that killing an innocent person and distributing his organs to save five lives is the right thing to do. In section 4, I consider, but ultimately reject, an alternative utilitarian view—"rule utilitarianism"—which seems to avoid this undesirable consequence. Finally, in section 5, I argue that act utilitarianism is *correct* to say that killing one person to save five is the right thing to do, as becomes clear when we consider other sorts of cases (involving runaway trolleys).

Before proceeding, let me clarify a couple things. First, act utilitarianism does *not* say that the right thing for a person to do is whatever makes *that person* the happiest. To help see this, consider the following case:

TERRORIST ATTACK
Kristian discovers that her girlfriend Demi is planning a terrorist attack. Kristian knows that if she calls the cops on Demi, it will end their relationship, Demi will never forgive her, and she'll feel incredibly guilty about turning Demi in. Kristian also knows that if she doesn't tell the cops, countless people will lose their lives or their loved ones. Kristian decides not to tell the cops, and Demi carries out the devastating attack. Demi is never caught. Kristian puts it out of her mind and feels no guilt or remorse about not preventing the attack.

Keeping the information to herself has a greater positive effect on *Kristian's* overall level of happiness than ratting out Demi would have. Still, act utilitarianism says that the right thing for Kristian to have done was to tell the cops. Why? Because act utilitarianism requires us to take into account the happiness of *everyone* affected by the action, not just the person who performed the action. The effects of withholding the information include not just Kristian and Demi's happiness but also the grief experienced by the victims' families and friends. The effects of telling the cops would include not just Kristian and Demi's unhappiness but also all the happy experiences that the victims and their families and friends would otherwise have enjoyed. Turning Demi in clearly would have had a greater positive effect on overall levels of happiness in the world. So, according to act utilitarianism, Kristian should have turned Demi in.

Second, I say that I am defending *a* utilitarian theory. What makes a view utilitarian is that it considers rightness and wrongness to be a function of how actions affect overall well-being, that is, a function of the things that make people better or worse off. I am assuming that people's well-being is entirely a matter of how happy or unhappy they are, though one could in principle defend a utilitarian theory on which well-being consists in something other than happiness (for instance, people getting what they want, even when it doesn't make them happy). Additionally, act utilitarianism describes *one* way in which morality might be a function of happiness, but there are other possible ways of saying what the function is. For instance, as we'll see in section 4, one could say that it's a function not simply of how one's specific actions affect people's happiness but rather of how the *rules* that one is following generally tend to affect people's happiness.

2. Why Accept Act Utilitarianism?

I'm not sure how to argue definitively for the truth of act utilitarianism. Still, I can give several reasons for taking it seriously as a theory of morality.

First, act utilitarianism delivers the right verdicts about which actions are right and wrong in a wide range of cases. Cheating on your romantic partner is wrong because it leads to so much emotional pain, in exchange for a comparably small and short-lived amount of sexual gratification. If I promise to drive you to the airport early in the morning and then I don't bother to show up because I don't feel like getting out of bed, I've done something wrong because your financial loss and distress over missing your

189

flight has a bigger negative effect on overall happiness (taking into account both yours and mine) than does dragging myself out of bed and getting you to the airport.

On the other hand, suppose I promise to drive you to the airport and I don't show up because, on the way out the door, I happen upon someone in desperate need of medical attention, and I drive him to the hospital. In that case, I did the right thing, even though I broke my promise. Why? Because leaving him to die would have had a greater negative effect on the overall level of happiness of all involved (including yours, mine, his, and his family and friends') than you missing your flight.

We'll consider some cases later where act utilitarianism may seem to get the wrong result. In the meantime, I would encourage you to think of cases from your own life where you judged that someone did the morally right or morally wrong thing, and see whether act utilitarianism delivers the same verdict about whether it was right or wrong. I bet it does.

Second, it's extremely plausible that morality is about making people better off and making the world a better place. If some action I perform increases the overall levels of happiness in the world more than any other action I could have performed, then I've done the best I can to make the world a better place. And surely, if I've done the best I can to make the world a better place, I've done the right thing. Or put it another way. Suppose, just for the sake of argument, that act utilitarianism is false. That means that there could be some action that, on the whole, makes people better off and makes the world a better place—more so than any other action I could have performed—and yet it's the wrong thing to do. And I could sometimes be doing the right thing by choosing the action that generates more unhappiness. Both of these things would be possible if act utilitarianism were false: it could be wrong to make the world a better place, and right to make the world a worse place. But that's absurd. So, act utilitarianism must be true.

Third, act utilitarianism is egalitarian. Act utilitarians are against sexist laws and practices. Since these practices have a dramatic negative effect on levels of happiness, by profoundly decreasing the levels of happiness for women, act utilitarianism rules them to be immoral. Act utilitarians oppose racist laws and practices for the same reason. Act utilitarians are against persecuting and discriminating against LGBTQ people for the same reason. These kinds of oppression are wrong, and act utilitarianism agrees that they're wrong. For, even though there are always those who benefit from the oppression, what they gain in happiness is far outweighed by the unhappiness experienced by the victims of the oppression. Act utilitarians have all along been saying that everyone's happiness has to be given equal weight, regardless of race, gender, or sexual orientation—even back when these were radical things to say.

Fourth, act utilitarianism makes good sense of the respects in which morality is, and isn't, a subjective matter. Morality is subjective insofar as the same action might affect one person's happiness differently from how it affects another's. For instance, suppose I tell you to close your eyes, and I feed you a bite of pepperoni pizza. Have I done something wrong? It depends. If you love pepperoni pizza and it makes you happy, then no. If you're a vegetarian and what I did makes you furious and nauseous, then yes. Act utilitarianism easily explains why what I did is right in the one situation and wrong in the other.

The same goes for cultural differences. In countries like the U.S., tipping your waiter is customary, whereas in countries like Japan it can be considered offensive. Accordingly, tipping is the right thing to do in the U.S. and the wrong thing to do in Japan. Act utilitarianism explains why the same action can be right in once place and wrong in another: because in the one place it makes people happy and in the other it makes them unhappy.

That's not to say that morality is entirely a subjective matter. We cannot change what's right or wrong just by *changing our minds* about what's right or wrong. To see this, consider the following case:

CONDONED LOBOTOMIES
The leaders of a certain oppressive country instituted a law that requires all newborn girls to be lobotomized. Dissenters were lobotomized as well. After a few generations, there are no more dissenters. The men are all happy with the arrangement, and the women are all lobotomized and have no opinion on the matter.

No one in this country thinks that it is wrong to lobotomize newborn girls. And yet obviously the leaders are doing something deeply immoral. Act utilitarianism explains why: the women of this country are deprived of the full range of intellectual and emotional enjoyments that they would otherwise have had. The fact that no one in the country *believes* that the practice is wrong is neither here nor there. What matters is how the practice affects the well-being of all involved, and (unlike tipping) the effects of lobotomies don't vary from one country to the next.

3. Killing One to Save Five

We saw that act utilitarianism tends to give the right answers to moral questions. But one might object that it at least *sometimes* gives the wrong answer, misidentifying a wrong action as the right thing to do. In other words, the objection is that there are counterexamples to act utilitarianism, examples in which one action does more than another to increase overall levels of happiness and yet is not the right thing to do. So, it is incumbent upon me, as a defender of act utilitarianism, to address all such cases and show that they are not genuine counterexamples.

One might wonder, though, why any such defense is needed. If act utilitarianism generally gives the correct verdicts, why does it matter if it doesn't get the answer right in *every single* case? It matters because I am trying to do more than just give a useful rule of thumb for answering moral questions. For suppose act utilitarianism *were* just a useful, but not exceptionless, rule of thumb. In that case, even if I could convince you beyond any doubt that legalizing polyamorous marriages would increase overall levels of happiness, that would not yet settle the question of whether legalizing them is the right thing to do. After all, maybe polyamorous marriage is one of the exceptions to the rule, where increasing overall levels of happiness isn't the right thing to do.

A merely useful rule of thumb for investigating moral questions ends up being useless for *settling* moral questions. For that reason, I want to defend the view that act utilitarianism provides the complete story of what makes actions right or wrong. I want to defend a theory on which showing that one action is better than any alternative at improving happiness levels definitively settles the question of whether it is the right thing to do. Accordingly, even one case in which my theory misclassifies the wrong thing to do as the right thing to do, or vice versa, would be enough to falsify the theory.

Here, then, is the case I want to discuss, which is meant to be a counterexample to act utilitarianism.

ORGAN DISTRIBUTION
Jonathan is a doctor, and his patient Nick is coming in for a routine physical. Looking over his past bloodwork, Jonathan realizes that Nick's organs are an exact match for five patients in critical condition upstairs in the Intensive Care Unit. When Nick arrives, Jonathan kills him (painlessly), making it look like an accident. Since Nick is an organ donor, his body is rushed upstairs, and his heart, lungs, liver, and each of his kidneys are successfully transplanted into those five patients, saving their lives. No other organs arrived that day, and the five patients would have died had Jonathan not killed Nick for his organs. The five patients all go on to lead long, happy lives. No one ever finds out that Nick's death was not an accident.

Some will say that what Jonathan did is immoral. And yet, killing Nick and saving the five patients results in higher overall levels of happiness than letting him live and allowing the five patients to die. After all, killing Nick results in the loss of one life's worth of happiness and one group of mourners, whereas letting the five patients die would have resulted in the loss of five lives' worth of happiness and five times as many mourners.

If all that is right, then act utilitarianism is false. The argument can be reconstructed as follows:

The Organ Distribution Argument
(OD1) Killing Nick has a greater positive effect on overall levels of happiness than letting him live
(OD2) If killing Nick has a greater positive effect on overall levels of happiness than letting him live, then: if act utilitarianism is true, then killing Nick was the right thing to do
(OD3) Killing Nick was not the right thing to do
(OD4) So, act utilitarianism is false

OD1 is true. There would have been more mourning and fewer happy lives if Jonathan hadn't killed Nick. OD2 is true as well: act utilitarianism says that, without exception, the action with the greatest positive effect on happiness levels is the right thing to do. And OD3 is supposed to simply be obvious. Even I agree that killing Nick *seems* to be morally wrong.

4. Rule Utilitarianism

One option for a utilitarian—which is worth exploring, but which I do not myself endorse—is to grant that the Organ Distribution Argument works and that act utilitarianism is false. The idea would then be to provide an alternative utilitarian view, one that won't deliver the result that Jonathan did the right thing in killing Nick. What would such an alternative view look like?

One idea would be to insist that doing the right thing isn't so much a matter of how a single action affects happiness levels, but rather a matter of how the *rules* one is following tend to affect happiness levels. Consider the following rules that one might choose to follow:

- Don't kill innocent people
- Don't steal
- Don't lie
- Don't break promises
- Treat people fairly

Even if following these rules doesn't *always* maximize happiness, it usually does, which is what makes them good rules.

With this in mind, one possibility for avoiding the implication that Jonathan did the right thing in killing Nick would be to reject act utilitarianism in favor of rule utilitarianism:

Rule Utilitarianism
Performing a certain action is the right thing to do if and only if it is prescribed by the collection of rules that, if adopted, would have the greatest positive effect on overall levels of happiness

194

Even though following the rules listed above won't have the greatest positive effect on overall levels of happiness in every single case, following them does more often than not have a positive effect on happiness. If so, they may well belong to the collection of rules that, if adopted, would have the greatest positive effect on overall levels of happiness—or, in short, "the best collection of rules."

Here is how rule utilitarianism is supposed to help with ORGAN DISTRIBUTION. According to rule utilitarianism, the right thing to do is to follow the best collection of rules. So, let us compare two rules: *don't kill an innocent person unless doing so saves multiple lives* and *don't ever kill any innocent people*. While it's true that following the first rule sometimes has a better effect on happiness levels (as in ORGAN DISTRIBUTION), typically it doesn't. If doctors were constantly killing healthy patients to distribute their organs, word would get out. There would be widespread panic. People would be terrified to go to the hospital, leading to all sorts of untreated illnesses and injuries. Even though five people would be saved for every one person killed, thousands of others would be sick, scared, and miserable.

Following the first rule tends, on the whole, to have a negative effect on happiness levels. Following the second rule, by contrast, tends on the whole to have a positive effect on happiness levels, even though in some rare cases it has a negative effect. Accordingly, the best collection of rules is going to include the second rule, not the first. Rule utilitarianism therefore tells us that the right thing for Jonathan to do is to let Nick live, since that's what's dictated by the better rule: *don't ever kill any innocent people*. Rule utilitarianism, unlike act utilitarianism, delivers what intuitively seems to be the right result in ORGAN DISTRIBUTION.

The problem with rule utilitarianism is that it faces counterexamples of its own—counterexamples that, to my mind, are even more damning than the alleged counterexample to act utilitarianism. For instance, recall the case mentioned in section 2 where I break my promise to take you to the airport because, on my way to get you, I find someone desperately in need of medical attention and decide to drive them to the hospital instead. Clearly, I am doing the right thing in that case. But rule utilitarianism says that I've done the wrong thing. After all, the rule I am following, *don't break promises unless something more important comes up*, tends on the whole to have a negative effect on overall happiness. If everyone broke their promises every time something more important came up, no one would trust anyone to keep their promises, and not being able to trust one another would have a huge negative impact on our emotional well-being.

By contrast, following the simpler rule *don't ever break promises* tends on the whole to have a positive effect on happiness levels, even though in some rare cases is has a negative effect. So, by the same logic as above, rule utilitarianism says that the right thing to do is to keep my promise and leave the needy person to die. But that clearly is not the right thing to do. So, rule utilitarianism is false.

Perhaps the rule utilitarian will respond that there's a rule I'm overlooking: *don't break promises unless you need to break them in order to drive a dying person to the hospital*. Following *that* rule will tend on the whole to have a positive effect on happiness levels, since it only allows promise-breaking in certain rare cases where promise-breaking really is the right thing to do. So, the rule utilitarian might say, it's this rule—and neither of the previous two rules about promises—that belongs to the best collection of rules.

But if the "rules" that the rule utilitarian has in mind can be that specific, then we need to reassess what rule utilitarianism says about ORGAN DISTRIBUTION. After all, Jonathan is following the rule *don't kill innocent people unless you're absolutely certain you can do it secretly and you'll save five people with the organs*. Following that rule will tend to have the greatest positive effect on the whole, since it only allows killing innocent people in rare cases where the killings save lives and don't lead to widespread panic (because they're done in secret). So, by rule utilitarianism, Jonathan *is* doing the right thing by killing Nick—exactly the consequence the rule utilitarian wanted to avoid!

The point here is that the rule utilitarian faces a dilemma. Either her rules are understood to be relatively general things, in which case rule utilitarianism has the absurd implication that I'm never allowed to break my promises, even in extreme cases. Or her rules can be highly specific, in which case rule utilitarianism *does* imply that killing Nick was the right thing to do, and switching from act utilitarianism to rule utilitarianism is no help in escaping that consequence. Since rule utilitarianism is either false or unhelpful, let's set it aside, return to act utilitarianism, and reassess whether act utilitarianism can be defended against the Organ Distribution Argument.

5. The Trolley Argument

Premise OD3 of the Organ Distribution Argument says that killing Nick was not the right thing to do. I admitted above that this premise seems true: it *seems* morally wrong for Jonathan to kill Nick. But things are not always as they seem. I will now argue that, despite appearances, OD3 is false.

My argument against OD3 involves considering a different case, one in which it *isn't* wrong to kill one person to save five. Here is the case:

TROLLEY DRIVER

Corrine is driving a trolley, which is hurtling down the tracks, faster than it should. Five pledges from a local fraternity have been tied to the tracks as part of an initiation ritual. By the time she sees them, it's too late to slow down. The only way to avoid killing them is to swerve the trolley onto a side track at an upcoming junction. But the pledge master, who is asleep on the side track, will be killed if she does. Corrine decides to steer the trolley onto the side track anyway, killing the pledge master. She then stops the trolley, unties the pledges, and they all go on to lead long, happy lives.

Corrine did the right thing: it was morally better to steer onto the side track, killing the pledge master, than to continue forward and kill the five pledges. And yet there would seem to be no morally relevant difference between what Corrine did and what Jonathan did. Both killed one person to save five. So, if it was right for Corrine to do what had to be done to save five people, how could it be wrong for Jonathan to do what had to be done to save five people?

Here, more explicitly, is the argument:

The Trolley Argument
(TR1) If there is no morally relevant difference between two actions A and B, and A is the right thing to do, then B is the right thing to do
(TR2) Diverting the trolley was the right thing to do
(TR3) There is no morally relevant difference between diverting the trolley and killing Nick
(TR4) So, killing Nick was the right thing to do

The idea behind TR1 is that, whenever there is some moral difference between two cases, there must always be some explanation of why they differ morally. Absent some such explanation, it would be arbitrary to say that the one action is wrong and the other isn't. TR2 is hopefully obvious; I'm not sure what more I could do to argue for it. And TR3 seems true as well: the cases are structurally identical, both being cases in which one person is sacrificed to save five. Thus, even though the act utilitarian conclusion that Jonathan did the right thing may strike you as counterintuitive, we nevertheless have excellent reason to think it's correct. Those who wish to say that it was wrong to kill Nick must find some flaw in the Trolley Argument.

I can imagine someone objecting to TR3, insisting that there is an important difference between the cases. Here's the idea. If Corrine hadn't swerved onto the other track, she would have killed those five pledges. By contrast, if Jonathan hadn't killed Nick, we wouldn't say that he *killed* the five needy patients. He merely *let them die*, and allowing people to die is not morally equivalent to actually killing them. Killing is worse, one might say, and that's why Jonathan's actions are worse than Corrine's: Corrine but not Jonathan had to do what she did in order to avoid *killing* five people.

I have my doubts about whether there is any morally relevant difference between killing and letting die. But let's suppose that there is. Even so, we can revise the trolley case so that it too involves a choice between killing and letting die.

TROLLEY LEVER
A runaway trolley with no driver is hurtling down the tracks towards five pledges from a local fraternity. Corrine is an

onlooker, standing beside the tracks. Next to her is a lever which can divert the trolley onto a side track. She could do nothing, and let the pledges die. But if she pulls the lever and diverts the trolley, it will kill the pledge master, who is asleep on the side track. Corrine decides to pull the lever, killing the pledge master and saving the pledges. She then unties the pledges, and they all go on to lead long, happy lives.

Again, Corrine intuitively did the right thing by pulling the lever and killing one person to save five. But the earlier objection no longer holds. For if she hadn't pulled the lever, *she* wouldn't thereby be killing anyone. She would merely be letting five people die. Just like Jonathan. So, the alleged morally relevant difference disappears, and the objection to TR3 disappears along with it. Importantly, TR2 remains plausible even once the case is revised: faced with a decision between killing one and letting five die, killing the one is the right thing to do.

6. Conclusion
I have defended a utilitarian theory of morality, according to which the right thing to do is always whatever will have the greatest positive effect on overall levels of happiness. We saw that there are powerful motivations for accepting utilitarianism, for instance that it is intuitive, that it is egalitarian, and that it respects the subjectivity and culture-relativity of morality without entailing an extreme subjectivism according to which what's right or wrong can be changed at whim. Finally, we saw some ways of defending utilitarianism against the objection that it wrongly condones killing one person to save five.

Reflection Questions
1. In section 2, I said that act utilitarianism is admirably egalitarian, opposing the mistreatment of women and minorities. But might it be egalitarian for the wrong reasons? Is the problem with oppression really that the oppressed group's suffering outweighs the benefits the oppressors derive from the oppression?

2. Can you defend rule utilitarianism against the objections raised in section 4?

3. In the trolley cases, the pledge master—who tied the pledges to the tracks—is morally responsible for the pledges being in harm's way. Is this a morally relevant difference between ORGAN DISTRIBUTION and the trolley cases? Can the cases be revised in a way that eliminates this difference?

4. Suppose act utilitarianism is true. In that case, in order to know whether something is the right thing to do, one would evidently have to know all of the different ways that the action might affect people's happiness, both in the short-term and long into the future. Is that a problem for act utilitarianism? How might a utilitarian respond?

5. What should an act utilitarian say about the morality of eating meat and other animal products?

Sources
Classic defenses of utilitarianism can be found in Jeremy Bentham's *Principles of Morals and Legislation* and John Stuart Mill's *Utilitarianism*. See Philippa Foot's "The Problem of Abortion and the Doctrine of Double Effect" and Judith Jarvis Thomson's "The Trolley Problem" for discussion of the organ distribution and trolley cases. See Russ Shafer-Landau's *The Fundamentals of Ethics* for a broader overview of theories of well-being and morality. See the opening chapter of Elinor Mason's *Feminist Philosophy* (titled 'Feminism in the Multicultural Context') on defending universal values in the face of cultural disagreement. Here are some additional resources:

- E.F. Carritt: Criticisms of Utilitarianism
- Crash Course Philosophy: Utilitarianism (youtube.com)
    https://www.youtube.com/watch?v=-a739VjqdSI
- Josh Harris: The Survival Lottery
- Ursula K. Le Guin: The Ones Who Walk Away from Omelas
- Julia Markovitz: Utilitarianism (wi-phi.com)
- Mozi: Universal Love

- Nicholas: A Solution to the Trolley Problem (youtube.com)
- Alastair Norcross: Consequences Make Actions Right
- J.C.C. Smart and Bernard Williams: *Utilitarianism: For and Against*
- Bernard Williams: Utilitarianism and Integrity

APPENDIX A
Logic

Throughout this book, I present arguments, defend their premises, and then claim that the conclusions of those arguments *follow from* the premises. In this appendix, I'll explain what it means for a conclusion to follow from some premises and how you can tell when a conclusion follows from some premises. In section 1, I introduce the notion of a *valid* argument, that is, an argument whose conclusion follows from its premises. Then, in section 2, I identify four types of valid arguments. Finally, in section 3—because nothing is sacred in philosophy—I show how even claims about which types of arguments are valid can be called into question.

1. Valid Arguments

Suppose you and I have gotten our hands on a live chicken. I want to keep it as a pet, and I've already even given it a name: 'Camilla'. You want to slaughter it and eat it. I'm trying to convince you that we shouldn't eat Camilla, and I give you the following two arguments:

The Cuteness Argument
(CA1) Camilla is cute
(CA2) It's wrong to eat cute things
(CA3) So, it's wrong to eat Camilla

The Feathers Argument
(FA1) Camilla has feathers
(FA2) Feathers are soft
(FA3) So, it's wrong to eat Camilla

You probably aren't convinced by either argument. Why not?

It's easy to say what goes wrong with the Cuteness Argument. You might say the first premise is false, because chickens are ugly. Or you might deny the second premise, saying that just because something is cute doesn't mean it's wrong to eat it. Or maybe you'll deny both. Either way, the problem with the argument is that its premises aren't true.

But what about the Feathers Argument? You probably don't find it any more convincing than the Cuteness Argument. But both of its premises are true. So, what *is* the problem with the Feathers Argument? The problem is that the conclusion doesn't *follow* from the premises. Or, as philosophers like to say, the argument is not valid.

A *valid* argument is an argument whose conclusion is a *logical consequence* of its premises. When an argument is valid, the premises guarantee the truth of the conclusion; it's impossible for the premises to be true without the conclusion being true. You would be contradicting yourself if you accepted all the premises but denied the conclusion.

The problem with the Feathers Argument is that it's invalid: it doesn't follow from Camilla's having feathers and feathers' being soft that it's wrong to eat her. There's no contradiction in accepting the premises of that argument while denying its conclusion. The Cuteness Argument, by contrast, is valid: the claim that it's wrong to eat Camilla *is* a logical consequence of the claim that Camilla is cute and the claim that it's wrong to eat cute things. Anyone who accepts the premises of the Cuteness Argument is logically required to accept the conclusion as well, on pain of contradicting themselves.

You might be surprised that I just called the Cuteness Argument 'valid'. But look again at my definition of 'valid'. That definition doesn't require the premises of a valid argument to be true, or even plausible. All that's required is that *if* the premises are true, then the conclusion is guaranteed to be true as well. An argument can be valid and still be a pretty bad argument, like the Cuteness Argument, because its premises are implausible. (Philosophers have a different word for arguments that are valid *and* all of whose premises are true. We call them *sound* arguments.) Also, as defined above, validity can only ever be a feature of *arguments*. So, at least in philosophical discussions, it's best to avoid calling premises or points 'valid'. Only arguments should be described as valid or invalid.

One more word of warning: don't confuse *following* and *following from*. To see what I have in mind, consider this argument from chapter 4:

Against Fearing Death
(FD1) You cease to be conscious when you die
(FD2) If you cease to be conscious when you die, then being dead isn't bad for you
(FD3) So, being dead isn't bad for you
(FD4) If being dead isn't bad for you, then you shouldn't fear death
(FD5) So, you shouldn't fear death

It's true that FD2 follows FD1. That is, it comes immediately after FD1. But FD2 does not follow *from* FD1. To say that it follows from FD1 is to say that there's a valid argument whose conclusion is FD2 and whose only premise is FD1. That, in turn, implies that you would be contradicting yourself if you accepted FD1 while at the same time denying FD2. But notice that this isn't at all contradictory. You can agree that you cease to be conscious when you die (FD1), and yet reject FD2 on the grounds that you don't have to be consciously aware of bad things in order for them to be bad for you. What *is* true is that FD3 follows from FD1 and FD2. But FD2 doesn't itself follow from FD1.

2. How to Check for Validity
Many of the arguments in this book have conclusions you won't like. If the arguments were invalid then, as with the Feathers Argument, you could just reject the conclusion without having to find a premise to reject. But since the arguments *are* all valid—I made sure of it!—rejecting the conclusion of any one of them always requires finding some premise to deny.

But what did I *do* to ensure that the arguments were all valid? How can you tell if an argument is valid? One way is to eyeball it: look at the premises, and check whether it seems like the conclusion follows from them. But we can do better than that. We can identify certain recurring forms or patterns whose presence guarantees that an argument is valid, regardless of what the argument is about. Accordingly, another way to check for validity is to see if the argument has one of these forms. If it does, then it's valid. I'll give four examples.

2.1 Modus Ponens

To see what I have in mind by a "form" of argument, compare these two arguments:

The Drinking Age Argument
(DK1) Kristina is twenty years old
(DK2) If Kristina is twenty years old, then Kristina is not
      allowed to buy alcohol in the US
(DK3) So, Kristina is not allowed to buy alcohol in the US

The Moral Argument
(MA1) There are objective moral values
(MA2) If there are objective moral values, then God exists
(MA3) So, God exists

In some ways, the arguments are pretty different: one is about Kristina and drinking, the other is about God and morality. But there's also something they have in common, something structural.

To see what they have in common, let's recall some vocabulary that we learned in section 3 of the Introduction to this textbook. Claims of the form 'if... then...', like DK2 and MA2, are called *conditionals*. The bit that comes between the 'if' and the 'then' is the *antecedent* of the conditional, and the bit that comes after the 'then' is the *consequent* of the conditional.

What the Drinking Age Argument and the Moral Argument have in common is that each contains one premise that's a conditional, another premise that's the same as the antecedent of that conditional, and a conclusion that's the same as the consequent of that conditional. In other words, they both have the following form:

Modus Ponens
P
If P, then Q
So, Q

Arguments with this form are called *modus ponens* arguments. ('Modus ponens' is Latin for *method of affirming*: you reach the conclusion by taking a conditional premise and combining it with a premise that affirms its antecedent.) Every modus ponens argument is a valid argument.

Here are two things to note about modus ponens arguments. First, it doesn't matter whether the conditional premise comes first or second. For example, this is also a modus ponens argument:

The Rearranged Drinking Age Argument
(RD1) If Kristina is twenty years old, then Kristina is not allowed to buy alcohol in the US
(RD2) Kristina is twenty years old
(RD3) So, Kristina is not allowed to buy alcohol in the US

That said, you do have to "mind your Ps and Qs" and how they're distributed in the argument. This, for instance, is *not* a modus ponens argument:

The Mangled Drinking Age Argument
(MD1) Jean Blanc is not allowed to buy alcohol in the US
(MD2) If Jean Blanc is twenty years old, then Jean Blanc is not allowed to buy alcohol in the US
(MD3) So, Jean Blanc is twenty years old

This one doesn't have the form "P, if P then Q, so Q" but rather "P, if Q then P, so Q." This other argument form is called 'affirming the consequent', and is clearly invalid. Think about it. You can consistently accept MD1 and MD2 while denying MD3, for instance if you thought Jean Blanc was 18 years old. (You'd still accept MD2, that *if* he's twenty, he's still not allowed to buy alcohol.) By contrast, you can't consistently accept RD1 and RD2 while denying RD3. That's because the argument for RD3 is valid, whereas the argument for MD3 is invalid.

2.2 *Modus Tollens*
Another form that guarantees the validity of an argument is what's called *modus tollens*, Latin for *method of denying*. A modus tollens argument is an argument with one premise that's a conditional, another premise that's a denial of the consequent of

that conditional, and whose conclusion is the denial of the conditional's antecedent. Using the '~' symbol to symbolize denial, we can display the form of modus tollens arguments as follows:

Modus Tollens
If P then Q
~Q
So, ~P

Here are some examples of modus tollens arguments:

Whales Aren't Fish
(WF1) If whales are fish, then whales use gills to breathe
(WF2) Whales don't use gills to breathe
(WF3) So whales aren't fish

The Flipped Moral Argument
(FM1) If God does not exist, then there are no objective
       moral values
(FM2) There are objective moral values
(FM3) So, God exists

Again, the arguments are about entirely different topics but share a common structure. Also, as with modus ponens arguments, the order of the premises doesn't matter: it would still be a modus tollens argument if WF2 came first and WF1 came second. But the order within the premises does matter. You've got to have the denial of the conditional's consequent as a premise and a denial of its antecedent as the conclusion, not vice versa.

One other thing to notice here is that the same basic line of thought can be presented either as a modus ponens or as a modus tollens argument. The Moral Argument (from section 2.1) and the Flipped Moral Argument (just above) are really just two ways of packaging one and the same idea: that God must exist because objective morality presupposes the existence of God.

With these two types of valid arguments in hand, one can also construct more complicated arguments that involve both. For instance:

The Foreknowledge Argument

(FK1) God knew before you were born that you were going to read this book

(FK2) If God knew before you were born that you were going to read this book, then you couldn't have chosen not to read this book

(FK3) So, you couldn't have chosen not to read this book

(FK4) If you freely choose to read this book, then you could have chosen not to read this book

(FK5) So, you didn't freely choose to read this book

This argument combines a modus ponens argument and a modus tollens argument. The subconclusion FK3 follows, by modus ponens, from FK1 and FK2. And the conclusion FK5 follows, by modus tollens, from FK3 and FK4. Looking back at the Against Fearing Death argument in section 1, you can see that that argument combines two instances of modus ponens: a modus ponens argument from FD1 and FD2 to FD3, and another modus ponens argument from FD3 and FD4 to FD5.

2.3 Chained Conditionals

Here is a third type of valid argument, which I'll call a *chained conditional*, since the conclusion chains together the antecedent of one conditional premise with the consequent of another conditional premise.

Chained Conditional
If P then Q
If Q then R
So, if P then R

This form of argument is especially useful when you want to argue for a conditional claim, that is, when you want to give an argument that has a whole conditional as its conclusion.

Here are two examples of arguments with this form:

Against Fearing Non-Existence

(FN1) If you stop existing when you die, then being dead is not bad for you

(FN2) If being dead is not bad for you, then you shouldn't fear death

(FN3) So, if you stop existing when you die, then you shouldn't fear death

The Right to the Womb Argument

(RW1) If the embryo has a right to life, then the embryo has a right to use the mother's womb

(RW2) If the embryo has a right to use the mother's womb, then abortion is immoral

(RW3) So, if the embryo has a right to life, then abortion is immoral

2.4 Universal Instantiation

I'll mention one more form that a valid argument can have. This one is called *universal instantiation,* since it involves a "universal" premise claiming that everything belonging to one category also belongs to some second category. Together with an additional premise that one or more particular things belong to the first category, what follows is that those particular things also belong to the second category. Here it is schematically:

Universal Instantiation
All Fs are Gs
o is F
So, o is G

To get a valid argument of this form, you plug in some category for 'F', some second category for 'G', and a person or object for 'o'. (This makes it unlike the previous three types of valid arguments, where you plug in whole sentences for the variables 'P', 'Q', and 'R'.)

Here's an example of an argument by universal instantiation:

The Philosophical Genius Argument
(PG1) All philosophers are geniuses
(PG2) Korman is a philosopher
(PG3) So, Korman is a genius

The argument is valid, and what makes the argument valid is not the truth or the plausibility of the premises, but rather that the conclusion is a logical consequence of the premises. If you affirm the premises and yet deny the conclusion, you've contradicted yourself.

Universal instantiation arguments don't always wear their form right on their sleeve. Take the Cuteness Argument:

The Cuteness Argument
(CA1) Camilla is cute
(CA2) It's wrong to eat cute things
(CA3) So, it's wrong to eat Camilla

Superficially, this doesn't match the form of a universal instantiation argument, specified above. But with just a bit of rewording and rearranging, we can see that it's a universal instantiation in disguise:

(CA2*) All cute things are things that are wrong to eat
(CA1*) Camilla is a cute thing
(CA3*) So, Camilla is a thing that is wrong to eat

3. Challenging Modus Ponens and Modus Tollens
We have now seen four types of valid arguments: modus ponens arguments, modus tollens arguments, chained conditionals, and universal instantiations. These are not the *only* types of valid argument, and there's some controversy (in the philosophy of logic) about what would go on a complete list of valid forms of argument. But when you're constructing arguments of your own, so long as they have one of these four forms—or combine together arguments of these forms in the way suggested in section 2.2— you can be confident that your own argument is valid.

That said, because I apparently cannot go ten pages without arguing for some outrageous conclusion, I'm now going to argue—contrary to what virtually every philosopher and logician will tell you—that modus ponens and modus tollens arguments are not always valid.

Let's start with modus tollens. Consider the following case:

FLIGHT CONFUSION
I know that Olivia is due to fly from New York to Chicago, but I can't remember if the flight was this morning, or if she's flying tomorrow. So, I know she's either in Chicago or New York right now, but I don't know which.

Now, consider the following argument, which looks to be a counterexample to the thesis that all modus tollens arguments are valid:

The Defective Tollens
(DT1) If Olivia is in Chicago, then Olivia must be in Illinois
(DT2) It's not the case that Olivia must be in Illinois
(DT3) So, Olivia isn't in Chicago

This does appear to be a modus tollens argument: the first premise is a conditional, the second is a denial of its consequent, and the conclusion is a denial of its antecedent. Moreover, the premises are both true. DT1 is true because Chicago is in Illinois, so Olivia can't very well be in Chicago without being in Illinois. DT2 is true too. If someone were to say "she must be in Illinois," I could rightly respond: no, she might still be in New York. So DT2 rightly denies that she *must* be in Illinois.

But surely the argument is not valid. If it were, then DT3 would follow from those premises, and I would be able to use this argument to figure out where she is: she isn't in Chicago, so she must be in New York. Clearly, though, I can't know that Olivia is not in Chicago by using this argument. So, the argument must not be valid. In other words, this looks to be a counterexample to the claim that all modus tollens arguments are valid.

Now for modus ponens. Consider the following case:

TALENT SHOW

Celeste, Grant, and Esmée are the three finalists in a talent show. Celeste's performance was a complete disaster. Grant did a pretty good job. Esmée gave the performance of a lifetime, and she receives a standing ovation from the audience as well as all the judges. The judges are about to announce the winner.

Now consider the following argument, which looks to be a counterexample to the thesis that all modus ponens arguments are valid.

The Defective Ponens

(DP1) A woman is going to win

(DP2) If a woman is going to win, then: if Esmée loses, then Celeste will win

(DP3) So, if Esmée loses, then Celeste will win

This is a modus ponens argument. One premise is a conditional (albeit one that has a whole conditional as its consequent); another premise affirms the antecedent of that conditional; and the conclusion is the consequent of the first conditional. Moreover, the premises are both true. Esmée is clearly going to win, and she is a woman. So DP1 is true. DP2 is true as well. If a woman wins and it isn't Esmée then it has to be Celeste, since she is the only other woman still in the running. But DP3 is false: if Esmée loses, then it's *Grant* who's going to win. Celeste's performance was a disaster, so if Esmée lost, it would certainly be because a majority of the judges voted for Grant, not because they voted for Celeste.

If the argument were valid, then the truth of the premises would guarantee the truth of the conclusion. But since the premises are true and the conclusion is false, the premises clearly *don't* guarantee the truth of the conclusion. So, the argument isn't valid. Thus, not all modus ponens arguments are valid.

I'll leave it to you to figure out what (if anything) goes wrong in these arguments against the validity of modus ponens and modus tollens.

212

Sources

The argument against modus tollens is drawn from Niko Kolodny and John MacFarlane's "Ifs and Oughts." The argument against modus ponens is drawn from Vann McGee's "A Counterexample to Modus Ponens." For more on the philosophy of logic, see Susan Haack's *Philosophy of Logics* or Mark Sainsbury's *Logical Forms*.

APPENDIX B
Writing

This appendix provides some advice for writing papers for philosophy courses. The advice primarily concerns assignments requiring you to critically assess some view or argument, though much of what I say applies equally to assignments only requiring you to explain some view, argument, or debate in your own words (without weighing in with your own view on the matter). Of course, you should follow all instructions you receive from your instructors and disregard anything I say here that conflicts with those instructions. Absent explicit conflicts, however, it's likely that your instructor is looking for the sort of paper I describe here.

If you follow the advice I offer below, the final result will be a paper with three numbered and labeled sections, with each section broken up into multiple paragraphs, just as I have done in the chapters of this book. The first section introduces the view or argument you're criticizing, the second advances your objections to that view or argument, and the third addresses possible responses to your objections. (Some instructors may expect a short concluding paragraph at the end of the paper, summarizing what you've argued for. Others may find it unnecessary, especially for very short papers. Check with your instructor.)

To be clear, there is nothing sacred about this three-section model. Depending on the content of your paper, it may be useful to organize it differently. For instance, if your plan is to advance two very different objections to some premise, then perhaps a better structure for you would be to introduce the argument you're criticizing in section 1; advance your first objection and address possible responses to it in section 2; and advance your second objection and address possible responses to it in section 3. Or perhaps you plan to *defend* some argument against a particular objection. In that case, you might opt for a four-section model: introduce the argument in section 1, introduce the objection you'll defend it against in section 2, respond to the objection in section 3, and defend your response against potential challenges in section 4. The main thing is just that your paper be clearly organized, and that you take the time not just to present your own perspective but also to demonstrate an appreciation of your opponent's perspective.

For purposes of illustration, I'll imagine that your assignment asks you to criticize the Argument from Suffering from chapter 1.

The Argument from Suffering
(AS1) There is suffering in the world
(AS2) If there is suffering in the world, then God does not exist
(AS3) So, God does not exist

Your plan, let's suppose, is to reject AS2 by arguing that God allows suffering in order to test our devotion.

1. Introducing Your Target
The point of section 1 of your paper is to introduce your target— the view or argument you plan to criticize—and indicate what you plan to do in the paper. There are five main elements you'll want to make sure to include in this section, though not necessarily in this order.

First, you'll identify the topic of the paper. In this case, that's the Argument from Suffering. So, you'll want to begin the paper by saying something like this: "My aim in this paper is to assess a certain argument against the existence of God." Beginning your paper with a straightforward sentence like that is preferable to a flowery opening sentence like, "For centuries upon centuries, men have debated the existence of God."

Second, you'll state the view or argument that you're targeting. In the case at hand, you can simply copy and paste my formulation of the Argument from Suffering into your paper, of course citing the book and the page where you found it. (Ask your instructor for their preferred method of citation.)

Third, you'll go through the premises of that argument, one by one, clarifying what each premise is saying and why it is supposed to be plausible. This will likely be the lengthiest part of section 1, and it's important to do the best job you can explaining, on your opponents' behalf, how their argument is supposed to work. You'll have your chance to criticize the argument in section 2. For now, your goal should be the make the argument look as *good* as possible. Ideally, you want your opponents to think "I couldn't have said it better myself!" and the rest of your readers to think, "how is anyone ever going to find a flaw in that argument?!" Keep in mind that part of what you'll be graded on is the extent to which you understand and appreciate your opponent's perspective. Failing to present your target in its best light may suggest to your instructor that you don't truly understand the argument or position you're criticizing.

Importantly, when you pause on the different premises, don't simply *restate* them in your own words, but also identify your opponent's *reasons* for accepting those premises. So, for instance, when you pause on AS2, don't just say: "According to AS2, there wouldn't be any suffering if God existed." That's just reiterating what AS2 is saying. You also need to spell out the reasoning behind AS2 by saying something like: "The idea behind AS2 is that God is supposed to be all-powerful, and thus would be able to eliminate suffering if he wanted to, and also perfectly benevolent, and thus *would* want to eliminate all suffering."

Fourth, state your thesis, that is, the conclusion that you are ultimately arguing for. For instance, you'll want to say something like this: "My aim is to show that the Argument from Suffering fails because AS2 is false: even an all-good God would want to allow suffering so that we could have the opportunity to prove our devotion." Here, you are only *stating* your thesis, not yet defending it (that's what section 2 is for). Also, here and throughout the paper, it is perfectly appropriate to use first-person pronouns like 'I' and 'my'.

Fifth, you'll give an outline of your paper. If you're using the three-section model, you'll say something like this: "In section 2, I will present my objection to AS2 of the Argument from Suffering. Then, in section 3, I will address two possible responses to my objection."

2. Advancing Your Argument

Section 2 is where you offer your own criticism of your target. In other words, this is where you present your argument for the thesis of your paper. We're imagining that your thesis is that God allows suffering in order to test our devotion. What you need to do now is offer some *reasons* for thinking that God would do this. For instance, you would need to explain why there would have to be suffering in order for our devotion to be tested, and why being able to test our devotion is sufficiently important that a good God would want to do it despite having to make us suffer.

Here are some further tips for section 2.

First, it's crucial that you deny a *premise* of the argument you want to resist, and it should be 100% clear *which* premise your objection is meant to be targeting. If your aim is to criticize the Argument from Suffering, you shouldn't be arguing directly against AS3, that God doesn't exist (for instance by arguing that God must exist because *someone* must have created the universe). Rather, your goal is to show where the Argument from Suffering goes wrong, and you do that by challenging one of its premises. Have a look at the discussion of the Uncertain Fate argument and the Afterlife Argument in section 4 of the Introduction to this textbook for a refresher on the difference between denying a premise and denying the conclusion of an argument.

Second, you need to do more than simply express your opinion that the premise in question is false. It's not enough just to say (repeatedly, but in five different ways) that you don't think that suffering is incompatible with God's existence. Rather, you need to be presenting *reasons* for thinking this. You're trying to persuade another person—your reader—to change their mind about something, not just recording your own personal views and opinions about the issue.

Third, in a short philosophy essay, "less is more." It's generally better to raise a single, well-developed objection to a single premise, than to raise multiple objections to that premise, or to raise objections to multiple premises.

Fourth, avoid nuclear options, that is, argumentative strategies that amount to very general critiques of philosophical or moral reasoning, and that have nothing in particular to do with the argument at hand. An example of a nuclear option would be challenging AS1—which says that there is suffering in the world—by arguing that it's impossible for anyone to really *know* anything about the world since (after all) we may just be dreaming this whole thing. Or challenging the claim (in chapter 10) that it's morally permissible to pull the lever in the trolley example by arguing that thought experiments are pointless, or that morality is just a myth and nothing is really right or wrong. There is a time and a place for such challenges, and philosophers do take them seriously. But, because these critiques are so general, advancing such a critique is unlikely to demonstrate comprehension of the material at hand—which is the main thing you need to do in a short paper assignment.

When you present your arguments against your target, should you present them in the same labeled and indented premise/conclusion format that I've used throughout the book? It depends. If you have read appendix A on logic and feel confident in your ability to tell the difference between valid and invalid arguments, then yes: presenting your own arguments in this format can add a good deal of clarity to the paper and demonstrate an advanced understanding of the dynamics of argumentation. If, on the other hand, you don't feel that you have a firm grip on how to ensure that your arguments are valid, then trying to frame your arguments as I have is likely to do more harm than good. In that case, it's better just to state your reasons plainly, in paragraph form.

What if you're having trouble coming up with an objection to use in section 2? My advice would be to read and re-read and re-re-read the chapter that you plan to criticize. (The chapters aren't *that* long.) If you have your choice of chapters to criticize, choose the one whose conclusion you are most inclined to disagree with. On the first reading, let it all wash over you. On the second reading, keep an eye out for claims that seem especially fishy. On the third reading, skim through the parts you agree with but slow down and very carefully read the parts that seemed fishy, trying to pinpoint the exact sentence where the reasoning go wrong. Having pinpointed where it goes wrong, try to articulate *why* you think it goes wrong, and use that as the basis for your section 2.

3. Anticipating Possible Responses
The point of section 3 of your paper is to address possible responses to the things you said in section 2. To understand what you're supposed to be doing in this section, consider an analogy. A governor is giving a televised speech, trying to convince his constituents to support a proposition abolishing the death penalty. His argument is that it should be abolished because the death penalty isn't actually effective in deterring people from

committing violent crimes. He knows that some people will be skeptical of his argument, but he also knows he can't talk to them all one on one. So, he tries to anticipate and address the most likely objections people will have. For instance, he says: "Look, a lot of people are going to say: what about Oklahoma? When they reinstated the death penalty, violent crime dropped by ten percent. But those statistics are misleading. It was actually the new gun laws they passed, not the reinstatement of the death penalty, that accounts for the drop in violent crime."

This is the sort of thing you'll be doing in section 3. Put yourself in the shoes of your readers, and try to identify one or two ways that they are likely to push back against the argument you gave in section 2. For instance, if you claimed in section 2 that God allows suffering in order to test our devotion, you might imagine someone objecting that God is supposed to be all-knowing, in which case he should already know how devoted people are without having to test their devotion. And then you should respond to that objection, for instance by explaining why it's important for God to test our devotion despite already knowing how devoted we are.

Keep in mind that the point of section 3 is to *defend the objection* you originally put forward in section 2. Accordingly, you should avoid introducing a brand-new line of objection to the target argument from section 1. To see what I mean, imagine two different students, both of whom have argued (in section 2) that God allows suffering in order to test our devotion. Now compare the following two responses (in section 3) to the complaint that God would already know how devoted people are without having to test their devotion.

> *Student A:* I would respond that even God can't know how people will behave when their devotion is tested. Here's why that doesn't entail that God isn't all-knowing...

> *Student B:* I would respond that if God prevented all suffering, then we wouldn't be able to appreciate the good things we have in life.

Notice that Student A is coming to the defense of the very objection that she was advancing in section 2. Student B, by contrast, has completely abandoned the devotion defense and shifted to an entirely new objection to the Argument from Suffering (what, in chapter 1, I called "The Appreciated Goods Defense"). Be like Student A.

A few additional tips about section 3 of your paper.

First, make sure to carefully and charitably lay out the objections you're anticipating before going on to address them. Ideally, you'll want to devote a whole paragraph, not just a single sentence, to explaining the anticipated objection and how it's supposed to be a problem for what you said in section 2. What I said about section 1 applies equally here: when your opponent sees your presentation of the anticipated objection, you want her to think "exactly, I couldn't have said it better myself!"

Second, make sure that the objections you anticipate actually advance the discussion. In particular, don't imagine your opponent simply reiterating the argument from section 1 in defense of the targeted premise. In the case at hand, that would look something like this: "One might respond to my objection to AS2 by insisting that God is supposed to be all-powerful and all-good and such a being cannot allow any suffering." But if one were to say that, one would just be ignoring your argument from section 2. Contrast this with the anticipated objection I suggested just above: that God wouldn't need to test us to know whether we're devoted. That isn't merely a defense of AS2. Rather, it challenges your stated reasons for rejecting AS2, and that's what makes it a good objection to address in section 3.

Third, one way for your opponents to respond to your objections from section 2 is to try to show that those objections fail. But that's not the only way. Another possibility is for them to concede that your objections work, but then try to revise their own argument in a way that makes it immune to your objections, perhaps by revising some of the premises. In section 3, you could consider some way that they might try to do that, and then respond by raising a new objection to their revised argument.

4. Editing

Make sure to leave yourself plenty of time to revise your paper after completing the initial draft. First drafts tend to be pretty messy and full of small mistakes, and cleaning up the mess and catching all these small mistakes will go a long way towards improving the paper.

Here is the procedure I would recommend for editing your paper. Go through the rough draft of your paper very slowly, at a snail's pace, lingering on every sentence. Read each sentence out loud, and ask yourself the following four questions about it.

1. Is this exactly what I meant to say?
2. How might someone challenge this?
3. Can I make the sentence clearer?
4. Can I make the sentence shorter?

Let me say a bit about each of these questions.

Is this exactly what I meant to say? Philosophers—including your instructor—care a great deal about getting the small details right, and you will be amazed by their laser-like focus on the exact wording of your sentences. You might write something like "Killing is always wrong," and they'll leave a comment like: "Even killing blades of grass?" Presumably what you meant was that killing *people* is always wrong. But it's not their job to read your mind; it's your job to say exactly what you mean. Getting the details right is especially important when you're explaining the views and arguments you plan to criticize. One or two small errors in your description of those views and arguments will often be enough to convince your instructor that you don't really understand them.

How might someone challenge this? This question is especially important in section 2, when you're advancing your own argument or objection. Thinking hard about every possible way someone might try to deny something you've said is a great strategy for identifying good responses to address in section 3. But you should also be on the lookout for "cheap" ways that someone might challenge the sentence, which can be addressed by simply rewording it. For instance, you might close off the "what about blades of grass?" objection above by changing "killing is always wrong" to "killing people is always wrong." But then of course you should be thinking about other challenges, for instance that killing in self-defense isn't wrong.

Can I make the sentence clearer? This is where reading the sentence out loud will be especially helpful. If it sounds like something no one would ever say in a normal conversation—and more like something a pretentious old geezer would say with his nose in the air—then you need to find a simpler way of saying it. You might find that the sentence is *so* complicated that you have trouble even reading it off the page. If so, simplify the wording, simplify the grammar, and consider breaking it into two smaller sentences. You might find that the sentence includes "vocabulary words" that you would never use in ordinary conversation. Replace them with ordinary words that mean the same thing. Don't let the point you're trying to make get obscured by needlessly complicated ways of saying it.

Can I make the sentence shorter? A philosophy paper should be a lean, mean, arguing machine. If a word or phrase isn't serving some clear purpose, cut it out. You might find that you've written "I will argue that God doesn't exists and that anyone who believes in God is mistaken." If so, you've said the same thing twice; you should delete the second half of the sentence. In some cases, the right way to make a sentence shorter is to delete *all* the words in it, getting rid of the sentence altogether. For instance, you might find that some sentence is just repeating the very same point you made earlier in the paragraph. In that case, choose the sentence you like best and delete the other one. Or you might find that the sentence is making a point that, although interesting, is actually just a digression that's irrelevant to your argument. Delete it.

Finally, when editing, make sure to give special attention to sentences starting with words like 'So' or 'Therefore' or 'Thus'. When your laser-focused instructor sees any of these words, her head is going to whip back to the previous sentence to see whether the current sentence really does follow from the previous one, or if it's just a separate point (in which case you shouldn't have said 'Therefore'). Likewise for 'That is' or 'In other words'. Suppose you say: "We weren't created by God. In other words, humans did not have an intelligent designer." The 'in other words' suggests that the sentences are saying the same thing. But they don't: saying that God didn't create us still leaves open that we had an intelligent designer other than God (maybe aliens). Since the two sentences don't say exactly the same thing, you shouldn't have said 'In other words'.

5. Likely Criteria for Grading

Even if your instructor does not have an explicit rubric for the assignment, it's likely that your grade will be largely determined by four criteria: comprehension, critical development, use (or misuse) of philosophical vocabulary, and quality of writing.

Comprehension

Your grade will likely be determined primarily by how well you demonstrate understanding of the philosophical concepts, views, and arguments you're discussing in your paper. Because you're being evaluated on whether you've *demonstrated* understanding of the material, you should try to explain things in such a way that any intelligent person would be able to understand your paper, particularly someone who is not in the class and has never encountered the argument or chapter you're talking about.

Among other things, this means you have to define any technical jargon you're using. For instance, if the argument includes terms like 'expected utility' or 'omnibeing', you have to explain what these terms mean. Even though your instructor of course already knows what they mean, she wants to see whether *you* know what they mean well enough to explain them in your own words. There typically is no need to define perfectly ordinary terms like 'suffering' or 'wrong'.

To check whether you've pitched the paper at the right level, show a draft to your smartest friends, and see what they do and don't understand.

Demonstrating comprehension of the material also requires explaining things *in your own words*. For this reason, it's important not to rely too heavily on quotations from the readings. As I mentioned earlier, it's fine to directly copy and paste the indented arguments used in the textbook. But when (in your section 1) you're trying to explain the idea behind some premise, don't simply quote the textbook's explanation of the premise and move on. My own advice would be to read and re-read the textbook's explanation until you're sure you understand it, and then set the textbook aside and explain in your own words what you've just read and understood. You may find it easier to find your *own* words when you don't have the textbook's words right in front of you.

Critical Development

Assuming that your assignment is to critically assess some view or argument, and not simply to explain it in your own words, your instructor will want to see you developing an interesting objection or response. As I emphasized in connection with section 2, it's important to do more than simply express your opinion. You need to give reasons for adopting the position you do. And as I emphasized in connection with section 3, it's important to be thinking about, and explicitly addressing, concerns that an imagined opponent might have about the way you've defended your position.

Additionally, remember that you're being evaluated for comprehension even in the critical development portion of your paper. If you "straw man" your opponents by downplaying or ignoring sensible things they might say in response to your objections, your instructor may take that as evidence that you haven't entirely understood their position. If you rush too quickly to developing your own position without first carefully laying out the view or argument that you're criticizing, your instructor may feel that you haven't demonstrated an understanding of the views under discussion. So, take the time to explain the views or arguments you're targeting before trying to respond to them.

Philosophical Terminology

Your instructor will be paying careful attention to how you use philosophical terminology like 'argument', 'conclusion', 'premise', 'counterexample', 'valid', and so on. Here are three things to be especially careful about. First, as I explain in appendix A, 'valid' has a special meaning in philosophy. Arguments are the only things that should be called 'valid' in a philosophy paper, and an argument does not necessarily count as invalid just because it has false or implausible premises. Second, the conclusion and subconclusions of an argument are not premises.

In the Argument from Suffering, only AS1 and AS2 are premises, not AS3. Third, the view that someone is defending isn't itself an argument. If someone is advancing the Argument from Suffering, you shouldn't say "her argument is that God doesn't exist." Rather, her *view* is that God doesn't exist, she *argues* that God doesn't exist, and her *argument* is the whole sequence of claims consisting of AS1, AS2, and AS3.

Quality of Writing

Your instructor likely won't be too fussy about whether your use of commas or semicolons is exactly right. Still, she will be unlikely to give you a good grade if your writing is full of typos and blatantly ungrammatical sentences, or if your writing is unclear or poorly organized. After all, this is a humanities class, and an "A" in such a class indicates, among other things, that you are a competent writer.

6. Citation and Plagiarism

When discussing this book in class assignments, remember that I don't myself endorse all of these arguments, so you shouldn't say "According to Korman, ..." Instead, you can say "According to The Author, ..." and then cite the page numbers where I made the statement or argument you are discussing.

You may wish to consult outside sources when writing your essays, for instance the sources listed at the end of each chapter or other things floating around online. But this is not something your instructor will typically expect you to do. Indeed, in my experience (especially in one's first philosophy course), reading through journal articles and other materials you find online—and trying to reproduce the advanced ideas you find in there—often does more harm than good. Your time is better spent closely reading and re-reading the assigned texts.

Most importantly, you must make sure to acknowledge any sources you're drawing from by promptly citing them in your paper. Otherwise, you may be charged with *plagiarism*, that is, presenting someone else's work as your own. This includes not only directly copying and pasting sentences from outside sources without putting them in quotation marks and citing the source, but also copying sentences from outside sources and changing around some of the words. Here are some examples of plagiarism that I've encountered in my own classes:

Student: In Dialogues Concerning Natural Religion, David Hume explores the basic fundamentals of religious belief, and whether they can be rational.

Website: In Dialogues Concerning Natural Religion, Hume explores whether religious belief can be rational.

Student: It is meaningless to assume an analogy between one part of the universe and the whole universe.

Website: It makes no sense to assume that one part of the universe is analogous to the whole of the universe.

Student: He excels in using the reference of FLO (future like ours) because it is reasonable to use emotional attachment in comparing the life of a fetus to that of the life that we experience and live out.

Website: Marquis is highly persuasive using this FLO method because he uses emotional attachment comparing the life of a fetus to a life that we may experience.

Even one such sentence is often enough to warrant a failing grade on the assignment. (The first two plagiarized passages are from Sparknotes study guides; the third is from Joe Bird's Acting Ethically blog.)

You may be charged with plagiarism even if you had no intention to plagiarize, even if the plagiarism appears only in the opening section of the paper where you're explaining the views or arguments you plan to criticize, and even if the plagiarism was the result of accidentally submitting the "wrong version" of the paper or "accidentally" memorizing and reproducing the wording from a website. Being charged with plagiarism or other academic infractions may seriously jeopardize your applications to law school, business school, or grad school, in addition to severely affecting your grade in the course and possibly resulting in suspension or expulsion from your college or university. So, you need to be very careful when working with outside sources.

APPENDIX C
Theses and Arguments

This document is meant to be used as an easy reference for the key arguments and theses that appear in the book. Print it out or keep it open on a separate tab.

CHAPTER 1: CAN GOD ALLOW SUFFERING?

The Argument from Suffering
(AS1) There is suffering in the world
(AS2) If there is suffering in the world, then God does not exist
(AS3) So, God does not exist

The Argument from Pointless Suffering
(PS1) There is pointless suffering in the world
(PS2) If there is pointless suffering in the world, then there is no omnibeing
(PS3) So, there is no omnibeing

The Argument for Disbelief
(DB1) You should not believe that all the suffering in Nornia is necessary for some unknown greater good that its ruler has in mind
(DB2) If you should not believe that all the suffering in Nornia is necessary for some unknown greater good that its ruler has in mind, then you should not believe that all the suffering in the actual world is necessary for some unknown greater good that an omnibeing has in mind
(DB3) So, you should not believe that all the suffering in the actual world is necessary for some unknown greater good that an omnibeing has in mind

CHAPTER 2: WHY YOU SHOULD BET ON GOD

The Argument for Betting on God

(BG1) One should always choose the option with the greatest expected utility

(BG2) Believing in God has a greater expected utility than not believing in God

(BG3) So you should believe in God

CHAPTER 3: WHAT MAKES YOU YOU

The Same Body Account

A at t is the same person as B at t* if and only if A has the same body as B

The Conjoined Twins Argument

(CT1) If the Same Body Account is true, then *either* Abby and Brittany have different bodies or Abby and Brittany are the same person

(CT2) Abby and Brittany have the same body

(CT3) Abby and Brittany are not the same person

(CT4) So, the Same Body Account is false

The Body Swap Argument

(BS1) $Male_T$ and $Male_W$ have the same body

(BS2) If $Male_T$ and $Male_W$ have the same body, then: if the Same Body Account is true, then $Male_T$ and $Male_W$ are the same person

(BS3) $Male_T$ and $Male_W$ are not the same person

(BS4) So, the Same Body Account is false

The Psychological Descendant Account

A at t is the same person as B at t* if and only if A is either a psychological ancestor or a psychological descendant of B.

The Blackout Argument

(BL1) The unconscious man is not a psychological descendant of the conscious man

(BL2) If the unconscious man is not a psychological descendant of the conscious man, then: if the Psychological Descendant Account is true, then the conscious man is not the same person as the unconscious man

(BL3) The conscious man is the same person as the unconscious man

(BL4) So, the Psychological Descendant Account is false

The Fission Argument

(FS1) If the Psychological Descendant Account is true, then JoJo is the same person as Chad$_{RW}$ *and* is the same person as Alex$_{RW}$

(FS2) If JoJo is the same person as Chad$_{RW}$ and the same person as Alex$_{RW}$, then Chad$_{RW}$ is the same person as Alex$_{RW}$

(FS3) So, if the Psychological Descendant Account is true, then Chad$_{RW}$ is the same person as Alex$_{RW}$

(FS4) Chad$_{RW}$ is not the same person as Alex$_{RW}$

(FS5) So the Psychological Descendant Account is false

CHAPTER 4: DON'T FEAR THE REAPER

Against Fearing Death

(FD1) You cease to be conscious when you die

(FD2) If you cease to be conscious when you die, then being dead is not bad for you

(FD3) So, being dead is not bad for you

(FD4) If being dead is not bad for you, then you should not fear death

(FD5) So, you should not fear death

The Argument from Hedonism

(AH1) If you cease to be conscious when you die, then being dead doesn't result in more pain than you would otherwise have had

(AH2) Something is bad for you if and only if it results in more pain than you would otherwise have had

(FD2) So, if you cease to be conscious when you die, then being dead isn't bad for you

(HD*) Something is bad for you if and only if it results in more pain than you would otherwise have had

(HD**) Something is bad for you if and only if it results in more pain *or less pleasure* than you would otherwise have had

The Unread Mail Argument

(UM1) Carly would have had more pleasure had she not met Evan

(UM2) If Carly would have had more pleasure had she not met Evan, then: if HD** is true, then meeting Evan was bad for her

(UM3) Meeting Evan was not bad for her

(UM4) So, HD** is false

Against Post-Mortem Consciousness

(PC1) If Animal ceases to be conscious when you die *and* you are Animal, then you cease to be conscious when you die

(PC2) Animal ceases to be conscious when you die

(PC3) You are Animal

(FD1) So, you cease to be conscious when you die

The Too Many Thinkers Argument

(TT1) Animal is in your chair and is thinking

(TT2) You are the only thing in your chair that is thinking

(PC3) So you are Animal

CHAPTER 5: NO FREEDOM

The Argument for Freedom
(FR1) Sometimes you perform an action after deciding to perform that action
(FR2) If one performs an action after deciding to perform it, then one performs that action freely
(FR3) So some of your actions are performed freely

The Desire Argument
(DS1) What you choose to do is always determined by your desires
(DS2) You can't control your desires
(DS3) So, what you choose to do is always determined by something you can't control
(DS4) If what you choose to do is always determined by something you can't control, then you never act freely
(DS5) So, you never act freely

The Argument from Determinism
(DT1) Determinism is true
(DT2) If determinism is true, then you are never able to do otherwise
(DT3) If you are never able to do otherwise, then none of your actions are free
(DT4) So, none of your actions are free

The Doomed Regardless Argument
(DM1) If an action is determined to happen, then you couldn't have done otherwise
(DM2) If you couldn't have done otherwise, then the action is not free
(DM3) So, if an action is determined to happen, then it is not free
(DM4) If an action happens randomly, then it is not free
(DM5) Every action you perform is either determined to happen or happens randomly
(DM6) So, none of your actions are free

The Consequence Argument

(CQ1) If determinism is true, then what you do is always a consequence of the laws of nature and the distant past

(CQ2) You have no control over the laws of nature or the distant past

(CQ3) So, if determinism is true, then what you do is always a consequence of things over which you have no control

(CQ4) If what you do is always a consequence of things over which you have no control, then you are never able to do otherwise

(DT2) So, if determinism is true, you are never able to do otherwise

CHAPTER 6: YOU KNOW NOTHING

(FLP) Future states of the world will be like past states of the world

Against Knowing the Future

(KF1) If you are not justified in believing that FLP is true, then your belief that the sun will set in the west tomorrow is unjustified

(KF2) You are not justified in believing that FLP is true

(KF3) So, your belief that the sun will set in the west tomorrow is unjustified

(KF4) If your belief that the sun will set in the west tomorrow is unjustified, then you don't know that the sun will set in the west tomorrow

(KF5) So, you don't know that the sun will set in the west tomorrow

The Faulty Foundation Argument

(FF1) Your belief that the sun will set in the west tomorrow is based on FLP

(FF2) If a belief is based on something that you aren't justified in believing, then that belief itself is unjustified

(KF1) So, if you are not justified in believing that FLP is true, then your belief that the sun will set in the west tomorrow is unjustified

FLP is Unjustified
(UJ1) If your belief in FLP is justified, then it is either justified by direct observation or by inductive reasoning
(UJ2) Your belief in FLP isn't justified by direct observation
(UJ3) Your belief in FLP isn't justified by inductive reasoning
(KF2) So, your belief in FLP is unjustified

The Anti-Circularity Argument
(AC1) All inductive reasoning about the future assumes the truth of FLP
(AC2) If all inductive reasoning about the future assumes the truth of FLP, then any inductive reasoning about FLP is circular
(AC3) No belief can be justified by circular reasoning
(UJ3) So, FLP isn't justified by inductive reasoning

(TDH) You are currently lying down in bed dreaming about sitting down reading a philosophy textbook

The Dreaming Argument
(DR1) If you have no way of knowing that TDH is false, then you don't know that you're sitting down reading
(DR2) You have no way of knowing that TDH is false
(DR3) So you don't know that you're sitting down reading

The Competing Hypotheses Argument
(CH1) One knows a certain thing only if one has some way of knowing that all competing hypotheses are false
(CH2) TDH is a hypothesis that competes with your belief that you're sitting down reading
(DR1) So, if you have no way of knowing that TDH is false, then you don't know that you're sitting down reading

The Argument from Deduction
(DE1) If you know you're sitting down reading, you can deduce that TDH is false from things you know
(DE2) If you can deduce something from things you know, then you have a way of knowing that thing
(DE3) So, if you know you're sitting down reading, then you have a way of knowing that TDH is false

The No Evidence Argument
(NE1) If you have no evidence against something, then you have no way of knowing it's false
(NE2) You have no evidence against TDH
(DR2) So, you have no way of knowing that TDH is false

CHAPTER 7: AGAINST PRISONS AND TAXES

Against Taxation and Imprisonment
(TX1) If there is no morally relevant difference between two actions A and B, and A is wrong, then B is wrong
(TX2) It is wrong for Jasmine to extort and kidnap her neighbors
(TX3) There is no morally relevant difference between Jasmine extorting and kidnapping her neighbors and the government taxing and imprisoning its citizens
(TX4) So, it is wrong for the government to tax and imprison its citizens

No Consent
(NC1) Someone tacitly consents to an arrangement only if (i) there is a reasonable way to opt out and (ii) explicit refusal to opt in is recognized
(NC2) There is no reasonable way to opt out of paying taxes and following laws, and explicit refusal to opt in is not recognized
(NC3) So, we have not tacitly consented to paying taxes and following laws

The Argument for Open Borders
(OB1) If there is no morally relevant difference between two actions A and B, and A is wrong, then B is wrong
(OB2) It is wrong for Jasmine to restrict access to the park
(OB3) There is no morally relevant difference between Jasmine restricting access to the park and the government restricting access to the country
(OB4) So, it is wrong for the government to restrict access to the country

CHAPTER 8: THE ETHICS OF ABORTION

The Right to Life Argument
(RL1) Emm has a right to life
(RL2) If Emm has a right to life, then it is seriously immoral to deprive Emm of Taylor's womb
(RL3) So, it's seriously immoral to deprive Emm of Taylor's womb

The Requirements of Life Argument
(RQ1) If something (or someone) has a right to life, and it needs a certain something in order to survive, then it has a right to that thing
(RQ2) Emm needs Taylor's womb in order to survive
(RQ3) So, if Emm has a right to life, then Emm has a right to Taylor's womb
(RQ4) If Emm has a right to Taylor's womb, then it is seriously immoral to deprive Emm of Taylor's womb
(RL2) So, if Emm has a right to life, then it is seriously immoral to deprive Emm of Taylor's womb

The Violinist Argument
(VA1) Maurissa has a right to life and needs Riley's blood in order to survive
(VA2) Maurissa does not have a right to Riley's blood
(VA3) So, someone who has a right to life does not thereby have a right to all the things they need in order to survive

The Known Risk Argument
(KR1) Taylor freely chose to have sex and knew that this could lead to Emm using her womb
(KR2) Whenever someone freely does something and knows that it could lead to certain consequences, one consents to those consequences
(KR3) So, Taylor consented to Emm using her womb
(KR4) If Taylor consented to Emm using her womb, then Emm has a right to Taylor's womb
(KR5) If Emm has a right to Taylor's womb, then it is seriously immoral to deprive Emm of Taylor's womb
(KR6) So, it is seriously immoral to deprive Emm of Taylor's womb

The Simple FLO Argument

(SF1) It is seriously immoral to kill something (or someone) if killing it deprives it of a future like ours

(SF2) Killing Emm deprives Emm of a future like ours

(SF3) So, it is seriously immoral to kill Emm

The Modified FLO Argument

(MF1) It is seriously immoral to kill something (or someone) if killing it deprives it of a future like ours *and* the killing does not involve any FLO-overriding factors

(MF2) Killing Emm deprives Emm of a future like ours

(MF3) Killing Emm does not involve any FLO-overriding factors

(MF4) So, it is seriously immoral to kill Emm

CHAPTER 9: EATING ANIMALS

The Argument from Precedent

(PR1) There have been people who eat meat throughout human history

(PR2) If there have been people doing a certain thing throughout human history, then it is morally permissible for you to do it

(PR3) So, it is morally permissible for you to eat meat

The Natural Order Argument

(NO1) Other animals eat meat

(NO2) If other animals do something, then it's morally permissible for you to do it

(NO3) So, it's morally permissible for you to eat meat

The Natural Capacity Argument

(CP1) You are naturally capable of eating meat

(CP2) If you are naturally capable of doing a certain thing, then it is morally permissible for you to do that thing

(CP3) So, it is morally permissible for you to eat meat

The Necessity of Protein Argument
(NP1) Eating meat is necessary for getting enough protein
(NP2) If doing something is necessary for getting enough
protein, then it is morally permissible for you to do it
(NP3) So, it is morally permissible for you to eat meat

The Argument from Fred's Puppies
(FP1) If there is no morally relevant difference between two
actions A and B, and A is immoral, then B is immoral
(FP2) What Fred does is immoral
(FP3) There is no morally relevant difference between what Fred
does and you buying and eating factory-farmed meat
(FP4) So, it is immoral for you to buy and eat factory-farmed
meat

CHAPTER 10: WHAT MAKES THINGS RIGHT

Act Utilitarianism
Performing a certain action is the right thing to do if and only if
it will have a more positive effect on overall levels of happiness
than any other available action

The Organ Distribution Argument
(OD1) Killing Nick has a greater positive effect on overall levels
of happiness than letting him live
(OD2) If killing Nick has a greater positive effect on overall
levels of happiness than letting him live, then: if act
utilitarianism is true, then killing Nick was the right thing
to do
(OD3) Killing Nick was not the right thing to do
(OD4) So, act utilitarianism is false

Rule Utilitarianism
Performing a certain action is the right thing to do if and only if
it is prescribed by the collection of rules that, if adopted, would
have the greatest positive effect on overall levels of happiness

The Trolley Argument

(TR1) If there is no morally relevant difference between two actions A and B, and A is the right thing to do, then B is the right thing to do

(TR2) Diverting the trolley was the right thing to do

(TR3) There is no morally relevant difference between diverting the trolley and killing Nick

(TR4) So, killing Nick was the right thing to do

Made in the USA
Monee, IL
26 August 2024

64586620R00136